Bloom's Modern Critical Interpretations

Alice's Adventures in
   Wonderland
The Adventures of
   Huckleberry Finn
All Quiet on the
   Western Front
As You Like It
The Ballad of the Sad
   Café
Beloved
Beowulf
Billy Budd, Benito
   Cereno, Bartleby the
   Scrivener, and Other
   Tales
Black Boy
The Bluest Eye
Cat on a Hot Tin
   Roof
The Catcher in the
   Rye
Catch-22
Cat's Cradle
The Color Purple
Crime and
   Punishment
The Crucible
Darkness at Noon
Death of a Salesman
The Death of Artemio
   Cruz
The Divine Comedy
Don Quixote
Dubliners
Emerson's Essays
Emma
Fahrenheit 451

Frankenstein
The Grapes of Wrath
Great Expectations
The Great Gatsby
Hamlet
The Handmaid's Tale
Heart of Darkness
I Know Why the
   Caged Bird Sings
The Iliad
Jane Eyre
The Joy Luck Club
The Jungle
Long Day's Journey
   Into Night
Lord of the Flies
The Lord of the Rings
Love in the Time of
   Cholera
Macbeth
The Man Without
   Qualities
The Metamorphosis
Miss Lonelyhearts
Moby-Dick
Night
1984
The Odyssey
Oedipus Rex
The Old Man and the
   Sea
On the Road
One Flew Over the
   Cuckoo's Nest
One Hundred Years of
   Solitude
The Pardoner's Tale

Persuasion
Portnoy's Complaint
A Portrait of the Artist
   as a Young Man
Pride and Prejudice
Ragtime
The Red Badge of
   Courage
The Rime of the
   Ancient Mariner
The Rubáiyát of Omar
   Khayyám
The Scarlet Letter
A Separate Peace
Silas Marner
Song of Myself
Song of Solomon
The Stranger
A Streetcar Named
   Desire
Sula
The Sun Also Rises
The Tale of Genji
A Tale of Two Cities
The Tales of Poe
The Tempest
Their Eyes Were
   Watching God
Things Fall Apart
To Kill a Mockingbird
Ulysses
Waiting for Godot
The Waste Land
White Noise
Wuthering Heights
Young Goodman
   Brown

Bloom's Modern Critical Interpretations

Mark Twain's
The Adventures of
Huckleberry Finn
Updated Edition

Edited and with an introduction by
Harold Bloom
Sterling Professor of the Humanities
Yale University

BLOOM'S
LITERARY CRITICISM
An imprint of Infobase Publishing

Bloom's Modern Critical Interpretations: The Adventures of Huckleberry Finn—Updated Edition

Copyright ©2007 Infobase Publishing

Introduction © 2007 by Harold Bloom

Bloom's Literary Criticism
An imprint of Infobase Publishing
132 West 31st Street
New York NY 10001

ISBN-10: 0-7910-9426-X
ISBN-13: 978-0-7910-9426-6

Library of Congress Cataloging-in-Publication Data
Mark Twain's The adventures of Huckleberry Finn / Harold Bloom, editor. — Updated ed.
    p. cm. — (Bloom's modern critical interpretations)
  Includes bibliographical references and index.
  ISBN 0-7910-9426-X (hardcover)
  1. Twain, Mark, 1835–1910. Adventures of Huckleberry Finn. 2. Finn, Huckleberry (Fictitious character) 3. Mississippi River—In literature. 4. Boys in literature. 5. Race relations in literature. I. Bloom, Harold. II. Title. III. Series.
  PS1305.M28 2007
  813'.4—dc22   2006036858

Contributing Editor: Pamela Loos

Cover designed by Ben Peterson

Cover image: Dover Publications

Printed in the United States of America

Bang EJB 10 9 8 7 6 5 4 3 2 1

This book is printed on acid-free paper.

Contents

Editor's Note   vii

Introduction   1
   Harold Bloom

The Realism of *Huckleberry Finn*   7
   Tom Quirk

Life Without Father:
The Role of the Paternal in
the Opening Chapters of *Huckleberry Finn*   27
   Harry G. Segal

Huck and Jim on
the Mississippi: Going with the Flow?   43
   Carl F. Wieck

Huck, Jim, and the "Black-and-White" Fallacy   55
   James S. Leonard

Huckleberry Finn and the Problem of Freedom   67
   Sanford Pinsker

Deadpan Huck: Or,
What's Funny about Interpretation   75
   Sacvan Bercovitch

Who Shot Tom Sawyer?   119
   Jeffrey Steinbrink

Huckleberry Finn and
Twain's Democratic Art of Writing   129
    Mary P. Nichols

The "Raftsmen's Passage,"
Huck's Crisis of Whiteness, and
Huckleberry Finn in U.S. Literary History   149
    Peter Schmidt

Reinventing the World and
Reinventing the Self in *Huck Finn*   171
    Bennett Kravitz

"That Night We Had Our Show":
Twain and Audience   193
    Todd Giles

Floating Capital: The Trouble with
Whiteness on Twain's Mississippi   203
    Stephanie Le Menager

Chronology   229
Contributors   233
Bibliography   237
Acknowledgments   241
Index   243

Editor's Note

My Introduction celebrates Huck Finn as the greatest American image of the storyteller's freedom—from time and from fact. The plotlessness of *Huckleberry Finn* is studied by Tom Quirk, after which Harry G. Segal examines the scary figure of Pap Finn, and Carl F. Wieck gives a fresh perspective upon the Mississippi's importance in the novel.

The Huck-Jim relationship is seen by James S. Leonard in terms of Twain's shrewd manipulation of inarticulateness and illogic to create a highly articulate narrative and clear thematic logic.

Sanford Pinsker persuasively argues that Twain's greatest novel is profoundly subversive because it is truly anti-racist and thus tells us truth about ourselves.

The distinguished historicist Sacvan Bercovitch paradoxically suggests that *Huckleberry Finn*'s humor "lies in its denial of comic relief," while Jeffrey Steinbrink wryly demonstrates an accurate distaste for Tom Sawyer, Huck's too-respectable sidekick.

Twain's democratic ethos of writing is found to be incarnated in Huck-as-narrator by Mary P. Nichols, after which Peter Schmidt traces the influence of "Huck's crisis of whiteness" upon subsequent critics and historians of American literature.

The Huck-Jim relationship is freshly elucidated by Bennet Kravitz, while Todd Giles finds a dramatic component in the novel.

Stephanie Le Menager concludes this volume with a mordant essay on Twain's deep awareness that his American West was just as much founded upon "international piracy and slavery" as was the American South.

HAROLD BLOOM

Introduction

I

After supper she got out her book and learned me about Moses and the Bulrushers, and I was in a sweat to find out all about him; but by-and-by she let it out that Moses had been dead a considerable long time; so then I didn't care no more about him; because I don't take stock in dead people.

Huck Finn's American vision has this in common with Captain Ahab's or Walt Whitman's, that Huck too would strike the sun if it insulted him. The three best American books—*Huckleberry Finn*, *Moby-Dick*, *Leaves of Grass*—have in common also that they are each the most American of books. Twain's masterpiece is essentially comic, Melville's is tragic, Whitman's is beyond characterization or categorization, except that despite its humor and its Emersonian hopes for America, we remember it best for its dark shadows. *Huckleberry Finn*, shrewd and grim as it is sometimes compelled to be, remains unique in our national literature for its affirmative force. Fecund in its progeny—as diverse as Kipling's *Kim*, Eliot's *The Dry Salvages*, Hemingway's *The Sun Also Rises*, and Mailer's *Why Are We in Vietnam?*—the book is likely to go on engendering our strongest writers, with only *Leaves of Grass* as a rival in that role.

What is the secret of an appeal that affected Eliot and Faulkner, Hemingway and Joyce, with almost equal intensity? Is it because the book tells the truth? That was the judgment of Lionel Trilling, and I am not moved to dismiss such a judgment lightly. The book tells a story which most Americans need to believe is a true representation of the way things were, are, and yet might be. Huck lives in a complex reality that nevertheless does not negate his freedom. Yet that freedom is also a solitude, and is purchased by a series of lies, noble in their intention, but lies nevertheless. Without a family, yet with a murderous father always apt to turn up again, Huck perpetually experiences a primal loneliness that he both welcomes and dreads:

> Miss Watson she kept pecking at me, and it got tiresome and lonesome. By-and-by they fetched the niggers in and had prayers, and then everybody was off to bed. I went up to my room with a piece of candle and put it on the table. Then I set down in a chair by the window and tried to think of something cheerful, but it warn't no use. I felt so lonesome I most wished I was dead. The stars was shining, and the leaves rustled in the woods ever so mournful; and I heard an owl, away off, who-whooing about somebody that was dead, and a whippowill and a dog crying about somebody that was going to die; and the wind was trying to whisper something to me and I couldn't make out what it was, and so it made the cold shivers run over me. Then away out in the woods I heard that kind of a sound that a ghost makes when it wants to tell about something that's on its mind and can't make itself understood, and so can't rest easy in its grave and has to go about that way every night grieving. I got so down-hearted and scared, I did wish I had some company. Pretty soon a spider went crawling up my shoulder, and I flipped it off and it lit in the candle; and before I could budge it was all shriveled up. I didn't need anybody to tell me that that was an awful bad sign and would fetch me some bad luck, so I was scared and most shook the clothes off of me. I got up and turned around in my tracks three times and crossed my breast every time; and then I tied up a little lock of my hair with a thread to keep witches away. But I hadn't no confidence. You do that when you've lost a horse-shoe that you've found, instead of nailing it up over the door, but I hadn't ever heard anybody say it was any way to keep off bad luck when you'd killed a spider.

Huck, like any American, does not feel free unless he is alone, and yet solitude makes him fear that he is no part of the creation, however the world happened or came about. His extraordinary pathos results from his ambivalence towards a freedom he necessarily cannot evade for very long at a time.

II

V. S. Pritchett found in *Adventures of Huckleberry Finn* evidence of an American limitation, when compared to the more civilized modes of European literature:

> It is not a book which grows spiritually, if we compare it to *Quixote*, *Dead Souls* or even *Pickwick*; and it is lacking in that civilised quality which you are bound to lose when you throw over civilisation—the quality of pity. One is left with the cruelty of American humor.

Pritchett perhaps forgot that throwing over civilization and its discontents is not so easily accomplished, Huck's discomfort with culture is acute, but he is hardly "a natural anarchist and bum" to whom ideas and ideals are "repugnant," as Pritchett thought. Nor is he "the servant of the river-god," which was Lionel Trilling's trope, a mythologization that derived Huck's supposedly "very intense moral life" from his "perpetual adoration of the Mississippi's power and charm." That is to compound Huck with T. S. Eliot, for whom "the Boy is also the spirit of the River." Huck indeed is now part of the American mythology, but hardly because he is the spirit of the river, which is not a god for Twain, whatever it was to be for Trilling and for Eliot. Twain tells us that the Mississippi is well worth reading about, is remarkable, and manifests many eccentricities. Huck too is well worth reading about, is quite remarkable, and is a wonderfully eccentric boy. Critics are fond of finding a moral in him, or at least want to see him as a kind of Sancho Panza to Tom Sawyer's Don Quixote. Tom Sawyer, alas, is something of a bore and not very quixotic, and Huck has little in common with the shrewd and pragmatic Sancho. There is however a touch of the quixotic in Huck, who is a great storyteller, a boy who lies merely to keep in practice.

Huck's fictions are lies *against* time, against an impossible father, against society and history; but not against reason and nature. They are not lies *for* anything; Huck does not seek benefits from them. Like the strong poets, Huck always has the desire to be different, the desire to be elsewhere. Change and travel are necessary for Huck; without them he cannot be independent. But we would do him wrong if we judged him as seeking freedom above everything else. Except for Joyce's Poldy Bloom, Huck Finn must be the most good-natured and tolerant representation of a human being in the fiction of the English language. The freedom he must have, because he is that freedom, is a freedom that he wants for everyone else. It is the freedom of the storyteller, Twain's own freedom.

That freedom, by common consent, has something to do with postponing death, with deferring the fear of dying. Divination, the sidestepping of dangers to the magic, occult, ontological self, is a fundamental component of the urge to tell stories. Huck of course is never going to be an adult, and so never will have to die. Yet that sounds wrong, because Huck rejects a maturation that is merely the death drive. The superego haunts Huck, yet cannot dominate him, because Huck will not surrender his gift for lying. "You don't know about me," Huck begins by saying, and he ends with the insistence that he will be out there ahead of the rest of us:

> But I reckon I got to light out for the Territory ahead of the rest, because Aunt Sally she's going to adopt me and sivilize me and I can't stand it. I been there before.

Huck's discomfort with civilization stems from his wholehearted rejection of guilt, sin, and solipsism, all of them Eliotic attributes, or should one say virtues? We can call Huck's attributes his virtues, because Huck, like his creator, is essentially an enlightened rationalist, though retaining considerable zest for the romance of superstitions. Unlike Eliot, Huck is not a Christian, and his prayer is not, "And let my cry come unto Thee," but something more naturalistic and buoyant:

> Sometimes we'd have that whole river all to ourselves for the longest time. Yonder was the banks and the islands, across the water; and maybe a spark—which was a candle in a cabin window—and sometimes on the water you could see a spark or two—on a raft or a scow, you know; and maybe you could hear a fiddle or a song coming over from one of them crafts. It's lovely to live on a raft. We had the sky, up there, all speckled with stars, and we used to lay on our backs and look up at them, and discuss about whether they was made, or only just happened. Jim he allowed they was made, but I allowed they happened; I judged it would have took too long to *make* so many. Jim said the moon could a *laid* them; well, that looked kind of reasonable, so I didn't say nothing against it, because I've seen a frog

lay most as many, so of course it could be done. We used to watch the stars that fell, too, and see them streak down. Jim allowed they'd got spoiled and was hove out of the nest.

This delightful compromise upon a myth of creation is "kind of reasonable," and wholly characteristic of Huck's cheerful skepticism. Even more characteristic is the joy of being that opens chapter 19 with what must be the most beautiful prose paragraph yet written by any American:

Two or three days and nights went by; I reckon I might say they swum by, they slid along so quiet and smooth and lovely. Here is the way we put in the time. It was a monstrous big river down there—sometimes a mile and a half wide; we run nights, and laid up and hid day-times; soon as night was most gone, we stopped navigating and tied up—nearly always in the dead water under a tow-head; and then cut young cottonwoods and willows and hid the raft with them. Then we set out the lines. Next we slid into the river and had a swim, so as to freshen up and cool off; then we set down on the sandy bottom where the water was about knee-deep, and watched the daylight come. Not a sound, anywheres—perfectly still—just like the whole world was asleep, only sometimes the bull-frogs a-cluttering, maybe. The first thing to see, looking away over the water, was a kind of dull line—that was the woods on t'other side—you couldn't make nothing else out; then a pale place in the sky; then more paleness, spreading around; then the river softened up, away off, and warn't black any more, but gray; you could see little dark spots drifting along, ever so far away—trading scows, and such things; and long black streaks—rafts; sometimes you could hear a sweep screaking; or jumbled up voices, it was so still, and sounds come so far; and by-and-by you could see a streak on the water which you know by the look of the streak that there's a snag there in a swift current which breaks on it and makes that streak look that way; and you see the mist curl up off of the water, and the east reddens up, and the river, and you make out a log cabin in the edge of the woods, away on the bank on t'other side of the river, being a wood-yard, likely, and piled by them cheats so you can throw a dog through it anywheres; then the nice breeze springs up, and comes fanning you from over there, so cool and fresh, and sweet to smell, on account of the woods and the flowers; but sometimes not that way, because they've left dead fish laying around, gars, and such, and they do get pretty rank; and next you've got the full day, and everything smiling in the sun, and the song-birds just going it!

This is a cosmos that was not made, but "only just happened." It is no part of romance or legend, not myth, but a representation of a natural reality seen in its best aspect, where the days and nights swim and slide by. We hesitate to call this a fiction, since it lacks any residual Platonism. Even Freud had his last touch of Platonism, the transcendentalism that he called the "reality principle." Twain and Huck tell us a story about reality, but without reference to any principle.

III

Eminent critics have disagreed vigorously over the way in which Twain chose to end his masterpiece. That something is seriously wrong with the conclusion is palpable, but what is wrong may only be that in this book no conclusion is possible anyway. T. S. Eliot and Lionel Trilling both argued the formal adequacy of the long episode at the Phelps place, in which Tom Sawyer arrives again to organize the "rescue" of Jim, the runaway slave who in some clear sense has become Huck's true family. But the critical decision here certainly goes to Leo Marx, who sees the novel's end as its self-defeat:

> Should Clemens have made Huck a tragic hero? Both Mr. Eliot and Mr. Trilling argue that that would have been a mistake, and they are very probably correct. But between the ending as we have it and tragedy in the fullest sense, there was vast room for invention. Clemens might have contrived an action which left Jim's fate as much in doubt as Huck's. Such an ending would have allowed us to assume that the principals were defeated but alive, and the quest unsuccessful but not abandoned. This, after all, would have been consonant with the symbols, the characters, and the theme as Clemens had created them—and with history.

Marx is aware that he asks for too much, but that is the lasting power of the book that Twain wrote until he reached the Phelps place episode. We are so transported by *Huckleberry Finn* that we cannot surrender our hopes, and of these the largest is a refusal to abandon the desire for a permanent image of freedom. Twain could not extend that image into a finality, but the image endures nevertheless, as a permanent token of something evermore about to be.

TOM QUIRK

The Realism of Huckleberry Finn

"Hast seen the White Whale?" gritted Ahab in reply.

"No; only heard of him; but don't believe in him at all," said the other good-humoredly "Come aboard!"

"Thou are too damned jolly. Sail on. Hast lost any men?"

"Not enough to speak of—two islanders, that's all; but come aboard."

—*Moby-Dick*, chapter 115, "The *Pequod* Meets the *Bachelor*"

"It warn't the grounding—that didn't keep us back but a little. We bowed out a cylinder-head."

"Good gracious! anybody hurt?"

"No'm. Killed a nigger."

"Well, it's lucky; because sometimes people do get hurt."

—*Adventures of Huckleberry Finn*, chapter 32

I

The second of these passages, too familiar to require much commentary, is frequently instanced as a dramatic rendering of much that is noteworthy about *Huckleberry Finn*: the centrality to the novel's purpose of questions of racial prejudice; the transparent irony disclosed in Aunt Sally's anxious question and her genuine relief that no "people" were injured; the canniness

---

From *Coming to Grips with Huckleberry Finn*, pp. 83–105. © 1993 by the Curators of the University of Missouri.

of Huck himself, who, though perplexed by this sudden relative who calls him "Tom," knows enough about human nature to invent yet another fictional experience and to adopt yet another persona on the instant, but who is totally unaware of the satire, irony, or humor of his own remark. Huck knows his audience *inside* the novel; time and again he sizes up his situation in an antagonistic adult world and plays to the several desires, fears, and biases of those who confront or question him. However (despite his amiable introduction to us in the opening paragraph, his final summary complaint about the "trouble" he has had telling his story, and his closing adieu, "YOURS TRULY, HUCK FINN"), Huck is often indifferent to or ignorant of his effects upon an audience *outside* the book, which is to say us as readers.

If realism depends upon a certain consensual understanding of the world, an understanding, that is, of what Henry James said we cannot, one way or another, "not know," then the realism of *Huckleberry Finn* stands in peculiar relation to other realist works. As Michael Davitt Bell has shown, Twain's attachment to the announced principles of literary realism is tenuous at best,[1] and what is true for Twain is even more true for his young narrator. For Huck not only does not knowingly participate in this consensus understanding, but he also is supremely unqualified to render it in his narrative. Time and again, Huck proves that he can readily adapt to the moves of the game, but no one has taught him the logic of it. The origins of feuds, the behavior of pirates and robbers, the decor of the Grangerford house, the prerogatives of royalty, all these remain obscure and mysterious to him, but he quickly sizes up the situation and plays his part as best he can.

The first passage comes from as famous a book. Yet so far as I know this exchange and its coincidentally parallel expression in *Huckleberry Finn* have gone virtually unnoticed. There may be several explanations for this. Among them, and one perhaps worth exploring, involves the difference between the romanticism of *Moby-Dick* and the realism of *Huckleberry Finn*. That difference may be as simple as the distinction between motive and action, the difference, that is, between quest and escape—between the pursuit (all defiant of necessity and contingency, fixed upon some insane object and driven by some overruling passion) and the "scrape" (the unanticipated event somehow managed, eluded, or negotiated). Ahab bends the will of his crew to his purpose and dispenses with genial observances and courtesies; Huck caters to whim and courts favor, always with an eye to the nearest exit. The unmarried captain of the *Bachelor*, as with most of Melville's bachelors, is an emblem of moral complacency and lavish good humor, in command of a full cargo and homeward bound. Aunt Sally is a type, an equal mixture of Christian goodwill, blind bigotry, and doting affection, glad to receive the boy whom she takes to be her nephew. *Moby-Dick* is characterized by its symbolic trappings, its metaphysical inquiries, its lyrical spontaneity, its Shakespearean "quick probings at the very axis of reality," as Melville said in "Hawthorne and His Mosses."

But *Huckleberry Finn* works by other means: It subverts the same high drama that promotes its episodes (Boggs's drunken swagger, for example, results in his murder, but the dramatic emphasis is upon the town's perverse fascination with his dying; a distempered gang calls for the lynching of Colonel Sherburn, but what they receive is an upbraiding lecture on mob cowardice). It indulges on the happiest terms in reflective moments through the benign auspices of folklore, superstition, and enviable credulity. Ishmael's crow's-nest reverie is blasted by the anxious recognition that he hovers over "Descartesian vortices," but Huck and Jim argue the origins of stars—the moon must have laid them after all—and no one gets hurt. *Huckleberry Finn* displays much less of the Melvillean interest in an "Anacharsis Clootz deputation" of humanity than in the solidarity of two, a "community of misfortune" as Twain would later describe the partnership of Huck and Jim. In the above cited passages, Melville's is a throwaway line, Twain's an epitome of vernacular realism.

Huckleberry Finn, like *Moby-Dick*, is a storyteller's story. In both books the teller and the tale vie for our attention. Ishmael, the yarn-spinner, is intent on chasing to their dens the significances of his experiences, though it is seldom the case that we as readers feel that these adventures are existentially his at all. Huck, too, is a receptacle of impressions, but they are filtered through a distinctively adolescent consciousness—quick to perceive, slow to comprehend.

But there are two "authors" of *Huckleberry Finn*, Mark Twain and Huck Finn, and there are also two distinct fictive worlds established by them. Twain presents us with a world that must be judged, Huck with a world that must be inhabited. If both authors are realists, however, their realism is of different orders of experience. Huckleberry Finn's story is primarily a record of feeling, not cognition, and as Twain once remarked, "emotions are among the toughest things in the world to manufacture out of whole cloth; it is easier to manufacture seven facts than one emotion."[2] The "quality of felt life" that Henry James claimed is central to the realist aesthetic is fulfilled in Huck's story; the deadly satirical thrusts of a man slightly outraged by life are largely the result of Twain's management of that same narrative.

The difference between Mark Twain's realism and Huck Finn's may be seen at a glance in comparable passages from *Life on the Mississippi* and *Huckleberry Finn*:

I had myself called with the four o'clock watch, mornings, for one cannot see too many summer sunrises on the Mississippi. They are enchanting. First, there is the eloquence of silence; for a deep hush broods everywhere. Next, there is the haunting sense of loneliness, isolation, remoteness from the worry and bustle of the world. The dawn creeps in stealthily; the solid walls of black forest soften to gray, and vast stretches of the river open up and reveal themselves; the water is glass-smooth, gives off spectral little wreaths of white mist, there is not the faintest breath of wind, nor stir of leaf; the tranquility is profound and infinitely satisfying. Then a bird pipes up, another follows, and soon the pipings develop into a jubilant riot of music.... When the light has become a little stronger, you have one of the fairest and softest pictures imaginable. You have the intense green of the massed and crowded foliage near by; you see it paling shade by shade in front of you; ... And all this stretch of river is a mirror, and you have the shadowy reflections of the leafage and the curving shores and the receding capes pictured in it. Well, that is all beautiful; soft and rich and beautiful; and when the sun gets well up, and distributes a pink flush here and a powder of gold yonder and a purple haze where it will yield the best effect, you grant that you have seen something that is worth remembering.[3]

In chapter 19, Huck and Jim watch "the daylight come":

Not a sound, anywheres—perfectly still—just like the whole world was asleep, only sometimes the bull-frogs a-cluttering, maybe. The first thing to see, looking away over the water, was a kind of dull line—that was the woods on t'other side—you couldn't make nothing else out; then a pale place in the sky; then more paleness, spreading around; then the river softened up, away off, and warn't black any more, but gray; you could see little dark spots drifting along, ever so far away—trading scows, and such things; and long black streaks—rafts; sometimes you could hear a sweep streaking; or jumbled up voices, it was so still, and sounds come so far; and by and by you could see a streak on the water which you know by the look of the streak that there's a snag there in a swift current which breaks on it and makes that streak look that way; and you see the mist curl up off of the water, and the east reddens up, and the river, and you make out a log cabin in the edge of the woods, away on the bank on t'other side of the river, being a wood-yard, likely, and piled by them cheats so you can throw a dog through it anywheres; then the nice breeze springs up, and comes fanning you from over there, so cool and fresh, and sweet to smell, on account of the woods and the flowers; but sometimes not that way, because they've left dead fish laying around, gars, and such, and they do get pretty rank; and next you've got the full day, and everything smiling in the sun, and the song-birds just going it! (156–57)

Disclosed here are the obvious differences to be expected between a genteel and a vernacular narrator, or more properly between an adult and a child. Twain's passage is deliberate—shaped by rhetorical motive, organized logically in homogenous time and space, varied in diction, consistent in tone, and obedient to the terms of its announced purpose. Descriptive detail corroborates the preordained sentiment; the hushed silence, the creeping mists, the massed color and softening light contribute to, even validate, the "enchantment" of the scene.

Huck's description moves by statement and correction—there is "not a sound," he says, "but only sometimes"; the air is "sweet to smell" but "sometimes" there is a dead gar laying around. There is in Huck's passage the unembarrassed monotony of phrasing—the word *streak* is used three times in the same clause. And Huck dispenses with explanatory remark. Twain's river is a mirror in which are to be found the reflections of wood and shore; but when Huck says "and the east reddens up, and the river" there is no authorial indication that the river reflects the red of the sky, for his world need not answer to the laws of optics. The phenomenon is local to his perception; it would not occur to him that the scene is an "effect." Huck's river at dawn is shifting impressions first and only incidentally a world of objects—the "little dark spots," we are told by way of an appositive, are trading scows; the "dull line," the woods; the "long black streaks," rafts. His world is populated by things, but they don't authorize his experience. And he does not belabor the mental corrections necessary to make such a world.

Twain's description is a "composition," a self-conscious act of language so constructed that we may grant that the scene is "worth remembering." Whether or not his depiction is memorably phrased, it stands as admiration of a natural event whose picturesque existence is independent of his rendering. Huck's scene is merely recalled, and one feels that without his consciousness to sustain it, the world itself might dissolve. For all that, however, Huck's landscape is the more tolerant; it admits the coexistence of the duplicity of cheats and stench of rotting fish with the music of birds. Huck is ever alert to treachery and snare, yet without condemning, he delivers an undiminished natural scene and exults in a privileged moment. Twain, by contrast, aims at a universal sentiment that is tonic relief from the "worry and bustle of the world."

Twain's presence pervades *Huckleberry Finn*, but with few exceptions, he is loyal to the terms of the book and favors Huck's unmediated world of feeling over his own often angry conviction.[4] That is, however strong Twain's own sentiments, he typically recognized that his first artistic responsibility was to a rendering of the authenticity of Huck's adolescent sensibility. The realism of *Huckleberry Finn* is disclosed alternately by the thread of Huck's consciousness, not yet come to full awareness of how fully implicated in events it is, and by the palpable events that seem randomly strung upon it, which is to say by the narrative itself. These are inevitably interwoven, and often tangled, but it is well to take up the teller and the tale separately.

II

One of the things to be observed about the realism of *Huckleberry Finn* is that Huck's voice functions much like Whitman's multivalent "I" in "Song of Myself"—he is the narrator of his chronicle and the author of his book; he is the chief witness of events and, emotionally at least, the principal victim of them; he is ruled and to a degree protected by the laws of the republic and the customs of place, but only accidentally a citizen of and never a voice in the dominant culture that so mystifies him.

Both as "author" and as narrator, Huck typically forgoes representational depiction. He himself has seen the Aunt Sallys of the world before, and he is far less interested in disclosing her character than in dealing with the situation. Huck's own considerable experience in the world (the result of having fended for himself most times, not of playing the detached observer of life), as remarkable as it is regrettable in a fourteen-year-old child, outfits him for his adventures. In this sense, the realism of the quoted passage above, and dozens of others like it, is presupposed in the telling itself.[5] Unlike Ahab, Huck takes the world on its terms, not his own, and experience has taught him how to best navigate its treacheries and to delight in its beauties.

Huck's wary canniness is frequently the source in *Huckleberry Finn* of the sort of narrative detachment so often associated with realist writing; it is also the source of a special pathos. When Huck sees the king and the duke tarred and feathered, men who "didn't look like nothing in the world that was human," he is incapable of hardening himself to their plight. Huck finally concludes, "Human beings can be awful cruel to one another" (290). This familiar scene is moving not because it effectively dramatizes Twain's attitudes toward the damned human race, nor for that matter because it serves as moral pronouncement (these two con men are scalawags through and through and deserve the sort of treatment they at long last receive). Nor, I believe, does it signal Huck's moral development, or as Leo Marx would have it, "a mature blending of his instinctive suspicion of human motives with his capacity for pity."[6] Instead, it is the unlooked for and disquieting revelation, somewhat surprising in a boy as familiar with the world as Huck is, that gives the moment force.

For Huck has witnessed earlier far greater and more disturbing cruelty than this: the murderous treatment of Jim Turner on the *Walter Scott*; the killing of Buck Grangerford, which still troubles his sleep; Boggs's gasping out his last breath under the weight of a family Bible; not to mention the thievery and calculated deceptions of the king and the duke themselves. What he hasn't before recognized, indeed does not fully recognize even as he speaks his sad conclusion, is the universal human condition of cruelty. Nor has he yet developed the righteous, which is to say the "civilized," indignation that would serve as defense against his own spontaneous impulses.

Huck and Tom have no opportunity to help these con men, and they go on home. But Huck is feeling "kind of ornery and humble," not so brash as before, even though he knows he hasn't done anything to cause the event he has just witnessed. Only two chapters earlier, in his famous decision to tear up the letter to Miss Watson and to "go to hell" and to help Jim, Huck's sympathies had prevailed against his training. Twain once observed in reference to a similar internal struggle in chapter 16, that this is a chapter "where a sound heart and a deformed conscience come into collision and conscience suffers defeat." His analogous moral decision in chapter 31 is a temporary triumph, however; as Harold H. Kolb, Jr., has remarked, "Huck never defeats his deformed conscience—it is we [as readers] who do that—he simply ignores it in relation to Jim."[7] When he sees the punished king and duke, however, Huck finds that a conscience, deformed or otherwise, has little to do with whether you do right or wrong or nothing at all. And precisely at that moment conscience moves in on him: "If I had a yaller dog that didn't know no more than a person's conscience, I would pison him. It takes up more room than all the rest of a person's insides, and yet ain't no good, nohow" (290).

Perhaps Huck is never so vulnerable as at this moment. His unwanted recognition, followed hard and fast by voracious conscience, has its inverted equivalent in *Moby-Dick* when Ahab realizes his quest is self-destructive but that he must press on nevertheless, and he drops his tear into the sea. For in Huck's response to the frenzied throng of townspeople exacting their revenge on these rapscallions and the image of the pair who do not look human, he concludes upon the human condition. Ahab is driven by interior impulses that extinguish all "natural" longings and lovings; but Huck, just as relentlessly, and simply by virtue of being alive and growing up, is being drawn into this inhuman, human world.

Robinson Jeffers, in "Shine, Perishing Republic," would have his children keep their distance from the "thickening center" of corruption:

> And boys, be in nothing so moderate as in love of man, a clever
>   servant, insufferable master.
> There is the trap that catches noblest spirits, that caught—they
>   say—God, when he walked the earth.

This is a belated wisdom, reduced to fatherly advice, that, boys being boys, will likely go all unheeded. But Twain (or Huck rather) dramatizes his troubled understanding at the moment of its birth; his conclusion is the unstudied remark, not yet a conviction, no longer a perception. For Huck, corruption has no center but spreads out evenly before him, just as he has left it behind in the wake of his flight; it presents no scrape to be mastered or outlived but the general human condition. And Huck is not yet wise; his insight yields instantly to vague, unaccountable feelings of guilt. And this, too, is a dimension of the realism of the book, for he is a boy more ruled by feeling than sober reflection.

Huckleberry Finn has sometimes been described as a picaresque novel without the picaro. This may be a meaningful statement if our understanding of the genre is qualified by the variations of it Cervantes accomplished in *Don Quixote*, a novel Twain read several times, Tom Sawyer at least once, and Huck not at all. Still, Huck is not quite an idealist, not yet a rogue. His mischievousness is typical of a boy his age, and it is combined with a special, sometimes ridiculous tenderness.

Huck is often capable of pseudomoralizing, citing his Pap as authority for lifting a chicken or borrowing a melon. This is also true when, in chapter 22, he dodges the watchman and dives under the circus tent: "I had my twenty-dollar gold piece and some other money, but I reckoned I better save it.... I ain't opposed to spending money on circuses, when there ain't no other way, but there ain't no use in *wasting* it on them" (191). Once inside, though the audience is hilarious, Huck is "all of a tremble" to see the danger of the drunken horseback rider. When, at length, he recognizes that he has been taken in by this performer, he is so admiring of him and the bully circus itself that he claims if he ever runs across it again, "it can have all of *my* custom, every time" (194).

In this relatively slight episode are compactly blended the multiple functions of Huck as author, character, narrator, and comic device. As author, he tries to make the circus scene vivid to us, but he is not equal to the task. His rendering of the performance is notable for its descriptive flatness. The passages are sprinkled with a few vernacular metaphors, but unlike his disturbing description of his Pap in chapter 5, Huck's language here is indefinite and vague. The men are dressed in their "drawers and undershirts," he says, and the ladies have lovely complexions and are "perfectly beautiful." What is vivid, however, is his faltering speech, his slightly breathless excitement. As narrator, he gropes for adjectives and falls into abstractions and platitudes. Huck is mastered by the spectacle, which is simultaneously his experience and his subject matter. But as boy, he is true to childlike enthusiasm and typically replaces descriptive detail with hyperbolic affidavits of his rapt attention: it was "the splendidest sight that ever was"; the women looked like "real sure-enough queens"; it was a "powerful fine sight"; "I never see anything so lovely"; "they done the most astonishing things" (191–92). At length, he becomes the straight man to his own joke. So pleased is he with the sight that he promises the circus can have his business any time, evidently unaware of the humor of the remark, that his "custom" has in no way damaged his purse.

Huck is worldly wise but never jaded, as this episode dramatizes, but the significance of his pranks are defined less by youthful motive than by the terms of the adventure. The charm of what Neil Schmitz calls his "Huckspeech" (speech "written as spoken, talked into prose")[8] can be, and is, radically redefined by narrative context. There is prankishness involved, for example, when Huck plays his joke on Jim after they have been separated in the fog, but he receives a tongue-lashing that so cuts him that he "humbles himself to a nigger." Huck's manufacture of his own murder in order to escape the potentially lethal abuse of his Pap is grotesque to be sure, but it is highly dramatic too, and Huck regrets that Tom is not handy to throw in "the fancy touches" (41). He laments Tom's absence as well in an episode that is a mixture of romantic escapade and existential urgency when, in chapter 12, he and Jim undertake to save Jim Turner from certain death. The same may be said for his efforts to preserve the Wilks girls' fortune from the hands of the king and the duke.

As humorist Huck is humorless, as hero he is only accidentally heroic, and as narrator he seems never quite to know where to place the accent. He is constitutionally incapable of distilling from his supposed experience either the ultimate conditions or the deeper significance of his adventures. Huck never doubts the existence of the "bad place" and the "good place"; in fact, he believes them to be all that Miss Watson has told him. However, while he can imagine the fires of hell and the monotony of playing harps and singing forever, he scarcely comprehends eternity and has little interest in it. His famous declaration "All right, then, I'll go to hell" (271) is not accompanied with an exclamation point. The statement is matter-of-fact and to be taken literally, for Huck is a literal-minded boy. He is temperamentally suited to the bad place (wickedness is in his line, he says), and he will give up trying to achieve the other place. But his decision is also the resignation of self-acceptance, a declaration, that is, of the acceptance of the world's judgment upon him, not the resolution to abide by some higher moral authority, as is sometimes claimed. It is just this quality that gives the scene its special pathos. Huck is not built right, and the fact that he is social and moral refuse is hardly arguable.

Huck is caught between stern rebuke ("Don't scrunch up like that, Huckleberry"; "Don't gap and stretch like that") and enforced social acceptance ("Pray every day, Huckleberry"; "Chew your food, Huckleberry"). But he remains the same boy the town allowed to sleep in a hogshead, stay away from school, and make do for himself. Caught on the horns of this dilemma, there is nevertheless a strong undercurrent of self-affirmation; Huck is filled with self-recrimination and self-condemnation, but never self-loathing: When Jim is bitten by the rattlesnake, he curses himself as a "fool" for not remembering that the mate was apt to join the dead one he had placed in Jim's blanket; he is sorry for the outcome and his stupidity but not the impulse. Huck devoutly tries to admire Emmeline's poetic "tributes" and drawings because he accepts the Grangerford family faith that she was a saint; he even steals up into her room and browses through her scrapbook when he begins to "sour" on her. He often regrets that Tom Sawyer is not around to throw some style into his plans, but Huck never fully accepts the world's corrections or refusals of him. And this same realistic disclosure of a young boy's self-consciousness, in the hands of Mark Twain, becomes a satirical vehicle as well.

Twain often employs a satirical strategy in Huck that he seems to have observed in himself and to have dramatized in *A Tramp Abroad*. The narrator of that book does not condemn violent alien customs (most particularly the revolting German student duels) but instead curses himself for failing to comprehend the wisdom of received tradition. The same is true of countless occasions in *Huckleberry Finn* where Twain's intent, as opposed to Huck's, is to expose sham, pretense, and outright silliness: Huck is perplexed that the widow makes him "grumble over the victuals" even though there is nothing wrong with them; he takes it on faith that Emmeline Grangerford's pictures are "nice," but they always give him the "fan-tods"; he goes to church with the Grangerfords and hears a sermon about brotherly love and "preforeordestination," and everyone agrees it was a good sermon, and it must be so because, for Huck, it proved to be "one of the roughest Sundays" he had ever run across.

Tom Sawyer variously describes Huck as a lunkhead, an idiot, or a saphead for failing to comprehend the observances required of pirates, robbers, or royalty. Huck never disputes Tom's basic superiority or his own cultural and moral ignorance; after all, Tom is "full of principle" (307). In fact, Huck is flabbergasted that Tom is willing and eager to help him free Jim, and he regrets his own betrayal of his friend for not insisting that he not sink so low:

> Here was a boy that was respectable, and well brung up; and had
> a character to lose; and folks at home that had characters; and he
> was bright and not leatherheaded; and knowing, and not ignorant;
> and not mean, but kind; and yet here he was, without any more
> pride, or rightness, or feeling, than to stoop to this business, and
> make himself a shame, and his family a shame, before everybody.
> I *couldn't* understand it, no way at all. (292–93)

As a realistic portrayal of one boy's concern for another, the statement is touching; as satire, it is deadly—all the more so when we learn that Miss Watson has already freed Jim in her will and that Tom knows it.

Twain once astutely remarked that, unlike *Tom Sawyer*, *Huckleberry Finn* is not a book for boys but for those who used to be boys. It is not altogether clear Twain recognized this distinction at the time of writing the novel, so strong was his identification with his created character, but the instinctive decision to have an unwashed fourteen-year-old outcast tell a story ultimately meant for readers whose own innocence was behind them proved to be an enabling one. As a character or narrative consciousness, Huck is pure possibility—his future casually spreads out before him, luxuriant in meandering adventures and antics, freedom and easiness. But he is doomed as well—for every adult reader knows (though because we are adults we are often reluctant to admit it) that his delightful caginess and high jinks depend less on moral purpose than on youthful energy; his escapes and accommodations are destined to become evasions and compromises in the end.[9] Huck does not know this, he hasn't even considered the issue; but we his grown-up readers do, and every vile specimen of humanity surveyed in this rich cross section of America confirms it. Huckleberry Finn set out to tell a story and did the best he could. By degrees, it became apparent to Mark Twain that the boy was writing a novel.

III

Perhaps *novel* is too narrow a word. In his "Notice," and apparently after some deliberation, Twain chose to describe his book as a "narrative." In any event, the tale Huck tells is all slapdash and Oh, by the way, as mixed up in its way as the king's recitation of Hamlet's soliloquy; the book Twain wrote is another matter.

Huckleberry Finn is a highly episodic book, and the arrangement of episodes observes no incontestable narrative logic. The feud chapters precede rather than follow the Boggs shooting not for self-evident artistic reasons but because we are to suppose that is the order in which Huck lived them. The episodic density of the book thins considerably as the narrative progresses, the last half being dominated by the lost heirs episode and the evasion chapters. But this is not because these events are more important than earlier ones but because in the several-year gestation of the book Twain himself had acquired the capacity to make more of less. That capacity, it is true, sometimes degenerates into artifice and burlesque, as in the strategy to acquire one of Aunt Sally's spoons, but it likewise betrays an author's professionally calculated attitude toward his material. Moreover, Twain had commercial as well as artistic motives impelling him to finish his book; undoubtedly, in the final burst of composition in 1883, he approached his narrative, in part, as a commodity that was too long in production. Besides, he had his own newly formed publishing company ready to print and promote it.

The *reason* some episodes follow others might be more confidently pursued by examining how the novel grew and took shape during the seven years of its intermittent composing. That is a story too complicated to tell here.[10] It is enough to say, perhaps, that Huck Finn, as character and voice, was a metaphor for Twain's mind: through his identification with the boy he might indulge nostalgically in vagrant thoughts and happy recollections, and particularly in the early stages of composition he might satisfy his own desire to escape the cares of a world that was too much with him. And when he was in more aggressive moods, through the satirical latitude Huck's perspective on events permitted him, Twain could deal scathingly with his several hatreds and annoyances—racial bigotry, mob violence, self-righteousness, aristocratic pretense, venality and duplicity, along with several lesser evils. His complaints about these and other matters found their way into Huck's narrative.

W. D. Howells once affectionately complained that he wished Mark Twain might rule his fancy better, and for his part, Twain contributed to the public image of him as a jackleg novelist. However, not since the work of such critics as Gladys Bellamy, Sydney Krause, William Gibson, Walter Blair, Victor Doyno, or Henry Nash Smith, to name only a few, has anyone been able to celebrate Twain's maverick genius at the expense of his literary art. Still, we cannot dismiss out of hand Mark Twain's claim that he merely served as the "amanuensis" to his creative imagination, and in fact on the first page of the manuscript of the novel he gave his book the working title "Huckleberry Finn/Reported by Mark Twain." By the end of the first paragraph, however, even that modest claim seems too much.

From the manuscript we know that Twain had at first begun his tale with "You will not know about me ..." before he fully accepted Huck's ungrammatical authenticity and, with it, all the multiplying implications of the decision. "You don't know about me," Huck begins, "without you have read a book by the name of 'The Adventures of Tom Sawyer.'" Clearly, Mark Twain cannot serve even as the reporter of Huck's narrative, and, besides, he is not to be trusted, for we have it on Huck's authority that he told some "stretchers" in recounting Tom's story. Within the first three sentences, Huck has politely dispensed with "Mr. Mark Twain" and introduced himself as an orphan in more ways than one.

Except perhaps for the opening lines of "Song of Myself," there may be no more audacious beginning to an extended work of the imagination. Mysteriously, we are forced, or rather agree, to assume what Huck assumes, not because we are in the seductive presence of someone afoot with his vision, but because Huck amuses us. He makes us laugh and, later, cry; we want to be with him and to hear him speak. Just as mysteriously, we assume, or rather never ask, how such a book written by a boy could come to be, nor do we require of it even the most fundamental elements of fictional probability.

Even without Kemble's illustration of Huck writing a letter to Mary Jane Wilks in chapter 28, we can easily imagine him in the act of writing itself—squinting one eye, holding his tongue between his teeth, tightly clenching his pencil as he begins to record his adventures. It is somewhat more difficult, however, to imagine when or why Huck tells his story. We know that he has finished it before he lights out for the Territory and that he has presumably spent about as much time writing as it took for Tom's bullet wound to heal. But the only apparent motive he has in the writing is to correct the forgivably exaggerated account of Tom and him that Mark Twain had published as "The Adventures of Tom Sawyer." (It would be out of character for Huck to assume that anyone might actually be interested in his thoughts or exploits.) More perplexing is the fact that Tom Sawyer was published in 1876, but the novel takes place in the 1830s or 1840s, and it never occurs to Huck that he ought to explain this curious discrepancy. It is equally unimaginable that Huck should have lit out for New York instead of the Indian Territory to seek a publisher for the completed manuscript. The very conditions of the fiction that is his book are perhaps the biggest stretcher of all.

It is not for nothing that Twain added the elaborate introductory apparatus to his novel—the heliotype image of him as a frontispiece, sternly presiding over his book; his parenthetical identification of Huck as "Tom Sawyer's Comrade"; his setting of the scene and the time of the novel; his "Notice" and his "Explanatory." These were no doubt, in part, attempts to reassert his own authorial presence in the narrative to follow, but Twain has also rather generously and succinctly made up for some of Huck's literary failings. Huck, after all, never tells us the when or where of this narrative, but Twain does—the Mississippi Valley, forty to fifty years ago. Perhaps Huck did not know, after all, that his story ought to display some interest in motive, plot, or moral, and Twain in his "Notice" somewhat protectively and very authoritatively warns us away from even noting their absence in the narrative. At the same time, in his "Explanatory," Twain calls attention to one of the book's chief virtues, the careful attention to and realistic rendering of dialect. We can imagine Huck straining to parse out a sentence, but we hardly expect him to have taken the same pains Twain did in fashioning the speech of his characters.

Huck's story as novel is impossibility followed by implausibility and linked together by unlikelihood. To give a merely incidental example, when in chapter 17 Huck wakes up after his first night at the Grangerford house, he has forgotten that he is now George Jackson. That much is realistic; the reader, too, is apt to get lost in the dizzying array of Huck's aliases. But Huck tricks Buck into giving the name away:

> "Can you spell, Buck?"
> "Yes," he says.
> "I bet you can't spell my name," says I.
> "I bet you what you dare I can," says he.
> "All right," says I, "go ahead."
> "G-o-r-g-e J-a-x-o-n—there now," he says. (136)

Then Huck privately writes the name down because "somebody might want *me* to spell it, next." One need not be a metafictionist to see the difficulty here. Huck, as narrator, has spelled George Jackson correctly from the beginning, along with any number of other, more difficult names—Harney Shepherdson, Emmeline Grangerford, Lafe Buckner, Silas Phelps, "Henry the Eight," Colonel Sherburn (how Huck was able to sound out *Colonel* is a permanent puzzle). Are we to suppose that in the few months since this exchange with Buck occurred that Huck has undergone some orthographically redemptive experience? My point here is not to indulge in fastidious fault-finding but rather to note that in the course of reading these sorts of questions simply don't come up. The enchantment, the atmosphere of mind, conveyed by Huck's narrative presence is too pleasing, too hypnotic, to permit skepticism. There is considerable magic in the realism of *Huckleberry Finn*.

However improvised and shapeless the boy's narrative is, it nonetheless miraculously coheres almost in spite of itself. More often than not, the plot thickens only to dissolve into another overlapping adventure. We expect Colonel Sherburn to get lynched; but he does not. What really happened to Buck Grangerford; Huck won't tell us. We become interested in the romance of Miss Sophia and Harney Shepherdson, but all we know of their star-crossed love affair is that they got across the river safely. We pity Boggs's sixteen-year-old daughter and ask for revenge; but what we get in her potential hero, Buck Harkness, is a coward and someone looking "tolerable cheap" at that. We hope that the king and duke get their just deserts, but then are made to feel sorry for them when they do. We wish to see the Wilks girls reunited with their money and their nearest kin, but in the climactic scene of this episode the crowd rushes forward to the coffin and Huck takes the opportunity amid the confusion to get away from there, and we, his readers, however much a part of us might want to linger, are willingly drawn after him. The Wilks girls' adventure is abruptly over, and Huck's has acquired new life.

And the two principal plot devices, it turns out, are false leads, Hitchcockean MaGuffins: Huck is fleeing from Pap, but Pap, we learn at last, was the dead man in the floating house thirty-four chapters and several hundred miles ago. Jim is escaping from the dreadful edict of Miss Watson to sell him down the river, but, again, we eventually discover that he had been freed two months earlier in her will. Time and again, the action that enlists our interest is discarded, diverted, or thwarted. In "Chapter the Last" Twain, through several disclosures made by several characters, goes about tying up the loose ends of the story as quickly and efficiently as a calf-roper with the rope clenched between his teeth: Jim owns himself, and his early prophecy that he will be a rich man is fulfilled; Pap is dead, and thus Huck has free use of his six thousand dollars to finance a trip west; Tom is recovered from his bullet wound, and we now know why he had consented to free Jim.

If there is no plot to speak of, there remain nevertheless discernible mythic, structural, and satirical patterns throughout the novel—patterns of flight and absorption, prophecy and fulfillment, retreat and return, death and rebirth, initiation and emergence, repetition and variation. And there are multiple themes and issues as well—of the comic and devastating effects of Christian piety and absurd sentimentality, of obnoxious aristocratic privilege and backwater vulgarity, of marginalization and co-optation, of intuitive sympathy and utilitarian conduct, of inflexible racist bigotry and the dignifying enlargements of open friendship. Then there is the clear advance over and inestimable contribution to the tradition of American humor that is accomplished in the example of the book itself. These patterns, themes, and achievements are certainly "there" within the novel to the extent that criticism and interpretation can make them so, but they would be invisible to Huck and likely hazy to Twain himself. All of them may be comprehended, perhaps, in the insightful remark of Henry Nash Smith: Twain's "technical accomplishment was of course inseparable from the process of discovering new meanings in his material. His development as a writer was a dialectic interplay in which the reach of his imagination imposed a constant strain on his technical resources, and innovations of method in turn opened up new vistas before his imagination."[11]

The four groups of working notes for the novel Twain jotted down between 1879 and 1883 nevertheless reveal that Twain's imaginative reach was at times blind groping. Among other things, Twain considered including in his narrative a Negro sermon, the legend of a Missouri earthquake, a house-raising, a village fire, a hazing, elocution lessons, an encounter with alligators, a quilting bee, a candy-pulling, a temperance lecture, a duel, a lynching, an accidental killing with an "unloaded" gun, an auction, a dog messenger, and (most improbably of all) an elephant given to Huck and Tom so that they might ride around the country and "make no end of trouble."[12] Twain was always tempted by burlesque, of course, and the fact that he resisted the several temptations suggested by this list of creative brainstorms testifies to more than a bit of artistic restraint. However, many have felt he so yielded to his fondness for burlesque in the final evasion episode that he irreparably damaged Huck's integrity and credibility, subjected Jim to a series of unnecessary degradations, subverted the terms of Huck and Jim's friendship he had so patiently developed, and ultimately betrayed his reader's confidence.

That is an issue individual readers will decide, but the working notes indicate at least the range of possibilities Huck's adventures suggested to the author, a range so vast as to become arbitrary. The only requirements of his then developing narrative, it seems, were that Huck should have been the witness to the events, or to a recitation of them by another, and that Huck narrate them. This is merely to say that Twain banked on the realism of a literary manner over and above the realism of subject matter. Any and all of the events recorded in his working notes conceivably could have happened along the Mississippi, of course, but they indicate no definite narrative direction. And many episodes he did dramatize are no less adventitious than those he contemplated. After all, he did choose to include witch pies and rope ladders, hidden treasure and secret tattoos, sideshows and soliloquies, feuds and romances, ghost stories and fistfights. And as palpable as the river is in the book, it is absolutely incredible that a runaway slave should be trying to get to Canada on its current.

If Twain did not in every instance manage to rule his fancy, he does seem to have tried to coordinate the several products of it. The most obvious example of this sort of artistic management is in the telling juxtaposition of the Boggs shooting with the drunken bareback rider at the circus. In the first episode, the actual physical suffering of Boggs and the emotional grief of his daughter are mixed with the sham of pious sentiment and the predictably perverse fascination of the townspeople, who shove each other aside to get a good look at a dying man. At the circus, Huck's worrying over the supposed drunk is sincere, but the man's peril is merely show business. There are other paired episodes or details as well: the actual deafness of Jim's daughter and the deaf-and-dumb hoax of the duke; the real rattlesnake on Jackson's Island that bites Jim and the garter snakes with buttons tied to their tails in the shed at the Phelps farm; Huck's captivity in his Pap's cabin and the gruesomely imagined evidence of his invented murder, and Jim's captivity in the shed on the Phelps farm and the ridiculous traces of Tom's romantic prescriptions that convince the townsfolk that Jim is a raving lunatic; Huck's efficient attempts to save Jim Turner aboard the *Walter Scott* and Tom's embroidered and leisurely efforts to rescue Jim in the evasion episode. Each of these correspondences, and others as well, mark with deadly satirical effect the difference between realistic urgency and contrived hoax. They also mark how artfully Twain blended the two.

Many of the characters and episodes in *Huckleberry Finn* can be explained as inspired narrative twists that keep the plot moving along, broaden the range of Huck and Jim's adventures, and permit the author to indulge in such imaginative improvisation as might occur to him. The most important of these are the introduction of the king and duke in chapter 19 and the reemergence of Tom Sawyer in chapter 33. When Twain allowed the king and duke to commandeer the raft, he violated the sanctity of the craft and the river itself. But it was also an enabling move, for now his characters could travel in daylight and the author could survey in freer fashion the manners and language of life along the river. The maneuver also helped explain away the difficulty of moving an escaped slave into the Deep South, since Huck and Jim now have considerably less say in events. The fantastic reintroduction of Tom Sawyer, who suddenly becomes the superintendent of affairs and relaxes the deadly serious consequences of Huck's decision in chapter 31 to help Jim, turned Huck's experiences and commitment into disappointingly fanciful pranks. But at least it provided a strategy, however improbable, for concluding a book that might have drifted along forever.

Huckleberry Finn was published in England in 1884; coincidentally, Henry James published his famous essay "The Art of Fiction" the same year. Twain's novel passes most of the tests for the art of the novel that James proposes there—that it be interesting, that it represent life and give the very "atmosphere of mind" in contact with experience, that it "catch the color, the relief, the expression, the surface, the substance of the human spectacle." It also happens to fulfill the requirements of some critics and the expectations of many readers that James holds up for skeptical scrutiny—that it have a "happy ending," that it be full of incident and movement, that it have an obvious moral purpose. Coincidentally, too, James compares in the same essay two novels he had at the time been reading—Robert Louis Stevenson's *Treasure Island* and Edmond de Goncourt's *Chérie*. The first, he notes, "treats of murders, mysteries, islands of dreadful renown, hairbreadth escapes, miraculous coincidences, and buried doubloons"; the second seeks to trace "the development of the moral consciousness of a child." James approves of Stevenson's novel because it achieves what it attempts, whereas De Goncourt's, in his estimation, does not. James probably did not imagine, even as he struck the comparison, that any writer, much less an American writer, might effectively fuse both attempts in a single project, but he certainly would have approved the attempt.

Not that Twain would have given a fig for James's approval. In such matters, W. D. Howells was Twain's admired comrade, as Hawthorne was Melville's. Even so, after Twain had finished his novel and was making revisions, he wrote Howells with a certain petulant self-confidence that he, at least, was happy with the result: "And *I* shall *like* it, whether anybody else does or not." Melville's summary remark to Hawthorne upon the achievement of *Moby-Dick*, to risk one final comparison, is similarly defiant: "I have written a wicked book, and feel spotless as a lamb." The wickedness of *Huckleberry Finn* is not the wickedness of *Moby-Dick*, of course, but it is the sort one might expect of Huck Finn, and maybe Mark Twain. For Huck had been brought up to it, and the rendering of it was right in Twain's line.

NOTES

1. "Mark Twain, 'Realism,' and *Huckleberry Finn*," in *New Essays on "Huckleberry Finn,"* ed. Louis J. Budd (Cambridge: Cambridge University Press, 1985), 35–59.

2. *Life on the Mississippi* (New York: Viking Penguin, 1986), 228–29.

3. Ibid.

4. Twain does speak his own mind from time to time—most obviously when he has Colonel Sherburn scold the mob in chapter 22, and perhaps most interestingly when he chooses to speak through Jim about the benefits of industry and progress in parts of chapter 14.

5. Shaped as he is by experience, however, Huck remains innocent in an important way. Unlike Colonel Sherburn, say, who has traveled in the North and lived in the South and is therefore able to proclaim on the cowardice of the "average" man (190), Huck's perspective has not frozen into an attitude. Not only is the narrative point of view of this novel presexual, as has so often been observed, but it is also prepolitical, even preideological. Huck, in his efforts to help Jim, may worry that he may become a "low-down Abolitionist," but the quality of that anxiety is rather more like a thousand childhood myths—e.g., the worry children have that, having made an ugly face, it will "stick."

6. "Mr. Eliot, Mr. Trilling, and Huckleberry Finn," *The American Scholar* 22 (Autumn 1953): 423–40.

7. Twain, quoted in Walter Blair, *Mark Twain and Huck Finn* (Berkeley and Los Angeles: University of California Press, 1960), 143; Kolb, "Mark Twain, Huck Finn, and Jacob Blivens: Gilt-Edged, Tree-Calf Morality in the *Adventures of Huckleberry Finn*," *The Virginia Quarterly Review* 55 (Autumn 1979): 658.

8. *Of Huck and Alice: Humorous Writing in American Literature* (Minneapolis: University of Minnesota Press, 1983), 96.

9. Twain knew this, too; in a cranky moment, he predicted that Huck would grow up to be just as low-down and mean as his Pap.

10. Walter Blair and, more recently, Victor A. Doyno have provided us with full and perceptive book-length studies of the evolution of the novel. See Blair, *Mark Twain and Huck Finn*, and Doyno, *Writing Huck Finn: Mark Twain's Creative Process* (Philadelphia: University of Pennsylvania Press, 1991).

11. *Mark Twain: The Development of a Writer* (Cambridge: Harvard University Press, 1962), 113.

12. The working notes for *Huckleberry Finn* are reproduced in the California-Iowa edition of the novel, 711–61.

HARRY G. SEGAL

Life Without Father:
The Role of the Paternal in the
Opening Chapters of Huckleberry Finn

Critics have argued for generations about the failure of the ending of *Huckleberry Finn*. Ernest Hemingway began the debate by characterizing the escapades at Silas Phelps' farm as "cheating"; his statement was soon followed by rhetorical volleys between Eliot, Trilling, Marx, and others whose writings, taken together, form a miniature canon all their own.[1] While the ending has been variously defended on formal, political, aesthetic, and moral grounds, the very presence of a debate sustained for more than sixty years bears witness to the "problem" of those closing chapters. Perhaps the most simple, and ultimately unanswerable, criticism of the ending is that the characters have grown inexplicably younger—that is, they appear to behave in ways which disregard or "undo" their earlier, more maturing experiences. It seems inconceivable that Huck would go along so easily with Tom's *Count of Monte Cristo* escapades after witnessing the Grangerfords' feud, just as Jim's childlike acquiescence to the escape plan cannot be reconciled with the wisdom and dignity he had earlier shown as Huck's surrogate parent. Despite the ingenuity of even the most brilliant supporters, no reading can provide the characters in the closing chapters with those psychological qualities they so palpably lack; instead, supporters are left in the more awkward position of arguing that the failure of the ending constitutes an ironic success.

From *Journal of American Studies* 27, no. 1 (April 1993), pp. 19–33. © 1993 by Cambridge University Press.

This essay is not intended as a late entry into the long-standing debate. Rather than justifying or attacking the constricted conventionality of the novel's ending, what follows is an explanation of why it occurs. I begin with this observation: the superficiality of the book's close does not abruptly follow an otherwise serious novel. Critics have been so distracted by the unsatisfying ending that they have failed to note that *Huckleberry Finn* begins with a series of evocative, dreamlike chapters which begins to give way to Twain's more conventional parodies of Southern society long before Huck is taken for Tom by Aunt Polly. This shift starts with the death of the Grangerfords and the arrival of the King and the Duke—from there the narrative unevenly divests itself of emotional resonance before culminating in the flat, parodic tone of the final chapters. In contrast, the most powerful passages of the novel may be found in the opening sequences where Huck awaits the arrival of his father, escapes him, and rushes off in a blaze of ambivalence with his alternate father, Jim. I believe the one is an avoidant answer to the other; that is, the difficulties of the novel's ending may be explained as a reaction to the depth of its beginning.

The novel's opening invokes a broad range of formal and psychological issues by its juxtaposition of character and novelist, fiction and reality, and ultimately, that of father and son. Huck's competitive relationship with "Mark Twain," his response to the sighting of pap's "corpse," and his flight to Judge Thatcher and Jim after recognizing pap's footprints, may be read together as a depiction of a son's turbulent struggle against intimacy with a threatening father. I will argue that the process of writing those beginning chapters, often interrupted by writing blocks, revealed to Twain, consciously or unconsciously, his disturbing issues of selfhood and fatherhood which thus made inevitable the ultimate emptying of the closing chapters. In addition, this relationship between Twain and the writing of his text is *itself* a subject of the images and tropes of Huck's early adventures; as the opening chapters turn on struggles with the father, they form, at the same time, a self-conscious commentary on how those struggles come into narrative being.

Implicit in such an explanation of the novel's structure is a psychodynamic model of the creative process which assumes that as authors free associate characters and endings, they gain momentary glimpses of the unconscious issues represented in their fiction. Since authors are always readers of their emerging text, they are continuously faced with the choice of pursuing unconscious feelings and memories evoked by the actions and experience of their characters or of moving onto "safer" narrative ground by choosing to avoid the emotionally-laden material. (They can do this by writing something psychologically neutral, and thus often uninteresting, or through the more neurotic compromise of the writing block.) I refer to analysis of this process as "psychoformalism" because it proposes that a literary work is itself a record of the dialogic relationship between writer and text—between *psyche* and form.[2]

When Huckleberry Finn first addresses the readers in his beguiling and provocative opening paragraph, he immediately confounds their understanding of who he is. By saying he has read *The Adventures of Tom Sawyer* and has an opinion about its worth, Finn suggests there is a fictional Huck who should not be confused with the real one. In fact, he strongly implies that the fictional Huck is irrelevant.

> You don't know about me, without you have read a book by the name of "The Adventures of Tom Sawyer," but that ain't no matter.[3] (p. 1).

This opening sentence may be read in two ways. It says that it doesn't matter if we have heard of Huck through *Tom Sawyer* or, taken literally, that *Tom Sawyer* doesn't matter. In either case, Finn's position on the other novel could not be more clear: knowing *The Adventures of Tom Sawyer* is not a prerequisite for reading *The Adventures of Huckleberry Finn*.

The emergence of Huck Finn the narrator has long been of interest to critics. Henry Nash Smith argued that the vernacular first person inadvertently led Twain to the creation of a tragic character, while Alan Trachtenberg believes that Huck is trapped by his author's need to use him as a comical figure.[4] Trachtenberg compares Huck's enslavement to Twain's satiric intentions with Jim's search for political freedom and insists that the novel's attack on society required that Huck remain undeveloped." Huck's character is stunted by his creator's need for him to serve as a technical device. The same devices of irony which liberate the reader by instructing him about civilization and human nature also repress Huck by using him" (p. 969). The opposed readings of Trachtenberg and Smith form, paradoxically, a continuum of discontinuity; namely, that Huck does "deepen" as a tragic character in the novel's opening and is indeed transformed into a "technical device" long before the ending of the novel.[5] I propose that Huck's inconsistent voice, at times deeply "autonomous" while at others mechanical and contrived, has to do with his role as narrator-heir to Mark Twain. By turning the fictional Huck into a fictionally "real" person who has read Tom Sawyer and hopes to improve on its quality, Twain unconsciously evoked the struggle between father and son which dominates the tropes and language of the novel's opening. Consider Huck's critique of *Tom Sawyer*:

That book was made by Mr. Mark Twain, and he told the truth, mainly. There was things which he stretched, but mainly he told the truth. That is nothing. I never seen anybody but lied, one time or another, without it was Aunt Polly—Tom's Aunt Polly, she is—and Mary, and the Widow Douglas, is all told about in that book—which is mostly a true book; with some stretchers, as I said before. (p. 1)

It is a powerful comma which separates "he told the truth" and "mainly" in the first sentence, for its pause implies that Twain is a liar. Finn may not condemn the famous author openly, but his contempt is never far from the surface. He forgives Twain by saying, "I never seen anybody but lied, one time or another," yet he twice makes it clear that Twain lied *often* in his narrative: there were "things which he stretched." It was "mostly a true book ... with some stretchers." This opening offers a stark contrast to *Tom Sawyer*. That novel began with an idyllic portrait of the Missouri town told by a benevolent narrator; Finn begins his book by attacking an established author.

This playful competition between Finn and Twain contains an unconscious rivalry between father and son—a rivalry implicit in Huck's attempt to write a sequel. One of the most problematic of artistic challenges, the sequel is a paradox because of the inherent demands on its form. A sequel must share some of the qualities of the first work without repeating them, extend the first work without violating its premises, and it must be good or better. In this way, the sequel is an escalation of the usual struggle for rhetorical identity—instead of evolving from an established genre while retaining some of its features as all first texts do, the sequel has a specific antecedent for which it must be simultaneously "self" and "other." This can be seen in the opening stance of *Huckleberry Finn*. A character born in work one (self) now introduces work two (other) and insists that work one is irrelevant. Even the vocabulary of those first two paragraphs points to the rhetorical dilemma. Finn says that Twain told the truth "mainly," except for some "stretchers." The question is which text is the "main one," and how can an author "stretch" it into a sequel?

Harold Bloom believes every creative act to be a battle between ambitious son-poets and canonical father-texts, yet there is an even closer relation between the writing of a sequel and oedipal phase anxiety.[6] A "strong" poet, according to Bloom, misreads earlier poems so as to achieve difference; an author writing a sequel must achieve differences *and* resemblance. Psychoanalytic accounts of adolescent development may be of use here.[7] The children who accommodate oedipal phase anxiety most successfully emerge neither as copies of their same-sex parents nor as opposite versions of them; instead, they enjoy resembling the parent in some ways while taking pride in the strengths which are theirs alone. This erewhonian version of the healthy oedipal child, found primarily in textbooks, encompasses the broadest definition of the word *success*. For such a child, the values and talents of her parents are not the only qualities she internalizes—her success may resemble her family's, but it will reflect her own culmination of insight and experience. This paradox of originality—that something is original because it treats inherited material in an original way—is reflected in the paradoxical meanings of *success*. Derived from the Latin *sequor, to follow*, *success* literally means something that succeeds something else, while our contemporary understanding of *success* implies if not an original event, at least one that is self-sufficient and enduring. The essence of the oedipal struggle dwells in these opposed meanings, for the successful child is always a successor. Since *sequel* is derived from *sequor*, it signifies a form where the dialectical meanings of *success* are equally immanent. To succeed is to follow; to follow a successful work with another is to write a sequel.

Since it is an expression of both meanings of *success*, the sequel is always about the oedipal struggle. Or put another way, sequels are always about being a sequel. To consider some examples, *Antony and Cleopatra* is a sequel to *Julius Caesar* and one of its principal themes is Antony's role, inherited from his "father" Caesar, of being Cleopatra's lover. In the second volume of *Don Quixote*, Cervantes' knight is no longer the foolish son struggling to join the long lost world of his chivalric fathers but has gained, instead, an obsolete dignity and even, at times, paternal wisdom.[8] (It is also, wonderfully, an attack on the false sequels published after his brilliant first novel.) *The Odyssey* begins with the plight of Telemachus and his need to protect his mother from suitors who carry the projections of his own desires. And perhaps the most dramatic example is the *New Testament* which, as an appendix to the *Old Testament*, describes Christ's oedipal relationship with God—Jesus, both Son and Father, embodies the Hebrew laws yet irrevocably changes them. So Finn's opening attack on Mark Twain should not be a surprise; it is an inspired announcement that a sequel has begun.[9]

The tension between first text and sequel, Huck Finn and Mark Twain, is nowhere more clear than in the content of Huck's accusation: he calls Mark Twain a liar. By doing so, he implies that his novel will be true while the last novel was false—yet his readers soon learn that Huckleberry Finn is perhaps the most accomplished liar in American literature. This is an evocative contradiction. The accusation suggests that this book will correct *Tom Sawyer* and reveal those characters as they truly are. However, the ironic narrator who claims to tell the truth while admitting that he tells falsehoods complicates his relationship with the reader. Like Iago who lies to the audience in his asides, Finn's compromised reliability leaves his text open to post-structuralist inquiries: are there fictional truths? are there truthful fictions? Finally, the taste for lying which Huck shares with Twain also returns us to the nature of the sequel, for here the son actively denies his obvious resemblance to the father.

A sequel is ultimately a response, and not an initial statement, if only by virtue of its successor status. If a first novel is defensively optimistic and happy, a place where mothers adopt stray boys and ideal fathers make them their proteges, then one can expect a second novel featuring the same landscape to undo those defenses in the services of difference—it may even present a world without kind mothers, where ideal fathers are powerless. While this paradigm is necessarily reductive, it provides a way into *Huckleberry Finn*. To start this search for difference, the St. Petersburg of Huck's novel is not the same one found in *The Adventures of Tom Sawyer*. The ultimately benevolent town in the first novel, conveyed through literary cliches, has been replaced by a less cohesive, less protective one. Its citizens may bear the same names, but they and their society are different. The saviour-mother of the first book, the Widow Douglas, is now a neglectful woman who grumbles over her meals and gives charge of Huckleberry over to her insensitive sister, Miss Watson. Tom Sawyer, who showed only moments of arrogance in the earlier text, is now openly contemptuous of Huck's "ignorance" and calls him a "numskull." These changes prove false the suggestion implicit in the ending of *Tom Sawyer* that society would save Huck. This St. Petersburg is not the nostalgic vision of the sleepy, antebellum South capable of rescuing the child in its readers; it is instead a sinister place where violence and isolation are ever present.

> I set down in a chair by the window and tried to think of something cheerful, but it warn't no use. I felt so lonesome I most wished I was dead. The stars was shining, and the leaves rustled in the woods ever so mournful; and I heard an owl, away off, who-whooing about somebody that was dead, and a whippowill and a dog crying about somebody that was going to die; and the wind was trying to whisper something to me and I couldn't make out what it was ... Then away out in the woods I heard that kind of a sound that a ghost makes when it wants to tell about something that's on its mind and can't make itself understood, and so can't rest easy in the grave and has to go about that way every night grieving. (p. 4)

This oft-quoted passage is the novel's first chapters in miniature, for it captures Huck's surreal isolation. Like moments in an unsettling dream, the boy hears vague messages of death but cannot answer back. Huck is, here and throughout, a witness to loss, and his testimony of the night casts his readers as fellow witnesses. For just as Huck cannot answer the ghost who "can't make itself understood," neither can we, locked on our side of the text, answer Huck.

Not only is the tone and location of this sequel different from its first text, it has a new psychological focus. In *Tom Sawyer*, Huckleberry Finn escorts Tom to nocturnal landscapes where father corpses are buried and exhumed, and where digging underground leads momentarily to unconscious wishes and fears. Those excursions were a side effect of Tom's gathering success: growing more powerful meant occasional confrontations with his urge to beat the father and his fear of paternal reprisal. In this work, the nocturnal landscape and confrontation with fathers are primary events; they overwhelm and dominate the daylit world. Thus, an understanding of the nature of the sequel reveals the psychoformal pressures on *The Adventures of Huckleberry Finn, Tom Sawyer's Comrade*. As a sequel, it must be about oedipal struggle; as a sequel to *Tom Sawyer*, a work which moved away from unconscious issues, this novel must move towards them; specifically, Huck must face that father in the graveyard from whom Tom Sawyer escaped to the idealized figure of Judge Thatcher. While these reversals have enormous consequences, their aggregate effect is this: since Huck Finn held back the world of the unconscious in *Tom Sawyer*, his sequel will dwell there.[10]

The unconscious of the novel is nowhere more apparent than when Huck first mentions his biological father. Ironically (or perhaps predictably), this first news of pap is an exaggerated account of his death, and yet pap's effect on his son and on the text is so powerful that even a false report about him intensifies the mood and structure of the early chapters.

> Well, about this time he was found in the river drowned, about twelve mile above town ... They judged it was him, anyway; said this drowned man was just his size and was ragged, and had uncommon long hair—which was all like pap—but they couldn't make nothing out of the face at all. They said he was floating on his back in the water. They took him and buried him on the bank. But I warn't comfortable for long, because I happened to think of something. I knowed mighty well that a drownded man won't float on his back, but on his face. So I knowed, then, that this warn't pap, but a woman dressed *up* in a man's clothes. (p. 14)

An analysis of this passage reveals pap's tremendous impact, for Huck's explanation raises more questions than it answers. If the floating corpse was a woman, why didn't anyone say so? Why does Huck so calmly present his theory without wondering why a woman would be dressed in man's clothes? But Huck's speculation is most intriguing, however, because it foreshadows his return trip to St. Petersburg dressed as a girl in a dress which he and Jim find next to the dead body of pap. This circling of the future into the present, as well as a face that cannot be recognized and a father who may be a woman, evoke the consciousness of dreaming where events and qualities are layered with echoes of alternate events and qualities. When critics have described *Tom Sawyer* as a dream of boyhood, they mean literary dreaminess—a nostalgic idealized landscape descended from Romance. True to the nature of the sequel which must be similar and different from its first text, the landscape of *Huckleberry Finn* is dreamlike in another way: it resembles psychological dreams where identity, impulse and action are neither fixed nor separate.[11]

The false report of pap's death may be a good example of a passage informed by dream logic (or primary process thinking), but it is one of a limited number. The dreamscape is an unstable part of this novel, one clearly difficult to sustain. While the last chapters of *Huckleberry Finn* fail because of the utter lack of unconscious depth so present in the beginning chapters, even the dreamscape of the novel's opening ebbs and flows like an unconscious tide, drawn, to fulfill the simile, by the waxing and waning of Huck's father. This tentative yet repercussive interchange between the novel's reality and its psychological issues may best be understood by analyzing the sequence of events following the first signs of pap's return.

> There was an inch of snow on the ground, and I seen somebody's tracks. They had come up from the quarry and stood around the stile a while, and then went on around the garden fence. It was funny they hadn't come in, after standing around so. I couldn't make it out. It was very curious, somehow. I didn't notice anything at first, but next I did. There was a cross in the left boot-heel with big nails, to keep off the devil. (p. 19)

By not sharing with the reader until several scenes later what that cross in the left boot heel meant—namely, that the tracks belong to his father—Huck's description adds suspense to the narrative. Aside from piquing the reader's interest, omitting the name of the early morning stalker also blurs his identity and allows his tracks to evoke a host of possibilities. Consider the second sentence: "*they* had come up from the quarry ..." Huck's persistent use of the third person plural only emphasizes the multiple referents of the pronoun. It suggests that there are many fathers who could be circling his house, and in a narrative where Huck adopts a series of men to father him, his use of "they" takes on a proleptic quality. Besides foreshadowing events in the narrative, this passage also harkens back to the false report of pap's death. That "they" have come "up from the quarry" sounds as though people have come up from underground or up from the grave, while the crossing of the fence suggests a return from the underworld. Within the passage, therefore, the wish that his father were dead is combined with the wish that he return.

Huck immediately responds to the sighting of his father's footprints by rushing to Judge Thatcher, the ideal father of Tom Sawyer, for help. In an exchange noted by one critic for its ambiguous treatment of Thatcher, Huck tries to give him his money.[12]

> He says:
> "Well I'm puzzled. Is something the matter?"
> "Please take it," says I, "and don't ask me nothing—then I won't have to tell no lies."
> He studied a while, and then he says:
> "Oho-o. I think I see. You want to sell all your property to me—not give it. That's the correct idea."
> Then he wrote something on a piece of paper and read it over and says:
> "There—you see it says 'for a consideration.' That means I have bought it of you and paid you for it. Here's a dollar for you. Now you sign it." (pp. 19–20)

A close look at this scene shows that Huck has not come to the Judge for help. Quite to the contrary, instead of telling him what happened Huck remains silent and insists that Thatcher take his gold. Although Huck never tells the reader why he does this, one plausible explanation is that he wishes to keep the money and assumes that his father will have a more difficult time getting it away from an adult than from a child. If so, by using him as an obstacle the boy has set up the Judge as effectively as any professional con man. And while his entrapment of Thatcher may seem unwarranted, the Judge's reaction appears to justify Huck's expectations of him. Like all good cons, success depends upon the greed of the mark. Although he returns Huck's money at the end of the novel, there is no suggestion in the present passage that Thatcher intends to do so. "He studied a while," Huck writes, and then says "Oho-o ... You want to *sell* all your property to me ... not give it." The King or the Duke would have been worthy of 'studying' for a moment before coming up with a discrimination as sophistical as that between giving away cash and selling it for a dollar ("That's the correct idea"). From a man looked up to as a god by the townspeople in *Tom Sawyer* to a lawyer contemplating taking money from a child in *Huckleberry Finn*, Thatcher sounds like a con man, too. In this sequel, ideal fathers are no longer ideal.

Huck's encounter with paternal figures does not stop with the Judge, for in the very next scene he seeks out a third and more welcoming father; he goes to Jim with the hope that Jim's hairball, "taken from the fourth stomach of an ox," might tell him something about pap. After trying to get it to roll on the floor, Jim announces that the hairball "sometimes wouldn't talk without money."

> I told him I had an old slick counterfeit quarter that warn't no good because the brass showed through the silver a little, and it wouldn't pass nohow, even if the brass didn't show, because it was so slick it felt greasy and so that it would tell on it every time. (I reckoned I wouldn't say nothing about the dollar I got from the judge.) I said it was pretty bad money, but maybe the hairball would take it, because maybe it wouldn't know the difference. Jim smelt it, and bit it, and rubbed it, and said he would manage so the hairball would think it was good. He said he would split open a raw Irish potato and stick the quarter in between and keep it there all night, and next morning you couldn't see no brass, and it wouldn't feel greasy no more, and so anybody in town would take it in a minute, let alone a hairball. (p. 21)

In its structure this scene is, literally, a new version of Huck's exchange with Judge Thatcher, but one sporting several important changes. In both instances the boy has gone to an older man for help and the man has charged him for services rendered. Yet in the second version, man and boy have found more trustworthy partners. Huck apparently feels comfortable enough to confide in Jim the signs of pap's imminent arrival, just as Jim generously lowers his price and accepts the false quarter for payment. (Of course, the exchange is not without an undertone of struggle: Jim still claims the hairball needs money, while Huck "reckoned" he wouldn't say anything about the dollar given him by the Judge.)

As a new version of the Thatcher meeting, Huck's scene with Jim serves as a reading of the earlier one. The central image of the "old counterfeit quarter that warn't no good" may be understood as representing the "counterfeit" transaction with the Judge (and by metonymy the coming relationship with pap). As the better father, Jim's remedy for the brass quarter is both magical and suggestive: the "raw Irish potato" will be "split open," and the quarter placed between the two halves and kept there "all night." This process, a kind of Missouri alchemy, strongly implies that father relationships, so fraught with fear and loathing, can be changed into something of value. That is, a more peaceful intimacy—such as floating down the Mississippi on a raft—may transform something "counterfeit" and violent into something real. Such a transformation needs a magic spell or, to decode the metaphor, it requires the unique range of literary form which can contain and generate a progressively redemptive series of fathers.

Still, solving the problem of the bad father is not as simple as merely moving from pap to Thatcher to Jim. If the "cure" for the quarter is examined more closely, it seems to cause as many problems as it is meant to solve. The potato is cut into two pieces and then put back together, suggesting a primitive scheme of identity where self and other are aspects of each other, where two selves forming a symbiotic whole are constantly split apart and rejoined. (This neatly predicts Huck's life with pap in the cabin.) It would appear, then, that for this text getting close to a good father is terrifying because it evokes, among other deep memories and wishes, the earlier, violent symbiosis. This explains why the loving relationship between Huck and Jim, forever strained by Huck's social guilt, is continually interrupted by arbitrary twists in the plot as well as by long writing blocks suffered by Mark Twain. Even the magic spell itself betrays the possibility of a real reconciliation with the father because the cure is ultimately cosmetic. After a night between the pieces of potato, the quarter will still be "bad money"—it will only seem genuine.

Since the sighting of the footprints, the meeting with Thatcher, and the conference with Jim are all about the psychological consequences of the father's approach, these scenes may also be read as a commentary on Huck's relationship with Mark Twain. Finn begins his narrative, after all, by challenging Twain, and the nature of the sequel, oedipal in form, makes a compelling case for considering Twain as an aspect of pap.

> There was an inch of snow on the ground, and I seen somebody's tracks. They bad come up from the quarry and stood around the stile a while, and then went on around the garden fence. It was funny they hadn't come in, after standing around so. I couldn't make it out.

Twain is present in a generalized way through the topology of this passage. It suggests a diagram of the creative process, with the idea or inspiration "coming up" from the imagination only to be shaped by "stile" and narrative limits, represented by the garden fences. (There is even a lingering pun in *quarry*, considering that Twain 'mined' his childhood for his fiction.[13]) To bring the creator directly into this metaphor of his writing process, let us assume that it is Twain himself who has come up from the quarry, who has encountered Huck's "stile," and who has circled the house without entering. Although Huck puzzles over why "they" hadn't come in, the answer may not be as mysterious as he thinks. If Twain had come into the house, then Huck would not have remained the narrator of *Huckleberry Finn*. Instead, the unentered house represents the "otherness" of the narrative, while its closed doors emphasize the distance between fiction and its author. The tracks in the snow, which showed that the man "stood around" for a long time, foreshadow the long eight years Twain will struggle to finish this disturbing narrative that he often tried to "pigeonhole" and once threatened to burn. The tracks show him circling his house of fiction and seeing within alien figurations which had emerged, somehow, from the dark passages of his quarry.

This circling of Huck by Twain, representing the inherent struggle of writing a sequel, is also figured within Jim's alchemical treatment of Huck's counterfeit quarter. This "bad money" that "wouldn't pass nohow ... because it was so slick it felt greasy and so that it would tell on it every time" stands for the dubious second text that must somehow pass for the original. Compromised by a first text written in an irretrievable confluence of imagination and recollection, and which may now seem foreign to him despite its faintly familiar strength, the author must coin a new text in the image of the older one. Cutting the potato in two symbolizes Twain's solution: there will be a second narrator, and a set of fathers to replace Judge Thatcher, and a new story that will, at least in its opening chapters, reveal the depths of unconscious feelings merely hinted at in the dark underground moments of *Tom Sawyer*. Keep that quarter "there all night," after a night of dreaming perhaps, and "anybody in town would take it in a minute."

The psychological price exacted for launching an alter ego narrator who claims, as textual material, narrative ground repressed in your first novel, is the rich but unsettled disorganization of poorly defended feelings so vividly represented by the floating female body of pap and his subsequent resurrection. As the historic controversy over the Phelps Farm escape sequence suggests, the unconscious depth claimed by the new author, Huck Finn, is only sustained until the old author, threatened finally by the reflection of his own aggression and longing for the father, hastens to restore to his novel the parodies, satires, and other literary devices which served him so well as a journalist and which ultimately take from *Huckleberry Finn* the temporary majesty of its opening chapters. The ending represents a desperate attempt to return to *The Adventures of Tom Sawyer*, to evade feelings conjured by the writing of its sequel; the claustrophobic quality and emotional vacancy of the Phelps Farm escape sequence suggests Twain succeeded in making his own escape.

After leaving Jim's consultation with the hairball, Huck walks home only to find his father waiting in his bedroom. It is not long after that pap wins custody of him, sues Thatcher for the money, and takes Huck away to a small cabin where he regularly beats him. The description of life in that cabin is perhaps the most powerful and dreamlike scene in the novel because it is the final and most prolonged encounter between son and father. Yet as we have seen, before it happens the tropes, images and events of the narrative seem preoccupied with it; it is as if the time with pap in the cabin left a proleptic impression on the narrative leading up to it. The coming relationship with pap exerts this influence because life without father is impossible for *Huckleberry Finn*; both Huck and his narrative are constituted by the race from and inevitable attraction to the paternal. This may be glimpsed nowhere more keenly than in this last look at Huck's discovering of his father's footprints:

> I didn't notice anything at first, but next I did. There was a cross in the left boot-heel with big nails, to keep off the devil.

The novel's collision of form and psychological force is so monolithic that its repercussions threaten to break the very frame of the text—for the cross placed in pap's left boot-heel, designed to "keep off the devil," shows that even the father of the narrative is running from a father.

NOTES

1. The series of essays about the ending of *Huckleberry Finn* have been referenced as a group many times and may be found collected in several critical anthologies as well as in an appendix to Norton's annotated edition of the novel. The following footnote is excerpted from "Mark Twain, 'Realism,' and *Huckleberry Finn*" in Louis Budd, ed., *New Essays on Huckleberry Finn* (Cambridge: Cambridge University Press, 1985):

> The *locus classicus* of the stand-off between proponents of the humorous and serious Twains is the famous debate about the ending ... beginning with Ernest Hemingway's declaration that "if you read it you must stop where the Nigger Jim is stolen from the boys. This is the real end. The rest is just cheating" (*Green Hills of Africa* [New York: Scribner's, 1935], p. 22). Leo Marx argues that the burlesque ending betrays the serious implications of the novel in "Mr. Eliot, Mr. Trilling and *Huckleberry Finn*," *American Scholar* 22 (1953): 423–40. His targets, on the basis of equally serious readings of the novel, *defend* the ending. See Lionel Trilling, "*Huckleberry Finn*" in *The Liberal Imagination* (New York: Scribner's, 1950), reprinted in

Claude M. Simpson, ed. *Twentieth Century Interpretations of Huckleberry Finn* (Englewood Cliffs, N.J.): Prentice-Hall, 1968), pp. 107–8. James Cox, to continue the available permutations and combinations, *defends* the ending as part of his attack on serious readings of the book. See *Mark Train: The Fate of Humor* (Princeton, N.J.: Princeton University Press, 1966), pp. 175–82. For a general discussion of this debate, see John Reichert, *Making Sense of Literature* (Chicago: University of Chicago Press, 1977), pp. 191–203.

2. Although "psychoformalism" is not an established term, the process to which it refers was first noted by Kenneth Burke who presented a technique he called "metaphorical psycho-analysis" along with an all-too-brief reading of Coleridge's pattern of images which served as an example, in *The Philosophy of Literary Form: Studies in Symbolic Action* (New York: Vintage Books, 1957), 62–76. See also his brilliant essay "Psychology and Form" in *Counterstatement* (Los Altos: Hermes, 1953). Other related theories include Ernst Kris' classic work on creativity and ego regression, *Psychoanalytic Explorations in Art* (New York: Schocken Books, 1964); Walter A. Davis' recent exposition of a "hermeneutics of engagement" in *Inwardness and Existence: Subjectivity in/and Hegel, Heidegger, Marx and Freud* (Madison: University of Wisconsin Press, 1989) could be applied to an author's dialectical relationship with his works; and the undercited work of Albert Rothenberg who argues that creativity is essentially the mechanism of dreamwork in reverse—see his *The Emerging Goddess: The Creative Process in Art, Science & Other Fields* (Chicago: Univ. of Chicago Press, 1979). A more extensive presentation of the psychoformal approach is in preparation; see also Harry G. Segal, *Mark Twain and the Power of the Paternal: A Psychoformal Analysis*, unpublished dissertation, English Department, Yale University, 1990, pp. 6–64, and Harry G. Segal, *The Effort After Meaning: Theoretical, Clinical, and Empirical Justifications for the Psychological Assessment of Narrative*, unpublished dissertation, Psychology Department, University of Michigan, 1990.

3. Mark Twain, *The Adventures of Huckleberry Finn, Tom Sawyer's Comrade* (Berkeley: The University of California press edition, 1985).

4. Henry Nash Smith, *Mark Twain: The Development of a Writer* (Cambridge: Harvard University Press, 1962); Alan Trachtenberg, "The Form of Freedom in *Adventures of Huckleberry Finn*," *Southern Review*, 6, (1970) 954–71.

5. More recently, Andrew Jay Hoffman, *Twain's Heroes, Twain's Worlds* (Philadelphia: University of Pennsylvania Press, 1988) claims that it is a "fruitless" critical task to separate Twain from Huck. "The character we identify as our hero cannot be fully separated from the character who writes him; the writing Huck cannot be fully separated from Mark Twain; the reader cannot be fully separated from the book" (31). Hoffman identifies the shifting tone and diction of the novel, decides that this quality necessitates a "holistic" reading, and insists that interpretations will falter if they privilege "only one of the several clearly interdependent parts of the novel" (p. 39). Certainly the contrast of Smith and Trachtenberg's individually influential readings would tend to support Hoffman's caution; Huck both "deepens" as a tragic character, yet seems trapped by the satiric frame surrounding him. However, Hoffman's solution is to step back from the novel and see it as an interplay of history, heroism, and textuality. (For him, Huck is a traditional Raglanian hero who is ultimately powerless at the novel's end because he has been taken from mythology and placed in a "realistic" novel determined by society and the writing of history.) His approach is an interesting extension of Robert Regan's work, but it effectively sidesteps the blurring of Twain and Huck by simply pointing out that it exists. He does not

attempt to explain why it is so, nor does he address the psychological factors which may have compelled such confusion.

6. After beginning his career by applying the mystical "I/thou" formulations of Martin Buber to romantic poetry, Bloom then embarked on his long and sometimes obscure project of positing a theory of literary succession *and* influence. See, of course, *The Anxiety of Influence* (London: Oxford University Press, 1975) and *The Map of Misreading* (New York: Oxford University Press, 1980).

7. See Anna Freud's major work, *The Ego and Mechanisms of Defense* (New York: International Universities Press, 1946) as well as that of Peter Blos *On Adolescence: A Psychoanalytic Interpretation* (New York: Free Press, 1862)—both classic treatises on the successful and unsuccessful outcome of the oedipal phase as first experienced by toddlers and re-evoked during adolescence.

8. See Rene Girard's perceptive argument on the roles of triangulation and desire in *Don Quixote* in *Deceit, Desire and the Novel* (Baltimore: Johns Hopkins University Press, 1963).

9. What makes Finn's novel rare, however, is that it is an especially strong sequel. Like the New Testament, read by more people than the Old Testament, *The Adventures of Huckleberry Finn* is no longer a sequel. For most readers, it is the first text.

10. To translate this idea into psychoanalytic terms, one could think of Huck Finn as the latent meaning of the manifest content of *Tom Sawyer*. See also Wayne Fields, "When the Fences are Down; Language and Order in *The Adventures of Tom Sawyer* and *Huckleberry Finn*," *Journal of American Studies*, 24 (1990), 3, 369–386, who argues that the world of Tom is one characterized by order and limits, while in Huck's narrative order is consistently undermined.

11. A beautiful description of this kind of awareness may be found in an early chapter of *The Magic Mountain*. As his grandfather once again shows Hans Castorp the family's baptismal bowl and recounts the young boy's christening, "a familiar feeling pervaded the child: a strange, dreamy, troubling sense: of change in the midst of duration, of time as both flowing and persisting, of recurrence in continuity—these were sensations he had felt before on the like occasion, and both expected and longed for again, whenever the heirloom was displayed." Thomas Mann, *The Magic Mountain*, trans. H. T. Lowe-Porter (New York: Knopf, 1949), 23.

12. Robert Regan, in his excellent book on Mark Twain, is the only critic I have found who questions the integrity of Judge Thatcher in this scene. Regan sees a "hint" of hypocrisy in Thatcher even in *Tom Sawyer* and argues that the Judge's redemptive act of returning Huck's money at the end of the novel takes place "several years and several hundred pages after the scene in which [he] gives Huck a dollar in return for his fortune." He goes on to speculate: "Perhaps the author had simply forgot the seed of doubt about the Judge's honesty he had planted so long before." Robert Regan, *Unpromising Heroes* (Berkeley: University of California Press, 1966), 135.

13. I am grateful to John Seelye for his comments as a reviewer on this manuscript. He suggests that the pun on quarry may be a triple pun: "Twain wrote much of *Huck Finn* while staying at Quarry Farm near Elmira—a place he associated with creativity." I am also grateful for the comments of Eric Sundquist, another reviewer.

CARL F. WIECK

Huck and Jim on the Mississippi: Going with the Flow?

The majestic Mississippi River is of central importance to Mark Twain's *Adventures of Huckleberry Finn* and, over the years since the novel first appeared, an impressive amount of scholarly effort has been expended in evaluating its role. While many perceptive observations and theories have been put forward to explain various aspects of the qualities that the river displays and embodies, relatively little consideration has been given to the fact that neither Huck nor Jim wish, or originally intend, to board a raft and float down the river with the current; for neither character is life on a southward-drifting raft a first choice. Nor is it certain that Twain himself had this in mind for his characters. According to Franklin R. Rogers, "[Bernard] DeVoto assumes that Twain planned from the beginning to take Huck and Jim on a journey downstream to the Phelps's farm, but if such had been Twain's original intent, he would not have destroyed the raft in the first place.... The resurrection of the raft is understandable only if one assumes that Twain had made changes in his plans for the novel."[1] Rogers further posits that

> in its early stages *Huckleberry Finn* was to be a burlesque detective story. Apparently its denouement was to feature Jim's trial for Huck's murder, a crime never committed; Pap's murder as well as

From *Refiguring Huckleberry Finn*, pp. 70–81. © 2000 by the University of Georgia Press.

the mock murder were to be connected with the Grangerford–Shepherdson feud in a plot-complex similar to that of *Simon Wheeler* ...

However, as Note A-10, urging the resurrection of the raft, indicates, Twain found the structural plan of his second work period insufficient for some reason, possibly because it was not readily expandable. Faced with the necessity of carrying on with a story he apparently had thought was almost finished he sought a means of adding to what he had already written. The device he adopted, as the resurrection of the raft suggests, is ... to drop the culmination which would coincide with the feud and to continue Huck's journey downstream in the company of two tramp printers.[2]

A realization of the fact that neither Jim and Huck nor their creator initially envisioned a raft journey down the Mississippi can thus contribute to our understanding of unplumbed depths in Twain's novel.

After Huck narrowly escapes being killed by his father during one of the old man's drunken binges, he decides to flee in a canoe he has found, informing us that "I judged I'd hide her good, and then, stead of taking to the woods when I run off, I'd go down the river about fifty mile and camp in one place for good, and not have such a rough time tramping on foot" (38). The words "for good" point to Huck's stopping more than temporarily, not to a continual push to put increasingly many miles between himself and his father. A little later, shortly after Huck escapes from the confinement imposed upon him by pap, we also learn that the boy's first act is to hide in his canoe, have a snack, and then "smoke a pipe and lay out a plan." His line of reasoning is clear:

> I says to myself, they'll follow the track of that sackful of rocks to the shore and then drag the river for me. And they'll follow that meal track to the lake and go browsing down the creek that leads out of it to find the robbers that killed me and took the things. They won't ever hunt the river for anything but my dead carcass. They'll soon get tired of that, and won't bother no more about me. All right; I can stop anywhere I want to. Jackson's Island is good enough for me; I know that island pretty well, and nobody ever comes there. And then I can paddle over to town, nights, and slink around and pick up things I want. Jackson's Island's the place. (41)

It is evident that Jackson's Island is to serve as a base and that Huck will depend on the town for necessary supplies. He has absolutely no intention of setting off on a river journey.

Jim is another who does not foresee risking his future on the river. His plan calls for him to travel by land rather than water. For Jim, the river is simply an impediment that must be dealt with in a manner that will not betray him. As he explains to Huck: "I'd made up my mine 'bout what I's agwyne to do. You see ef I kep' on tryin' to git away afoot, de dogs 'ud track me; ef I stole a skift to cross over, dey'd miss dat skift, you see, en dey'd know 'bout whah I'd lan' on de yuther side en whah to pick up my track. So I says, a raff is what I's arter; it doan' *make* no track" (53). Jim at this point decides to swim out to the middle of the river in order to hitch a surreptitious ride on a passing raft; and when he finally manages to catch hold of one and clamber aboard, he "reck'n'd 'at by fo' in de mawnin' I'd be twenty-five mile down de river, en den I'd slip in, jis' b'fo' daylight, en swim asho' en take to de woods on de Illinoi side" (54).[3] When one of the raftsmen approaches with a lantern, however, Jim's plan to completely abandon the river goes awry. He is forced to slide overboard, swim to Jackson's Island, and survive as best he can for the moment, encircled by the waters of the Mississippi.

It is by this circuitous course that Jim and Huck happen to be thrown together on an island refuge in a manner that owes much to Daniel Defoe's *Robinson Crusoe*.[4] The island itself, however, is depicted as much more than a refuge from the storms of life or from the natural storm from which Jim's knowledge of the actions of birds saves Huck. From Huck's description of the island during the spring rise of the river, we are led to see it as a combination of Paradise and Noah's Ark.

> Daytimes we paddled all over the island in the canoe. It was mighty cool and shady in the deep woods even if the sun was blazing outside. We went winding in and out amongst the trees; and sometimes the vines hung so thick we had to back away and go some other way. Well, on every old broken-down tree, you could see rabbits, and snakes, and such things; and when the island had been overflowed a day or two, they got so tame, on account of being hungry, that you could paddle right up and put your hand on them if you wanted to; but not the snakes and turtles—they would slide off in the water. The ridge our cavern was in, was full of them. We could a had pets enough if we'd wanted them. (60)

Even the catfish Jim and Huck catch while living on the island is a fisherman's dream of almost miraculous proportions. As Huck describes it, the catfish "was as big as a man, being six foot two inches long, and weighed over two hundred pounds.... It was as big a fish as was ever catched in the Mississippi, I reckon. Jim said he hadn't ever seen a bigger one" (65–66).

But Huck has also informed us that there are untamed serpents in this "Paradise," and the boy's joke with the dead snake, whose mate bites Jim and endangers his life, harbingers the finish to the two friends' idyll. It is, in the end, Huck's desire for knowledge that leads to departure from "Paradise." Huck, disguised as a girl, decides to "slip over the river and find out what ... [is] going on" (66). And the fact that a woman, in this case Mrs. Judith Loftus, is at the source of the information about the impending threat to Jim's freedom, posed by her husband, is not surprising when we consider the many biblical features of Twain's story. Understandably, it is the knowledge obtained from Mrs. Loftus that requires Huck and Jim to flee "Paradise."

At this stage in the novel Huck and Jim are forced to begin continually using the flow of the river to avoid capture, and only after this is the plan of abandoning the raft and the Mississippi at Cairo, with the intention of boarding a steamboat in order to go counter to the flow of the Ohio and *toward* freedom, adopted as a new strategy. The critical decision to leave Jackson's Island and drift down the Mississippi is taken unwillingly, is seen at best as a temporary state of affairs, and can by no means be construed as a propitious choice.

The mode of escape opted for by the two runaways must also be considered as less than ideal, since the piece of raft they utilize in making their departure has the major disadvantage of being distressingly sluggish as a means of travel. Huck tells us that "it must a been close onto one o'clock when we got below the island at last, and the raft did seem to go mighty slow" (77). At a later stage of the narrative, it is just this torpid movement that allows the king and the duke in a skiff to catch up with Jim and Huck only shortly after the raft has cast off. The lack of speed at that moment proves crucial as well as frustrating, since Huck believes he and Jim are at last rid of the two frauds and is already rejoicing in the fact that "it *did* seem so good to be free again and all by ourselves on the big river and nobody to bother us" (259). When the king and the duke manage to reach the raft, however, Huck feels crushed: "So I wilted right down onto the planks, then, and give up; and it was all I could do to keep from crying" (260).

Although we witness several idyllic scenes in the novel in connection with life on a raft, we gradually come to realize that the raft is a dangerously slow, unwieldy object. Even worse, it is subject to being torn from its moorings at critical moments, such as during the risky "adventure" on the sinking *Walter Scott* or in the frightening fog episode. And, as if the disadvantages already mentioned were not enough, Huck and Jim are also fully aware, in particular after having "watched the rafts and steamboats spin down the Missouri shore, and up-bound steamboats fight the big river in the middle" (77), and after unintentionally missing Cairo in the fog, that it is well nigh impossible to "take the raft up the stream of course" (129). A raft, despite certain agreeable qualities, represents a powerless conveyance always at the mercy of the weather and the current, and, what is more, continually in danger of being destroyed by a steamboat. Despite Huck's claim that there "warn't no home like a raft, after all" (155), existence on the drifting and uncertain collection of logs never quite measures up to the stable, calm contentment that Jim and Huck shared in their lost "Paradise." For want of an energy source that would enable it to oppose the movement of the current, a raft is only capable of going with the flow.

Nor is the river itself always the most hospitable of places. Beginning with the decomposed body mistakenly identified as pap, Twain populates the river at frequent intervals with hapless victims. There is, of course, pap's own body, found in the floating house, as well as that of Huck's proxy pig. And Buck Grangerford along with his cousin Joe also quickly become lifeless corpses when they seek refuge in the nonpartisan river. Instead of providing them protection, the Mississippi helps make them easy targets for their pursuers by slowing rather than speeding their escape: once in the water they immediately become "sitting ducks" for the men on shore. The three criminals aboard the *Walter Scott* represent additional sacrifices to the river's relentless flow, while Mary Jane Wilks points to another potential source of victims when she indicates that the usual fate of scoundrels in her town is what she thinks ought to be done to the king and the duke: "we'll have them tarred and feathered, and flung in the river" (240).[5]

At times it might seem that Twain overemphasizes the connection the river has with death, unless we take into consideration the importance of the assorted myths to which he refers, myths that serve as a commentary on the ways in which human beings attempt to relate to the river and its bodies. Huck, for example, "knows" the body found in the river and taken to be pap's has been falsely identified since it was discovered floating face upward. According to the myth, in which Huck firmly believes, women's bodies always float face upward while men's float face downward.[6] Then, too, there is the belief that bread containing some quicksilver will, in Huck's words, "always go right to the drownded carcass and stop there" (46).[7] Firing a cannon in the general area where a corpse is suspected to be located is also shown to be a method presumed effective for causing a body to come to the surface (45). All of these beliefs are scientifically unfounded, but the fact that they existed and are mentioned by Twain points to the need that people had for them, a need that must have been based on a sufficiently regular occurrence of death by, or in some way coupled with, the river.

Rivers are not, however, seen from only one point of view in the book. As Mark Twain well understood, rivers represented major thoroughfares in the years preceding the advent of railroads and paved highways. Dirt roads could become impassable during certain seasons or in certain kinds of weather, while rivers, because of their movement, usually remained navigable even in winter, hence the frequency with which towns were built along rivers and, consequently, the importance of the river as a means of linking places and experiences during the period covered in Twain's novel. Lionel Trilling points to that importance in suggesting that

> The form of the book is based on the simplest of all novel-forms, the so-called picaresque novel, or novel of the road, which strings its incidents on the line of the hero's travels. But, as Pascal says, "rivers are roads that move," and the movement of the road in its own mysterious life transmutes the primitive simplicity of the form: the road itself is the greatest character in this novel of the road, and the hero's departures from the river and his returns to it compose a subtle and significant pattern.[8]

Whether or not one accepts Trilling's view concerning the comparative significance of the river as a "character," his conception of the complexity that Twain's use of the river contributed to the form merits noting.

Careful examination of *Huckleberry Finn* reveals that Twain's attitude toward the river is certainly not simplistic or one-dimensional. This irresistible flow carries objects and people with it indiscriminately, shows no favoritism, and has parameters that seem much broader than any perception of the river as the embodiment of a single god might offer. It displays, among its myriad qualities, beauty, mystery, power, gentleness, generosity, constant threats, and an often deceptively benign surface, covering an interior that is not easy to fathom. Nor are its islands presented simplistically. Generally they are seen in the novel as safe havens, but Twain does not hesitate to represent them either as a sort of earthly paradise that can serve to bring humans and other creatures together in peaceful harmony, as noted earlier, or as a formidable hindrance to a fervently wished for reunion, as in the fog episode when Jim and Huck drift along opposite sides of an island.

Even crossing the river can be viewed as problematic. Jim, for example, is thwarted in his attempt to escape across the river and leave the threat of enslavement completely behind; this inexorably leads to a multiplicity of difficulties and a "loss of time" for him as he lives on the river in a sort of limbo, neither completely slave nor completely free. Harney Shepherdson and Sophia Grangerford, on the other hand, succeed in crossing the river and thereby escape becoming slaves to an ancient feud mentality.

The river also takes Jim and Huck past Cairo and safety and ever deeper into slave country, but for this it is in no way to blame, unless it is seen in an anthropomorphic light. Huck never sees the river in such a light, however, and his uncomplicated attitude toward this powerful entity seems apparent in a brief comment he makes shortly after the dissipating of the fog, along with its fears. Displaying awe and his habitual lack of prejudice, Huck remarks, "It was a monstrous big river here" (102). For anyone who has ever experienced a feeling of insecurity at being alone in a small craft far from shore, these words are probably not devoid of meaning.[9]

As Huck and Jim drift down the Mississippi toward adventures that would make Tom Sawyer's mouth water, were he only aware of them, we may therefore wonder if our heroes are really going to "go with the flow" of that mighty river. Is their fate to move through life and, like a raft, "make no track"? Or will they, like a steamboat or a canoe, be able to go counter to the flow when and where necessary?

The contention of this essay is that the primary thrust of Twain's novel is against "going with the flow" and that Huck's character is defined, and Jim's revealed, step by step as these two chance comrades find themselves in successive situations that require them to act or make a decision in some way running counter to major pressures being brought to bear on one or both of them.

Huck, for example, gradually finds the ways of the widow and Miss Watson, as well as Tom's imaginary "adventures," wearing on him and feels pressure building in himself to break away, when pap suddenly steps in and momentarily resolves the dilemma by removing him from the claustrophobic environment of the town. Prior to being kidnapped by his own father, however, Huck already gives a hint of what is to come when he realizes, immediately after pap's return to town, that "I warn't scared of him worth bothering about" (23). When pap challenges him with the comment "You think you're a good deal of a big-bug, *don't* you?" we see the spirit of teenage revolt rise to the surface in the reply, "Maybe I am, maybe I ain't" (23–24). A few pages later Huck expresses similar defiance in explaining that "I didn't want to go to school much, before, but I reckoned I'd go now to spite pap" (29). It therefore comes as no surprise that when pap becomes an actual danger to Huck's existence, the boy is willing to go against both pap and the flow of events by taking his pretended "suicide" into his own hands.

At almost exactly the same moment, back at the widow's, Jim, too, feels compelled to go against a flow of events; in his case it is one that could take him to New Orleans and a worse form of slavery than he has ever before experienced. Huck and Jim thus fortuitously break away from the grasp of a powerful current of circumstances almost simultaneously, and they continue to have this spirit of opposition in common throughout the book.

Huck again evinces his willingness to go against the flow when he makes an attempt at humor in the Raftsmen episode by claiming to be Charles William Allbright, the long-dead subject of one of the tall tales being told. In mocking his own identity, Huck not only challenges the essence of the tale but also makes a wry comment on what he thinks of all the blustery balderdash he has just heard. It is a risky maneuver for a young boy amidst men, but he dares to take the risk, just as he dared to flout pap's authority. He chooses to test his strength at this juncture and does not completely accommodate himself to the flow, unless we see his decision as one that he is certain will produce mirth in the tall-tale tellers by fitting in with the spirit of the moment. Given the situation, however, it would not seem to be a foregone conclusion that the reaction of the men will necessarily be what Huck could conceivably hope for. What does appear evident is that the fourteen-year-old Huck is constitutionally unable to accommodate himself easily to a situation that requires him to submit to an adult authority for which he obviously feels little respect.

Huck's father is also incapable of accommodating himself easily to society for more than brief moments, and his pattern of not doing things according to "reasonable" ground rules, such as not collecting and selling more driftwood at one time than is necessary to enable him to purchase enough liquor for a binge, can be seen as setting a pattern for his son. Huck has difficulty in understanding what he deems to be pap's shortsighted attitude toward the driftwood, but he comes much closer to making peace with society than pap ever does. Huck is, however, pap's son in not hesitating to go counter to the flow whenever his craw gets too full. Just as pap allows the new judge in town to go only to a certain limit in "converting" him before reverting to form, Huck also possesses definite limits as to what he is willing to tolerate.

Evidence of this may be seen in the Wilks episode when Huck sees the misery that the Wilks girls experience after a family of three of their "niggers" is split up and sold by the king and the duke. Huck is able to look on in silence only because he possesses secret knowledge:

> The girls said they hadn't ever dreamed of seeing the family
> separated or sold away from the town. I can't ever get it out of

my memory, the sight of them poor miserable girls and niggers hanging around each other's necks and crying; and I reckon I couldn't a stood it all but would a had to bust out and tell on our gang if I hadn't knowed the sale warn't no account and the niggers would be back home in a week or two. (234)

The kindness that the girls had shown the boy at an earlier moment in the novel stirred him at that point to steal the six-thousand-dollar bag of gold coins from the king and the duke; and this latest display of greed infuriates him enough to cause him to take things into his own hands once again and initiate a plan to once more counter the flow of the situation. Huck's clear revolt against the members of what he calls "our gang" comes about in spite of pap, who has shown by bad example that "the best way to get along with his kind of people is to let them have their own way" (165). In this instance, Huck decides not to let the king and duke "have their own way" and manages to stand firm against the twin flow of forces represented by their direct acts and by pap's indirect teaching.

In what are often considered some of the most dramatic episodes in the novel, Huck goes against the flow of society in trying to save Jim from slavery, and his decisions in this connection all run counter to the practice of the period. In taking his stand, Huck is, as we know, required to oppose received religious beliefs that could find justification in the Bible for holding slaves. He must also go counter to received political practice, which, according to the stipulations of the Constitution, required slaves to be returned to their masters. Huck's opposition to this dual flow exposes him, he believes, to being condemned at death to hell and condemned in life to being regarded as a "low-down Ablitionist" (52), but he cannot find it within himself to accept either the religious or the political precepts that might allow him to avoid such a fate.

With Huck, it is clearly his humane nature that gets in the way when it conflicts with the inhumanity he encounters. He feels that he should oppose the seemingly just hand of nemesis in order to try to save the criminals on the drifting and doomed *Walter Scott* "so they can be hung when their time comes" (87), and he goes to a good bit of trouble for them. It is against the flow of common sense, perhaps, but Huck cannot completely abandon either the men or his natural instinct to save life. Significantly, he goes with his *own* flow in an attempt to counteract what the flow of the river threatens to produce. He realizes only too well that he too could be hung one day and thus identifies with the murderers. Such an unexpected reaction reflects a tolerant ability to identify with all levels of imperfect humanity, contradicts the norm, and contributes in a major way to making Huck the universal symbol he has become. He can even find it within himself to try to counter the flow of lynch-mob justice and attempt to warn the king and the duke of their impending tarring and feathering, despite the fact that they have sold his friend Jim into slavery for a paltry "forty dirty dollars." In both of the above cases Huck applies his own sense of a more humane level of fair play to situations that apparently have already been decided by some power greater than himself. In each set of circumstances he displays the individual strength to resist the flow of what is seemingly preordained.

Twain also indicates that Jim, no less than Huck, ceaselessly strives to counter the flow. This begins early in the book when Jim seeks to carry out his escape by hitching a ride on a raft and must first swim to the middle of the river where, in a symbolic indication of his need and willingness to go against the flow, he significantly tells Huck that he "kinder swum agin de current tell de raff come along" (54). But Jim's opposition to the flow is not displayed solely in physical resistance to the river itself. He firmly opposes the movement of the current in spirit through never abandoning his goal of becoming free all the while he and Huck are drifting south. Jim's overtly rebellious acts, such as challenging Huck's "white" authority in the "Sollermun" and "Frenchman" arguments or daring to indicate that Huck is "trash" in the follow-up events to the fog scene, also add supporting evidence of Jim's strength of character.[10] Jim has the courage to oppose the flow of events as long as will be necessary for him to reach his goal of freeing not only himself but also his wife and children. At no point does he alter his stance or display the least inclination to waver on this issue, despite the mistreatment he undergoes at the hands of almost all of the whites with whom he comes in contact. In this manner, Jim is portrayed as just as stubborn as Huck in steadfastly, if quietly, going against what he feels to be the frustrating flow of events.

There are several other characters besides Huck and Jim who also display a willingness to resist the flow of events. Colonel Sherburn, for instance, coolly faces down a lynch mob that has flowed in a seemingly unstoppable mass toward his home. The doctor in the Wilks section dares to go counter to the crowd, the king and the duke, and even the Wilks girls themselves in his attempt to expose fraud. And, whether or not the gesture is seen as a deus ex machina, Miss Watson, who was originally planning to sell Jim, decides instead to oppose the practice of the day and liberate her slave, despite the fact that he ran away and thereby failed to honor the code of obedience that could have been expected to earn him his freedom. In each of these cases, individual courage claims the ultimate prize.

The final break with the flow occurs on the last page of the novel when Huck, after once again trying to find an acceptable existence in living according to Tom Sawyer's "style" and rules, realizes that Tom, with his "bullet around his neck on a watch-guard for a watch," will, for too long to come, always be "seeing what time it is" (362). That Huck notes and mentions Tom's vanity allows us to understand that at some level he is disturbed by the dreary implication of the new habit.[11] The ramifications of that fact and the possibility of having Aunt Sally as a surrogate for the widow Douglas and Miss Watson provide the motivation for Huck to once again oppose the flow. Huck valiantly attempts to diplomatically say no to further "adventures" with Tom over in the Territory by claiming not to have the "money for to buy the outfit" (361). But when Tom counters with the fact that Huck actually has more than six thousand dollars at his disposal, the scene is set for Huck to react once more in the only way he can conceive of to the kinds of pressures he experienced once before in the early pages of the novel.

In the end, the Mississippi must finally be left behind by both Huck and Jim. Neither character wished at the outset to be on the river, and neither now expresses regret at abandoning it. During a trip that has largely been defined by the current of this "road that moves," they more often than not have found themselves in conflict with the deceptively "comfortable" but unrelenting motion of its flow. Huck's final decision is a resolute rejection of life on and along the river in favor of the obvious risk involved in heading west onto dry land and into an un-"civilized" world where, contrary to the flow of accepted logic, the unknown appears less threatening than the known. It seems plain that neither the raft nor the river can offer Huck or Jim an acceptable future, and this should come as no revelation after watching the two friends struggle, each in his own way, so long against the downstream flow.

It is therefore back on terra firma, but in terra incognita, that Huck's struggle promises to continue; Jim's plans for the future, which have long been apparent, also exclude both raft and river. Neither character would appear at this juncture to harbor any illusions, romantic or otherwise, about the Mississippi, but it would not seem beyond imagining that memories of their recent experiences together might not be forgotten in the years to come. For Mark Twain could never forget the Mississippi he came to understand so well as a young man, despite the fact that the flow of his life ultimately separated him physically—although never spiritually—from the movement of that restless river. As a former steamboat captain he never forgot the difficulties involved in traveling upstream against the current, all the while clearly realizing that the responsibility for facing and overcoming those difficulties belonged in the end to only one person on the boat. When *Adventures of Huckleberry Finn* is regarded from this vantage point, the novel would appear to bear permanent witness to its author's understanding of the continual and complex challenge involved in not going only with the flow.

NOTES

1. Rogers, *Mark Twain's Burlesque Patterns*, 129.

2. Ibid., 135–36.

3. Twain's spelling of Illinois as Illinoi would seem to have at its root the fact that the word is seen to be spoken by Jim, and can thus be considered eye dialect. Since the *s* in Illinois is silent, however, there would appear to be no other justification for this misspelling.

4. See Gribben, *Mark Twain's Library*, 1:180–82.

5. In line with the theme of death by water, it is of tangential interest here that the hero of Emmeline Grangerford's poem "Ode to Stephen Dowling Bots, Dec'd" also undergoes death by drowning; in that case, however, the culprit is a well he falls into and not the Mississippi.

6. See explanatory notes 14.24–25 in Twain, *Adventures of Huckleberry Finn*, ed. Blair and Fischer, for Twain's possible source for this belief, as well as for Dr. Alvin Tarlov's statement concerning his observation of the fact that the bodies of "men, women, boys and girls—they all float face down."

7. See ibid., 46.3–4. It is also worth noting that on page C-3 of Mark Twain's working notes for *Huckleberry Finn* ("Appendix A," in Twain, *Adventures of Huckleberry Finn*, ed. Blair and Fischer, 739, 752), there is a clear indication that Twain was fully conscious of the potential of having bread "cast upon the waters" serve a purpose in his novel: "And bread cast returns—which it don't & can't, less'n you heave it upstream—you let cast your bread downstream once, & see. It can't stem the current; so it can't come back no more. But the widow she didn't know no better than to believe it, & it warn't my business to correct my betters. There's a heap of ignorance like that, around." The editors' comment on Twain's note points out: "This note suggests that Mark Twain considered revising or expanding the passage in chapter 8, where Huck eats the bread that has been set afloat to find his corpse and reflects on the efficacy of prayer" (45.27–47.7 [752]). It might be added that from all indications the speaker of the first-quoted passage is clearly Huck.

8. Trilling, introduction to *Adventures of Huckleberry Finn*, xvi.

9. Twain's working notes for his novel reveal other destructive displays he had planned for the river: in the notes for A-6 we find "An overflowed Arkansaw town. River booms up in the night," and on page B-2 we read "(overflowed banks?)" ("Appendix A," in Twain, *Adventures of Huckleberry Finn*, ed. Blair and Fischer, 728, 735).

10. Andrew Solomon suggests in regard to the "Sollermun" debate that

> Jim's words here are as much an act of mutiny as running away from Miss Watson was, and the penalty could have been, in fact, just as severe. Jim has now started to break his psychological enslavement, just as he had recently broken from physical enslavement; the importance of this break must not be ignored. It could even be argued that the black man's severing of the identification with a Biblical Hebrew, an identification based on their mutual slavery, is in itself his first step toward psychological freedom. ("Jim and Huck," 21)

11. See Oehlschlaeger, "'Gwyne to Git Hung,'" 124–25.

JAMES S. LEONARD

Huck, Jim, and the "Black-and-White" Fallacy

A function of logic—from Aristotle to Descartes and on to the present—has been to establish certainty of knowledge. By logical processes we discover what we can possess as knowledge beyond doubt. The function of literature has been somewhat different, as evidenced by its frequently acknowledged recourse to the irrational—by which we usually mean the emotional or otherwise subjective. There are narratives, of course, that evoke a sort of ultrarationality as a means of overcoming the normal fallibility of human perceptions. One thinks, for instance, of the detective stories of Edgar Allan Poe, Arthur Conan Doyle, and Agatha Christie. But overall, literature is more likely to dwell on the human discomforts or anxieties of *living with* doubt than to find ways to dispel it. Mark Twain, though he did dabble occasionally in the genre of the detective story (for example, *Pudd'nhead Wilson* and "Tom Sawyer, Detective"), is not one of those whom we would readily number among the celebrants of logical processes. Yet, he did have his uses for those processes. A notable example is the pervasive presence of logical or pseudological structures in his most admired novel, *Adventures of Huckleberry Finn*. These seem especially prevalent, interestingly enough, when the subject is race.

We are all well acquainted with the moment when Huck Finn resolves his great moral and emotional struggle in chapter 31 of his narrative with

From *Constructing Mark Twain: New Directions in Scholarship*, edited by Laura E. Skandera Trombley and Michael J. Kiskis: 139–150. © 2001 by the Curators of the University of Missouri.

55

the devastating formulation, "All right, then, I'll *go* to hell"—that is, he will accept damnation rather than work against Jim's efforts for freedom.[1] And we recognize that the dramatic force of this decision depends, at least partly, on the way Huck's movingly right conclusion is couched in the terms of a clearly false dilemma: to do what Huck's slaveholding society says he must do, or be damned for his failure to comply. By having Huck lead up to the climactic pronouncement with "I'd got to decide, forever, betwixt two things" (*AHF*, 270), Twain (his pseudonym rhetorically appropriate here) has made certain that we will not miss the logically fallacious structure. It is obvious that the structure of "false dilemma"—also known as the "black-and-white" fallacy—rests on the unwarranted assumption that only two choices are possible. But Huck's dilemma contains a second-order unwarranted assumption: the "hasty conclusion" that societal ethics and legal codes are built on natural law—God's law—and that a crime is thus inevitably a sin. So when we applaud Huck for the moral insight that drives his choice, we are in some sense endorsing the inverse of that proposition. Society's laws are shown, by our appreciation of the fallacious nature of Huck's reasoning, to be unrelated to divine law, or maybe even at odds with it—a subversive notion indeed.

And then there's the conversation with Aunt Sally (in chapter 32) in which Huck is claiming to have experienced a steamboat mishap. Aunt Sally humanely exclaims, "Good gracious! Anybody hurt?" And when Huck replies, "No'm. Killed a nigger," she comments with satisfaction, "Well, it's lucky; because sometimes people do get hurt" (*AHF*, 279). Although Huck's narration gives us no definitive assurance at this point that he disagrees with Aunt Sally's fallacious categorization of blacks as nonhuman—again both technically and literally a "black-and-white" fallacy—we assume that he does disagree. And on that basis we can congratulate him for using Aunt Sally's prejudice to play her like a fiddle. We see him here mastering what his society considers the "right" responses in order to conceal his "wrong" (in that society's view) intentions. Notice the difference between this instance and Huck's "I'll go to hell" soliloquy. In the conversation with Aunt Sally, Huck is in full rhetorical control of the situation. He arrives at the false conclusion knowingly without really giving himself over to it. In the "I'll go to hell" speech, he reaches the "true" conclusion by means of a specious logical process. But both scenes are high ethical moments for Huck.

Let's flash back, though, to consider at somewhat greater length a couple of Huck's ethically lower moments earlier in his narrative. First, the why-don't-a-Frenchman-talk-like-a-man? scene in chapter 14. This is a rich passage, deserving close attention because (1) it is funny, (2) it displays the racial dynamic between Huck and Jim, (3) it demonstrates the importance of Huck's first-person narration, (4) it provides a beautiful example of painstakingly constructed structural logic concealed beneath a burlesque surface, and (5) it's sufficiently self-contained to be appreciated in itself yet vitally connected in terms of theme and character development to the totality of the novel.

The scene consists of a conversation between Jim and Huck that some commentators have taken as a telling example of Jim's "minstrel-show darky" syndrome, but others have seen as a glowing triumph of Jim's native insightfulness over Huck's greater knowledge but lesser shrewdness. The exchange takes place on the raft during the idyllic interlude when Huck and Jim are alone, before they have encountered the troublesome (to say the least) King and Duke. They have escaped for the moment not just from Miss Watson and Pap but from all connection to societal complication—or so it seems. The question at issue in their conversation is why Frenchmen persist in the annoying habit of speaking French when, as Jim says, "Dey ain' no sense in it." Asked by Huck what he would do if someone approached him and said "*Polly-voo-franzy*," Jim gives a minstrel-show response that not only displays foolishness but also clearly establishes an attitude of subservience to whites: "I'd take en bust him over de head. Dat is, if he warn't white. I wouldn't 'low no nigger to call me dat" (*AHF*, 97).

Which way do the ironies fall here? With Jim's appalling ignorance on one side and his misplaced aggression toward members of his own race on the other, the reader is trapped in an unthinkable bind between pathos and low comedy, which is hardly helped (perhaps aggravated, in fact) by Huck's subsequent rhetorically sophisticated, though somewhat misguided, Socratic interrogation of Jim. Huck begins his logical assault by asking,

> "Looky here, Jim; does a cat talk like we do?"
>
> "No, a cat don't."
>
> "Well, does a cow?"
>
> "No, a cow don't, nuther."
>
> "Does a cat talk like a cow, or a cow talk like a cat?"
>
> "No, dey don't."
>
> "It's natural and right for 'em to talk different from each other, ain't it?"
>
> "'Course."
>
> "And ain't it natural and right for a cat and a cow to talk different from *us*?"
>
> "Why, mos' sholy it is."
>
> "Well, then, why ain't it natural and right for a *Frenchman* to talk different from us? You answer me that." (*AHF*, 97)

From Huck's insistent appeal to the "natural and right," it is, of course, only a short step to the submerged proposition that slavery—the subservience of the black man to the white man—is likewise "natural and right," based in differences as indisputable as the difference between a cat and a cow. This conclusion is suggested as well by the tone of Huck's explanation, beginning with patient simplicity, in recognition of the "natural" childlikeness of Jim's mind, then suddenly, triumphantly (one might even say viciously), springing the logical trap by which he demonstrates Jim's insufficiency in the realm of adult (which here means "white") logic. Notice, too, how the ratios have shifted. The original comparisons were American–Frenchman and English language–French language. These seem harmless comparisons, relying on the distinction between the familiar and the strange to suggest only difference and not hierarchy—even taking into account Twain's assertion elsewhere that his only prejudice was against the French. But Jim's remark about his possible responses to a speaker of French has shifted the ground to the far more pertinent and potent question of white speaker versus black speaker—for whom Jim uses the conspicuously pejorative term *nigger*. Huck, on the other hand, showing the white man's predilection for taking refuge in abstract analogies, has raised the rhetorical ante but at the same time redomesticated the conversation by changing the subject to cats and cows.

By this time, however, Jim has learned his logical and rhetorical lesson and is ready to show that the black man can play the white man's game with equal or greater adroitness. Tired of serving as Glaucon to Huck's homely version of Socrates, he decides to turn the tables—to rise up, one might say, and overthrow his rhetorical master. Instead of giving in to Huck's demand— "You answer me that"—Jim counters with a Socratic strategy of his own: "Is a cat a man, Huck?" Notice how closely this corresponds in form to the opening of Huck's aggressive interrogation ("Looky here, Jim; does a cat talk like we do?"), including the power play of using Huck's name (as Huck did to Jim) as direct address in the rhetorical question. Just as Jim had to do before, now Huck is forced to respond "No"—to which Jim replies,

> "Well, den, dey ain't no sense in a cat talkin' like a man. Is a cow a man?—er is a cow a cat?"
> "No, she ain't either of them."
> "Well, den, she ain' got no business to talk like either one er the yuther of 'em. Is a Frenchman a man?"
> "Yes."
> "*Well*, den! Dad blame it, why doan' he *talk* like a man? You answer me *dat!*" (*AHF*, 97–98)

What has happened in this latter part of the conversation? First, Jim has trumped Huck's false analogy (cat is to cow as Frenchman is to American) with an unwarranted assumption (a "man" speaks English), complicated by a pointedly thematic equivocation on the word *man* itself. Although Jim's argument is equally fallacious, it is rhetorically superior because it not only successfully appropriates Huck's own rhetorical strategy (in both form and phrasing) but also takes up his carefully contrived analogy and turns the blade, as it were, back against its owner. Second (though it happened at the same time), Jim has done something more remarkable than simply prove himself Huck's intellectual equal (at least within the bounds of this limited engagement). He has come, for the moment, to understand what it means to *be* Huck. Early in the discussion he declared his timidity in the face of a hypothetical confrontation with a white man. After all, Jim is a slave (albeit a runaway) in a slaveholding society; he would be a fool to risk a violent confrontation with a white man—or even a white boy. But he has been a remarkably quick study in his encounter with white—that is, European—logic (and shall we include that cornerstone of rationalism, the Frenchman Descartes, in our equation?). To the extent that such logic defines European and American culture, Jim has shown himself to be more "white" than Huck—foreshadowing Huck's later double-edged declaration (to which I will return later in my discussion): "I knowed he was white inside" (*AHF*, 341). The sense of power from Jim's revelation of inner likeness is apparent in the vehemence of his closing challenge: "You answer me *dat!*" (*AHF*, 98).

In the face of Jim's vehemence and the baffling closure of his logic, Huck attempts no further rejoinder. Instead, he falls back on a different kind of clout, the white man's final refuge in the slaveholding South—his ascribed status. For the slaveholder, or even the nonslaveholding Southerner, this was a legal status. For Huck, reflecting the power of European-American culture generally to justify its domination by force of nonwhite, non-European populations, it is the status of narrator. When he sees no further recourse against Jim's argument, Huck, as narrator, retains the prerogative (a prerogative external to the argument itself) to pronounce the final judgment, including the right to refer to Jim generically as "a nigger." He ends his description of the scene, "I see it warn't no use wasting words—you can't learn a nigger to argue. So I quit" (*AHF*, 98). It is this power—the power of the white man's self-proclaimed status as narrator of the events of American history—that has "colored" our view so as to blind us to the events and (as we see in this scene) the rhetoric that are contrary to his perceived interest. But beyond Huck, the still higher authority of Mark Twain has first limited Huck's reach (by, for a moment, handing the authorial reins to Jim), then has undercut Huck's closing ad hominem by means of conspicuous irony.

Now let's pair this analysis of the Frenchman argument with a look at the incident from the next chapter (chap. 15) in which Huck, after being separated and lost overnight in the fog and then finally reunited with Jim on the raft, immediately plays a trick on him. Here Huck, on returning to the raft, finds Jim sleeping; he pretends to have been asleep himself and, like Jim, to be just waking. Huck then manages to persuade Jim, principally by bald insistence, that in fact they were never separated. Jim has merely dreamed it all. He even suckers Jim into concocting an elaborate interpretation of the supposed dream, drawing on Jim's credentials as dream interpreter established earlier in their relationship. But then on the heels of Jim's gullible acceptance of the fallacious account, Huck turns the tables by questioning Jim's "interpretation": "'Oh, well, that's all interpreted well enough, as far as it goes, Jim,' I says, 'but what does *these* things stand for?' It was the leaves and rubbish on the raft, and the smashed oar. You could see them first-rate, now" (*AHF*, 104). Here Jim's abilities as "interpreter" have worked against him, as he, with Huck's strong encouragement, has made the fatal mistake of believing in his imagination and his white companion's assurances more than he believed his own eyes and memory. He can see the debris "*now*," but only after Huck has sanctioned its visibility. Jim takes the reversal hard, but he does not take it lying down. As before, he rallies to deliver a blow against his tormentor: "'What' do dey stan' for? I's gwyne to tell you.... Dat truck dah is *trash*; en trash is what people is dat puts dirt on de head er dey fren's en makes 'em ashamed" (*AHF*, 105).[2] This is a forceful response that once again demolishes what had seemed to be Huck's ascendancy over Jim. The power lies in Jim's sense of justice and in the depth of feeling he displays. But it also lies once again in cleverness. Although Jim speaks gravely to Huck, he again takes Huck's own argument (just as he did in the Frenchman conversation) and turns it against him. Huck points to the "leaves and rubbish" and smugly asks the rhetorical question, "but what does *these* things stand for?" And just as before, Jim, seeing that he has been abused, refuses to give in to Huck's bullying. He turns the question to his own uses.

This time Huck's major recourse to fallacious logic (other than suppression of the evidence of the "leaves and rubbish") comes at the end of his prank: the inconsistency by which, after luring Jim into belief in his unsupported account of what has happened, Huck disproves the account himself. Jim immediately falls back on his old standby, equivocation, but this time the equivocation is more a literary figure than a logical fallacy. He takes the literal "trash" (the leaves, and so on) and makes it the emblem of figurative "trash"—here, people who humiliate their friends. "Trash" is, of course, a category that Huck is all too prone, as Pap Finn's son, to being placed in. But Jim's point, by no means irrelevant to the novel's moral matrix, is that trash is as trash does. Still, it is not the insult to Huck that is crucial. More important is the facing down (the saying that enough is enough by saying what's what, again momentarily overwhelming, or taking over, the narration) confrontation that includes the use of the word *trash*, Jim's most potent available equivalent for combating his own vulnerability to the term *nigger*: one ad hominem at war with another.

This is a dangerous turn for a man in Jim's position, as Huck reminds us in his narration by the racial epithet he uses for Jim and the invocation of the hierarchy that accompanies it. Here Jim is no longer Jim. As at the conclusion of the Frenchman argument, he is "a nigger," the embodiment of a category that signifies disenfranchisement. The "who" has become a "what." However, whereas Huck's closure in the Frenchman argument was dismissive, this time, in the face of Jim's sincerity and the risk taking involved in his man-to-man confrontation with Huck, Huck genuinely recants: "It was fifteen minutes before I could work myself up to go and humble myself to a nigger—but I done it, and I warn't ever sorry for it afterwards, neither" (*AHF*, 105). This bottom line rewrites the one from the previous chapter, "you can't learn a nigger to argue," and in the process redeems Huck, whose credibility has been sagging a bit in these two head-to-head encounters with Jim. This exchange unravels the bitter comedy of the previous encounter and reweaves it thematically, supplying the happy ending withheld from us before and reestablishing the sympathy for Huck that was damaged somewhat by his brutal treatment of Jim in that prior incident.

Twain's mixing of the logical and the rhetorical creates what I referred to earlier as "pseudological" structures. The arguments between Jim and Huck are, in fact, exercises in sophistry—rhetorical push disguised as logic. When Huck, by his example, "teaches" Jim to argue (in the face of his contradictory insistence that it is impossible to do so), what he actually accomplishes is the "sophist-ication" of Jim. For a moment, Huck leaves his role as repository of natural virtue and assumes the role of society at large, and in that capacity his first act is the corruption of Jim. But his creation turns out to be a "Frankenstein's monster" that threatens its creator and (ultimately) society as a whole. The interactions between Huck and Jim graphically illustrate the slaveholding society's need to keep its slave population "ignorant," that is, unsophisticated.

Huck and Jim are "noble savage" figures whose contacts with civilization, in moral terms, work only to undermine their natural virtue. Nonetheless, the progress they make in the art of sophistry is not purely a matter of either moral decline or comic confusion. It is a deftness necessary to deal with society on, and in, its own terms. In the Edenic setting of the raft, it is no accident (both in the usual meaning of the term and in the

Aristotelian meaning of "nonessential") that Huck and Jim take healthy (again, in both meanings of the term) bites of the fruit of the tree of knowledge. Instead of the primal simplicity of innocent language use, they learn to put language to uses that bring its more complexly practical (and moral) possibilities into play.

In an earlier scene in the novel, as Jim and Huck grappled with Jim's mystically gifted hair ball and, in the process, with one another, they established a cordial version of the sophistic fencing that is played out more fiercely in the two raft scenes. After the latter two engagements, they have no need for another such confrontation. Although neither says so, they have together learned the art of argumentation, which, putting Huck's heart-versus-conscience dilemma into different terms, is the necessary foundation for articulating one's ethical independence. They are no longer bound by the "logic" of their society's ethical formulations, but can subversively and self-consciously establish an ethical subtext of their own design. Jim can decide for himself what to do about the wounded Tom Sawyer. And though society's highest praise for his action is that he is a "good nigger," Huck has his own formulation: Jim is "white inside."

I earlier referred to this as a "double-edged declaration," by which I meant that although Huck intends it as high praise, it nonetheless retains the degrading assumption that "whiteness" is superior to "blackness." But the ethical dimension is not the only relevant consideration here. Jim has also learned to be "white inside" in terms of his mastery of rhetorical nuance; he is no longer a *slave* to the false assumptions of white society. Among characters in the novel, only Huck is in a position to understand this—thanks to his exchanges with Jim on the raft. But we readers—by virtue of our comprehension of the totality of Twain's narrative, which exposes not only Huck's comprehensions but also those embedded in the ironic space between Huck Finn and Mark Twain—can understand it still better. Twain, by his use of pseudological devices, has forced us to use our own logical powers in sound ways to discover the ironically established premises of his narrative. We see the rhetoric as rhetoric; we are not to be fooled by its disguise as logic. And we see that Jim is, indeed, "white inside"—since his achievement of rhetorical mastery, sophistic though it may at times be, is a major step toward playing society's games on equal terms.

We have seen earlier in the novel that Jim is willing to evoke "black magic" as a force for manipulation of both blacks and whites. It is less clear that Jim himself actually "believes in" the magic in the usual meaning of "belief," but he certainly believes in it as a means for getting what he wants. In his conversations with Huck, he has learned to make similar use of "white magic"—by which I (somewhat equivocally) mean the power of logical forms.

Again, the degree to which Jim "believes in" the potency of these forms as representations of truth is unclear. But as he gains power over them, he can believe in them as substantial tools. As I have suggested, he is "white inside" in that he can manipulate argumentation. We might think here of Frederick Douglass, a contemporary of slaves like Jim, who evidently made a strong impression on Sam Clemens. Douglass, an escaped slave, no doubt found acceptance in "white" society partly on the basis of moral uprightness and a devotion to truth. But what really made him "white inside" was his ability to control the rhetorical situation—a more powerful version of what Jim does in *Adventures of Huckleberry Finn*.

In the slaveholding United States the ability to read and write was withheld from slaves not only to limit their ability to communicate and thus conspire but also to prevent their demonstrating humanness by means of language mastery. Jim's gains in his arguments with Huck have little to do directly with learning to read and write, but they have a great deal to do with a demonstration of humanness by the alternative route of rhetorical power—which for Douglass was an important validating adjunct to literacy. In this sense, Jim's accomplishment also points toward the alogical literary art by which Douglass—along with William Wells Brown, Harriet Jacobs, Harriet Wilson, and others (including white writers such as Harriet Beecher Stowe)—moved public opinion in the direction of outrage against slavery.

As for the phrase "white inside" itself, its seeming reinforcement of nineteenth-century assumptions about the inferiority of African Americans is finally outweighed in *Adventures of Huckleberry Finn* by the way it ironically thwarts the straightforwardness of the black-versus-white dichotomy. In the minds of white Southerners (and probably most Northerners as well) and in the eyes of the law of the United States, the difference between European Americans and African Americans was as unproblematic as the distinction between black and white. That is, either one was an African American, and therefore eligible for slavery and the legal restraints it entailed, or one was not. This was clearly an illogical situation since there were by Huck Finn's time many Americans of mixed African and European ancestry. The law dealt with this situation by the still more illogical expedient of maintaining that the presence of *any* African genetic inheritance made an individual "black." This was the equivocal legal and social context within which Twain's narrative was born.

There is nothing in *Adventures of Huckleberry Finn* to suggest that "white inside" had any meaning related to Jim's genetic makeup. He was evidently an African American slave, "pure and simple." But the notion that he could be "black" on the outside and "white" on the inside cannot help entailing a breaking down of the inviolability of the "black" and "white" categories as they were understood in Huck's time. If black and white were not totally separate, unmixable categories established and unchangeable from birth, then the whole foundation of slavery, and of white-versus-black prejudice in general, must rest on insubstantial ground. The white community's first response to Huck's "white inside" exclamation may be agreement: Jim has proved himself worthy of the unqualified approbation of white society. The counterresponse of the reader sensitive to the nuances of the situation is then a reaction against Huck's terminology, leading one to ask, "How is this a compliment, since Jim is obviously morally superior to virtually every white in the novel?" The third level of our response should be to reflect on the sleight of hand by which Mark Twain, through his quicker-than-the-eye prestidigitation, has pulled out of the hat a gem of literary logic—a "rarebit" of magic by which the hidden assumptions are made breathtakingly visible. That "slavery is wrong" is not a conclusion that we find very startling today; it was hardly surprising in Samuel Clemens's time either. But for all the literary-critical sophistication we have gained in recent centuries, there remains an element of truth in Alexander Pope's contention that literature gives us "What oft was thought, but ne'er so well expressed."

As we ponder the arguments on the raft, we should note that they are the two occasions in *Adventures of Huckleberry Finn* when Jim and Huck confront one another with real ferocity. In these arguments, which in terms of plot structure seem mainly a matter of killing time, something extraordinary happens with respect to Huck's narration. Although the episodes are recounted by Huck and from his point of view, it is Jim's point of view—Jim's "narration" vis-à-vis Huck's—that captures us. Jim's responses in both scenes are showcase examples of controlled articulateness, masked by signs of inarticulateness, which Huck does not exceed even in his highest moments. And more generally, does not this blatancy alert us to the tactical mastery of articulation by way of what seems inarticulate, or of textual (or literary) logic by means of what is patently illogical, as precisely the power play Twain uses on us throughout—a principal outcome of his successful employment of a sparsely educated fourteen-year-old boy as narrator?

Throughout Huck's narrative the landscape is littered with rhetorical ploys and logical fallacies. Their prevalence at heated moments such as those discussed here argues for a more thoughtful revision of Huck's crafty question: what does this rubbish stand for? First, and obviously, the ingenious way Mark Twain has brought logical fallacies (and other questionable articulations) to bear in Huck's narrative—varying the degree of self-consciousness with which the characters use them—creates an array of effects that deftly dismantles what for Huck and Jim's society is a simple matter of black and white. The novel's curious magic (in this realm, too, thwarting the distinction between black and white) rests largely on the use of inarticulateness to produce a movingly articulate narrative and on illogic to create a crystalline thematic logic. On a more theoretical (but, for the astute reader, no more remote) level, Twain has brought us face-to-face with the essentially alogical nature of literary narrative.

NOTES

1. Twain, *Adventures of Huckleberry Finn*, ed. Blair and Fischer, 271. Hereafter referred to as *AHF*.

2. Twain's manuscript casts some light on intention here. The large number of revisions he made in writing this scene (especially to Jim's climactic speech), trying evidently to get the articulations in this scene just right, suggests that he considered it a thematically pivotal moment.

SANFORD PINSKER

Huckleberry Finn *and*
the Problem of Freedom

"... he ain't no slave; he's as free as any cretur that walks this earth."
    —Tom Sawyer spilling the beans about Jim

"We're free... We're free..."
                    Linda Loman at Willy's graveside

Freedom is America's abiding subject, as well as its deepest problem.
I realize full well that I am hardly the first person to ruminate about the
yawning gap between our country's large promises and, its less-than-perfect
practice, much less the first to comment on the ways in which 19th-century
America struggled with the "peculiar institution" known as slavery. But I am
convinced that the way these large topics find a local habitation in the pages
of *Adventures of Huckleberry Finn* is yet another instance in which George
Orwell's prophetic words ring true: "It is the first duty of intelligent men to
restate the obvious." What Twain means to test out in Huck's idiosyncratic
telling of how he and Jim made their way down the river is nothing less than
what freedom in America means, and does not mean.

Critics of Twain's novel generally shy away from what makes it
simultaneously disturbing and important. So, let me offer the following
proposition in the spirit of plain Orwellian speech: *Adventures of Huckleberry
Finn* is a novel that does not blink about all that militates to keep genuine

From the *Virginia Quarterly Review* 77, no. 4 (Autumn 2001): 642–649. © 2001 by the *Virginia Quarterly Review*, The University of Virginia.

freedom under wraps and in control. Just as the book is as wide as the Mississippi on which many of its most memorable moments are set, it is also wide enough to take on the full range of American culture—from those elements out to elevate to those which run the gamut from the lower-browed to the downright coarse.

At this point, a thumbnail sketch of how the novel has been read, and misread, may be helpful. *Adventures of Huckleberry Finn* began its long, complicated history as America's most controversial novel shortly after its publication in 1885, when the well-meaning members of the Concord (Mass.) Public Library committee decided to exclude the book from its shelves on the grounds that the story was, in their words, "trashy and vicious." The trouble with Mr. Clemens, they went on to say, was that he had "no reliable sense of propriety." They were, of course, right about this, even if their rightness rather resembles that of a busted watch that tells correct time twice a day. What they worried about, between the words of their carefully crafted objections, is that Twain's novel would corrupt the young—of Concord and, presumably points west and south. The charge is a very old one and has been leveled against those, from Socrates onward, who were regarded as corrupters of the young.

In Twain's case, what he did that so upset the moral arbiters of Concord is boldly announced in the novel's second sentence: "That book [*The Adventures of Tom Sawyer*], Huck tells us by way of introduction] was made by Mr. Mark Twain, and he told the truth, mainly." The operative word is *truth*, although we get a pretty good idea about who Huck is and what he stands for by way of his qualifying "mainly." I shall have more to say about the "mainly" later, but for the moment, let me concentrate on what it means to tell the truth and thus begin our journey down a long, complicated path. One should be aware, for example, that truth-telling, properly understood, is not always what Huck had in mind or what many of Twain's readers imagined when they went about separating lies from the truth. *Truth*, in short, is one of those words—slippery, troublesome, but nonetheless, of great importance. This is even truer, as it were, at a time when many thinkers positioned on theory's cutting edge confidently insist that "truth" be surrounded by sneer quotes and interrogated until all that remains are the easy certainties of nihilism. Twain would have found this brand of postmodernism very strange indeed, although I hasten to add that the "pursuit of truth" in his novel leads to darker conclusions than theory has yet dreamt of.

One way to explain the difference between versions of truth-telling is to sharply distinguish between small-t truths of the sort that conform to observable "facts" and the large-T Truths that philosophers worry about and writers explore in fiction and poetry. In this latter sense, to tell the truth about the world requires more than a careful attention to realistic detail, however much this was certainly part of Twain's aesthetic agenda. Rather, it is a matter of burning away the social conditioning that puts layers of fat around the soul and that covers the eyes with motes.

In the late 1940's Lionel Trilling, perhaps the most influential critic of his time, famously declared that Huck and Tom Sawyer may tell the lies of children but they do not, in Trilling's words, "tell the ultimate lie of adults: they do not lie to themselves." These characters, who (rightly) believe that "the world is in a conspiracy to lie to [them]," are thus swaddled, Trilling argues, in "moral sensitivity."

In general T.S. Eliot is right about the way that Huck, Twain's satiric persona, works, but there are moments when Huck is not quite all that Eliot claims on his behalf. Take, for example, the moment in which Colonel Sherburn beats back a potential lynch mob by standing up to bullies and taking their cowardly measure. Huck describes the last, tail-between-their-legs moments this way: "The crowd washed back sudden, and then broke all apart and went tearing off every which way, ... I could a staid, if I'd a wanted to, but I didn't want to." Here, despite Eliot's large pronouncement, is a moment where Huck, in his own term, heaves off a "stretcher." In plainer language, he clearly lies to himself; moreover, we see his feeble rationalization as the sham it surely is.

Why, one wonders, would Twain so embarrass his otherwise savvy protagonist? My hunch is that he means to remind us that Huck is a very young, young boy, despite his sound heart and outbursts of good sense. He is, in short, given to backsliding of the human sort. This often overlooked point deserves emphasis if only because so many readers, including quite intelligent ones, fall into fits of disappointment whenever Huck—or by extension, Twain—lets them down. This usually occurs when Tom Sawyer enters the scene and bullies poor Huck with his insider knowledge of romance novels, but it can also happen when such readers tire of satire, even of dark, uncompromising satire, and prefer that the novel head off to other, more morally soothing directions.

Eliot makes much the same point about Huck's honesty when he talks about his "vision." He sees the real world, Eliot argues, but "he does not judge it—he allows it to judge itself." Enter Leo Marx's "Mr. Eliot, Mr. Trilling, and Huckleberry Finn," a 1953 essay that attacks both critics as "tender-minded" because they substitute structural arguments (Eliot's paean to the mythic river) or easy platitudes (Trilling's magisterial assertions about Huck's honesty) for the more sober recognition that Twain's novel ends in shambles and failure.

At this point, let me drag in Huck's comment about Mr. Twain telling the truth, *mainly*. Huck is not especially bothered by this—certainly he is not as lathered up about it as Mr. Marx will be—because, as he puts it, "I never seen anybody but lied, one time or another, without it was Aunt Polly, or the widow, or maybe Mary," Everybody else is given to heaving in "stretchers"; as far as Huck is concerned, they come with the territory. What the novel dramatizes, however, is how dangerous, and indeed, how deadly, certain "stretchers" can become—especially if they are generated by the small-r romantic wish to make quotidian life more glamorous than it in fact is. That romanticism of the sort behind the blood-curdling oaths taken by would-be members of Tom Sawyer's gang is one thing; when it generates the ongoing feud of the Shepherdsons and the Grangerfords, however, this is another matter altogether.

In much the same way that Twain, in *Life on the Mississippi*, argues that the novels of Sir Walter Scott were singularly responsible for the Civil War, *Adventures of Huckleberry Finn* presents one episode after another in which romance tromps his ignorant protagonist. For early generations of believers, Satan was the force to reckon with. He was cunning, shape-shifting, and always threatening to steal away with one's soul. Calvinists took his power seriously; no measures were too stern when it came to resisting the many forms his temptations took, whether it be packaged in a whiskey bottle or a pack of playing cards. Twain may have rather enjoyed kicking Christians in the slats when they refused to act as proper Christians or when their hypocrisy poked out like a sore thumb, but he did not see Satan lurking around every corner. Rather, it was the endless versions of small-r romanticism that got Twain's dander up. They lied—not as simple "stretchers," but as lies. And the biggest lie of all is that anyone, black or white, could be genuinely free.

This is why the current obsession with Twain's failure to address the implications of slavery comes to half a loaf. Yes, slavery was the most visible manifestation of man's inhumanity to man—not just the shackles and the beatings, but also in the systematic way in which an entire people was reduced to chattel property. Jim's line about being a rich man if he owned himself cracks the heart, and I would add, goes a long way to counter those arguments in which Jim is reduced to minstrel clown. Granted, the tone drips out of Twain's pen, just as it does when Tom dramatically proclaims that Jim is as "free as any cretur that walks the earth." Attentive readers cannot help but ask themselves, given all that the book has demonstrated, "How free is this?"—for not only the newly freed Jim, but also for Huck, for Tom, for everyone on the Phelps plantation and for everybody back home.

Granted, no American writer can match Twain when it comes to giving vivid expression to the great abiding dream of being free:

> Soon as it was night, out we shoved; when we got her out to about the middle, we let her alone, and let her float wherever the current wanted her to; then we lit the pipes, and dangled our legs in the water and talked about all kinds of things—we was always naked, day and night, whenever the mosquitoes would let us .... Sometimes we'd have that whole river all to ourselves for the longest time... It's lovely to live on a raft. We had the sky, up there, all speckled with stars, and we used to lay on our backs and look up at them, and discuss about whether they was made, or only just happened.

The dream, alas, cannot last, however much it remains lodged in the head of every reader with an ear for the music that language at its most supple can make. As my grandfather used to say about the America he both loved and quarreled with, "You could live if they'll let you." No remark better sums up the history of the Jews, or, with a snip here a tuck there, the necessary fate of Huck and Jim. Huck's instinctive goodness turns out to be no match for Tom's book-learning and charisma. Indeed, how could it? After all, it is Tom, not Huck, who knows how a proper "evasion" should be conducted, and how to give Jim the theatrical homecoming his protracted suffering deserves. Huck goes along with the former because, well, that is Huck's modus operandi, but he balks at the latter because he's had a bellyful of Tom foolishness. Granted, Twain knew full well that lighting out for the Territory would put Huck in harm's way, and that the lawlessness of the West was an exaggerated mirror of the more "sivilized" lawlessness of the East. Pursue it as Huck will, freedom remains an elusive promise, one that F. Scott Fitzgerald would later characterize as the boats that forever recede into the past no matter how hard one paddles.

Seen one way, Huck is a survivor, with an eye on a warm meal and a trundle bed; seen from another angle, he is the satiric lens through which we see the world's endless capacity for cruelty. That is why Huck's deadpan descriptions of, say, the Duke and the King are so effective. They know—or think they know—all that con men need to work a crowd—namely, that you can't cheat an honest man and, better yet, that there's a sucker born every minute. The same thing applies to Huck's account of the drunks who populate the shore towns and who take an enormous pleasure in setting dogs on fire. Freedom, for these folks, consists of inflicting as much cruelty as they can. Pap is squarely in their camp. He would vote for slavery if it were on all the ballots—that is, if he could stagger to the local polling place. He is, of course, not alone in this sentiment. Indeed, which voter in the world of Twain's novel felt otherwise?

Small wonder, then, that Leo Marx was so infuriated when he took Trilling and Eliot to task in the early 1950's or that Jane Smiley, a novelist of some reputation, recently argued that Harriet Beecher Stowe's *Uncle Tom's Cabin* is in every way superior to *Adventures of Huckleberry Finn*. Marx is a critic worth taking seriously. Smiley, unfortunately, is not. She sides with propaganda rather than with art, preferring a work that confirms her politically correct certainties rather than one which questions her unquestioned beliefs. For her, it is not enough that Huck *feels* a certain way toward Jim, he needs to act—and it is precisely on the level of action (or more precisely still, *non* action) that Twain's novel so badly fails in Smiley's opinion:

> To invest *The Adventures of Huckleberry Finn* with "greatness" is to underwrite a very simplistic and evasive theory of what racism is and to promulgate it, philosophically, in schools and the media as well as in academic journals. Surely the discomfort of many readers, black and white, and the censorship battles that have dogged Huck Finn in the last twenty years are understandable in this context. No matter how often the critics "place in context" Huck's use of the word 'nigger,' they can never fully excuse or fully hide the deeper racism of the novel—the way Twain and Huck use Jim because they really don't care enough about his desire for freedom to let that desire change their plans.

Smiley much prefers *Uncle Tom's Cabin* because it is full of people acting against slavery, because it is, unashamedly, an Abolitionist manifesto. But after the Civil War resolved the matter at the end of the rifle barrel, after oceans of blood had been spilled, Stowe's novel no longer packed the same immediacy it once did. True enough, *Uncle Tom's Cabin* retains an importance as an historical novel, but not, I think, as a living (which is to say, disturbing) piece of literature.

As Americans, we bow to no one in our official regard for freedom, but we are also a country whose Pledge of Allegiance insists that, here, there will be "liberty and justice for all." School children mouth the words without ever quite realizing that they are a contradiction, that if there is unbridled liberty there cannot be endless liberty. The contradiction also lies at the very heart of *Huckleberry Finn*. Twain wrote well before Sigmund Freud's *Civilization and Its Discontents* explained the small-print costs, in repression, deferred gratification, and neurosis, that inevitably come with the clear benefits of civilization. Huck does not want to return to a world that will insist that what he calls "sivilization" be spelled with a *c*—and moreover that such people are expected to wear shoes and have clean fingernails.

Huck prefers freer space and a separate peace. In this sense, his dream of freedom is the antithesis of Linda Loman's painful recognition that the American Dream of a paid-off house does not, alas, make one "free and clear." Arthur Miller's play is an indictment of a life lived in noisy, manic-depressive desperation. Willy, alas, was a man who never knew who he was, a man who bought into a world where Success lies just around the corner and where "being well liked" will eventually carry the day. But powerful as Miller's play clearly is, it does not limn freedom as darkly as Twain's novel does. For the problem of freedom in *Huckleberry Finn* so co-exists with its humor that readers forget just how broad the brush that Twain uses is. Jim's slavery and gradual movement toward freedom is at best only a small part of what the novel is about. Rather, it is Huck's understanding that, unlike Tom, he can never fit into society, added to our growing realization that he will never be free—even should he make it to the Territory and manage to survive—that makes Twain's novel so problematic. In short, *Adventures of Huckleberry Finn* is a deeply subversive book, not because it is peppered with the N-word or even because some see racism in what is the most anti-racist book ever written in America, but because it tells the Truth not "mainly," but right down to the core.

SACVAN BERCOVITCH

Deadpan Huck:
Or, What's Funny about Interpretation

"I am never serious [said K.], and therefore I have to make jokes do duty
for both jest and earnest. But I was arrested in earnest."
—Franz Kafka, deleted fragment from *The Trial*

It is a truth universally acknowledged that Mark Twain's *Adventures of
Huckleberry Finn* is funny. That's one of the few points of consensus, amidst
all controversies over its meaning. But *what's* funny about the book? We
may ask (as many critics have) if we *should* laugh at certain jokes, but that's
a different, *prescriptive* order of inquiry. Whether we should or shouldn't,
the fact is we cannot help but laugh at Huck's adventures, and the question
is why. A simple question, and it warrants a simple answer. What's funny
about *Huckleberry Finn* is that it's a humorous story. But then again, what's
humorous? Here's the way Twain himself defined the term, in a late essay
entitled "How to Tell a Story":

The humorous story is American, the comic story is English....
The humorous story bubbles gently along, the other bursts.

   The humorous story is strictly a work of art—high and delicate
art—and only an artist can tell it; but no art is necessary in telling
the comic ... story; anybody can do it.

From *The Kenyon Review* 24, nos. 3 and 4 (Summer/Fall 2002): 90–134. © 2002 by Kenyon
College.

The humorous story is told gravely; the teller does his best to conceal the fact that he even dimly suspects that there is anything funny about it; but the teller of the comic story tells you beforehand that it is one of the funniest things he has ever heard, then tells it with an eager delight, and is the first person to laugh when he gets through.

Very often ... [the] humorous story finishes with a nub, point, snapper, or whatever you like to call it. Then the listener must be alert, for in many cases the teller will divert attention from the nub by dropping it in a carefully casual and indifferent way, with the pretense that he does not know it is a nub.[1]

My essay is about the nubs or snappers in *Huckleberry Finn*, and more broadly about a distinctive and (according to Twain) a uniquely American mode of being funny. My focus, that is, is not on humor in general—not on theories of humor, from Aristotle through Northrop Frye—but on a mode of humor which Twain developed over the course of his career and perfected in his greatest work. My concerns are historical and critical: the practice of "the humorous story" as Twain conceived it (in contrast to the "comic story"), within the particular context of late-nineteenth-century America.

So considered, Twain's concept of humor refers above all to what we have come to call deadpan, an "orig[inal] US slang" term[2] that covers a wide range of American folklore, from Yankee Peddler to riverboat Confidence-Man and the Western tall tale. There are differences of course between these forms—deadpan, the con game, and the tall tale—but within the tradition of American humor I just spoke of, all three types are fundamentally related. The basic formula is standard throughout. The story is told "gravely," as Twain says; the teller is straightfaced—he recounts in earnest detail how Davy Crockett at age eight killed the biggest bear in Arkansas (a tall tale) or how you can get the Brooklyn Bridge dirt-cheap (a con job)—and what's funny is the listener who believes.

Of the three forms, the tall tale is the most cheerful: its exaggerations express and celebrate the values of the social group. The con game is relatively serious, sometimes dangerous: it evokes shared values in order to prey on the social group. But here too the rules of the game express a shared community. As in satire, the con game presupposes that those rules are normative, universal.

Deadpan is the loosest and most malleable of these forms. It denies all claims of the normative, and so refuses to indicate how the listener is supposed to receive the story (except as funny in *some* way). No signals are given—no winks or smiles, as in the tall tale; no changes of attitude, bearing, or expression, as (for example) in Melville's *Confidence-Man*. In deadpan, all clues are repressed, strategically concealed in the flow of humor. Thus the narrative centers on the listening or reading audience rather than on the gull in the tale. Or more accurately, we are the gulls in the tale; the larger text, so to speak, includes its reader or listeners as the suckers. Our interpretation becomes the subject of the story, and, so construed, the flexibility of deadpan allows it to go one crucial step further than the tall tale or con game. The humorist's exaggeration and satire (incorporated from the tall tale and the con game) may issue in a savage mockery of belief itself, a form of nihilism whose nubs stretch laughter at social norms and ideals beyond the breaking point.

The term "deadpan" was the last of the three branches of indigenous humor I've described to be officially labeled. Although we know that it had long before been current as slang, its first recorded appearance comes in the November 1927 issue of *Vanity Fair*, where it is defined by analogy to a card-shark who is "holding four aces and you wouldn't suspect it," and as late as March 1957, the English *Sunday Times* found it necessary to explain that "what is known [in the USA] as 'dead pan' humor [requires a] ... facial expression [which] gives no warning of the thrust to come."[3] For reasons I suggest later, it is a remarkable coincidence that, in the mainstream American literary tradition, the first official entry of deadpan (in its full threatening implication of the "thrust to come") appears in Nathanael West's *Miss Lonelyhearts* (1933), in a chapter entitled "Miss Lonelyhearts and the Dead Pan," where, as we shall see, the pun—"pan" as "face" and as the joking, death-threatening Greek god—is entirely appropriate to the method of *Huckleberry Finn*.

In relation to Mark Twain, then, deadpan is a definition from hindsight. I highlight it nonetheless as an illuminating perspective on forms of the past. I would call it historicist hindsight, an exemplary case where the contemporary view, far from being anachronistic, was and remains part and parcel of its subject—more so, I daresay, than the terms then in vogue. As a rule, such terms are descriptive; the view from hindsight is analytical. It helps illuminate what we now recognize as important cultural continuities. Thus what I mean by deadpan is an analytic category that is neither abstract, universalist, nor comprehensive, but, on the contrary, culturally conditioned, socially grounded, and aesthetically specific. It emerges out of the history of the genre or mode it represents, as being inherent in the origins and evolution of that genre or mode. It offers a temporal, non-transcendent vantage point from which to explore the creative forms at issue: in this case, the fluid, volatile qualities of a certain kind of humor which was dominant in Twain's time—which, indeed, bridged all areas of nineteenth-century

America, East and West, North and South, rural and urban, and all periods, from the Federalist and Jacksonian through the Gilded Age, from Timothy Dwight to Artemus Ward, George Washington Harris, James Kirk Paulding, and Owen Wister—and which has persisted ever since, on every level of culture, from literary classics to stand-up comics (or as Twain would have it, stand-up humorists).

* * *

Tall tale, con game, deadpan: in all three cases, the humor that Twain inherited reflects the particular conditions of the southwestern frontier. These are well known but worth rehearsing, since they help explain the distinctive connections *within the deadpan mode* between the tall tale and the con game. Consider first Henry Wonham's description of the turbulent context of the tall tale:

> Tall [Tale] Humor is American not because it is incongruous—all humor is that—but because it articulates incongruities that are embedded in the American experience. A country founded, settled, and closely observed by men and women with extraordinary expectations, both exalted and depraved, could not help but appreciate the distance that separated the ideal from the real, the 'language of culture' from the 'language of sweat,' the democratic dream from the social and economic reality of the early American republic.[4]

The social group, then, which the tall tale expresses and celebrates, is characterized by instability, defined by extreme alternations between exaltation and despair. Its rampant incongruities, its raw discrepancies between real and ideal, make it a con-man's paradise. Recently, Hilton Obenzinger has amplified Wonham's description in a way that extends this link between con man and tall tale and clarifies the relation of both to the deadpan mode. Following Wonham, he points out that the

> "gap" between culture and sweat found in frontier experiences— which characteristically included Indian wars, slave-dealing, *herrenvolk* white racial solidarity, endemic violence, economic instability, fluidity, humbuggery, and speculative fantasy— cultivated a vernacular humor of extremes, along with pleasure in horror and depravity....

Tall [tale] humor was a form of initiation and survival in response to radical physical and social uncertainties on the edge of settler-colonial expansion. This humor thrived at the borderland of displacement, migration, and violence, finding much of its pleasure in dethroning the condescension of gentility at the thickly settled Eastern core, while at the same time reproducing the radical incongruities and discrepancies at the root of all American experience.[5]

These are the social and psychological uncertainties of a new capitalist nation in the process of emergence. It makes for a world of physical turbulence and shifting identities where one way of being funny slides naturally into another.

A handy way to see the different kinds of fun involved in this process is through what (according to the *OED* and the *American Heritage Dictionary*) are the three basic meanings of the word: (1) *Funny* as in "just plain fun"—the childlike humor we designate as "kidding around," a humor commensurate with the traditional tall tale, "designed to amuse." (2) *Funny* in its antiquated meaning of "befool," as in "tricky or deceitful"—a satiric form of humor that plays upon social norms, and thus relates closely to the confidence game. (3) *Funny* as in "strangely or suspiciously odd, curious," the chilling sense of some sinister hidden meaning, as when we say there's "something funny" about that con man; he might be a killer. This sinister humor, which characterizes a certain form of deadpan, and which is latent in all deadpan modes, tends towards "horror and depravity." In our post-frontier times (the era of *Beavis and Butt-Head* and *Pulp Fiction*) it's the pleasure we take in sick jokes and the absurd.

Usually humorists specialize in one way or another of being funny—let us call them cheerful, satirical, and sinister. But as we've seen, these modes slip readily into one another; and American deadpan reaches its highest pitch, the finest turn of its "high and delicate art," when the joke reverberates with all three layers of fun, from (laughingly) "*that's* funny" to (suspiciously) "that's funny."

Mark Twain's humor is deadpan at its best, and *Huckleberry Finn* is his funniest book, in all three senses of the term. Accordingly, in what follows I use the terms tall tale, con man, and deadpan reciprocally, fluidly, on the grounds that Twain's deadpan—the third, sinister, "odd or curious" sense of funny—incorporates (without submerging, indeed while deliberately drawing out) the other two forms of humor.

His method involves a drastic turnabout in deadpan effect. In order to enlist the tall tale and con game in the service of deadpan, Twain actually reverses conventional techniques. That is to say, the novel *overturns the very tradition of deadpan that it builds upon*. As a rule, that tradition belongs to the narrator. Huck has often been said to speak deadpan-style; but the funny thing is, he is not a humorist, not even when he's putting someone on (as he does Aunt Sally, when he pretends to be Tom Sawyer). In fact, he rarely has fun; he's usually "in a sweat"[6]; and on the rare occasion when he does try to kid around (as when he tells Jim they were not separated in the fog) the joke turns back on itself to humiliate him. Huck's voice may be described as pseudo-deadpan; it *sounds* comic, but actually it's troubled, earnest. The real deadpan artist is Mark Twain of course, and what's remarkable, what makes for the inversion I just spoke of, is that this con man is not straight-faced (as Huck is), but smiling. To recall Twain's distinction between the English comic story and the American humorous story, the author is wearing the Mask of Comedy. He hides his humor, we might say, behind a comic facade. The humor, a vehicle of deceit, is directed against the audience. The tale itself, however, is constantly entertaining, often amusing, sometimes hilarious; apparently the storyteller is having a wonderful time, laughing through it all—and actually so are we.

So here's the odd or curious setup of *Huckleberry Finn*: the deadpan artist is Mark Twain, wearing the Comic Mask, doing his best to conceal the fact that he suspects that there's anything grave, let alone sinister, about his story, and he succeeds famously. Then, as we laugh, or after we've laughed, we may realize, if we're alert, that there's something we've overlooked. We haven't seen what's funny about the fact that we've found it funny. This artist has gulled us. He has diverted our attention away from the real point, and we have to go back over his story in order to recognize its nub.

The nature of re-cognition in this sense (understanding something all over again, doing a double take) may be simply illustrated. Consider a culture like the late nineteenth-century Southwest, which was both racist and egalitarian. The minstrel show was a genre born out of precisely that contradiction. So imagine a deadpan minstrel act that goes like this. The audience hears a funny story about a stereotype "darkie" and they smile and laugh along. The nub of course is that they are being laughed at; they've been taken in and made the butt of a joke. Once they see that, if they do, they understand what's truly funny about the story, and they're free to laugh at themselves for having laughed in the first place. That freedom may be compared to the shock of the funny bone. It's a complex sensation, engaging all three meanings of funny, not unlike the odd tingling vibration you feel when you're hit on the funny bone. A light touch might mean no more than a bit of healthy fun—say, the wake-up call of the tall tale (the joke reminds you of your egalitarian principles). A sharp touch might be unnerving—a satire directed against the system at large (you recognize that this self-proclaimed egalitarian society is fundamentally racist). A direct and vicious cut would be painful, a sensation of violence, as in the sinister sense of "funny" (you realize that egalitarianism itself is a joke and that you're a sucker for having believed in it).

Twain's humor, to repeat, spans all three forms. *Huckleberry Finn* is the apotheosis of American deadpan, a masterfully coordinated synthesis of all three layers of the meaning of funny, with the emphasis on the sinister. It is worth remarking that the novel is unique in this regard. Twain achieved this feat only once. His earlier works are rarely sinister, not even when they're brimful of violence, as in *Roughing It* (1872), or for that matter *Tom Sawyer* (1876). His later works are rarely funny, not even when they're brimful of jokes, as in *Pudd'nhead Wilson* (1892) or the tales of terror collected posthumously as *The Great Dark*. *Adventures of Huckleberry Finn* is Twain's great synthetic work, incorporating every stage of his development as "America's Humorist," from the unalloyed cheer of "The Celebrated Jumping Frog of Calaveras County" through the fierce satire of *The Gilded Age* to the David Lynch- (or Robert Crum-) like world of "The Man Who Corrupted Hadleyburg." Twain's mode of coordination in *Huckleberry Finn*, the dialectic behind his fantastic synthesis, is a drastic reversal of effect: the deadpan artist with the Comic Mask. And the procession of nubs or snappers he delivers constitutes the most severe shocks in our literature to the American funny bone.

The first shock is that the novel is funny at all. The slave hunt serves as both metaphor and metonymy for the world it portrays: *Huckleberry Finn* describes a slave hunt undertaken literally, collectively, by a society which is itself enslaved—a culture in bondage to all the Seven Deadly Sins (in addition to the sin of chattel slavery), and accordingly characterized by violence, mean-spiritedness, ignorance, and deceit. A fair example is Pikesville, a shanty town somewhere along the river:

> All the streets and lanes was just mud; they warnt nothing else
> *but* mud—mud as black as tar and nigh about a foot deep in some
> places, and two or three inches deep in *all* the places. The hogs
> loafed and grunted around, everywheres. You'd see a muddy sow
> and a litter of pigs come lazying along the street and whollop
> herself right down in the way, where folks had to walk around her,
> and she'd stretch out, and shut her eyes, and wave her ears, whilst
> the pigs was milking her, and look as happy as if she was on salary.
> And pretty soon you'd hear a loafer sing out, "Hi! so boy! sick
> him, Tige!" and away the sow would go, squealing most horrible,

with a dog or two swinging to each ear, and three or four dozen
more a-coming; and then you would see all the loafers get up
and watch the thing out of sight, and laugh at the fun and look
grateful for the noise. Then they'd settle back again till there was
a dog-fight. There couldn't anything wake them up all over, and
make them happy all over, like a dog-fight—unless it might be
putting turpentine on a stray dog and setting fire to him, or tying
a tin pan to his tail and see him turn himself to death. (183)

Readers of the novel remember Pikesville not for that bit of "fun" (though
that's the town's main source of laughter), but for the Shakespearean
soliloquy delivered there by the Duke and the King:

To be or not to be; that is the bare bodkin
That makes calamity of so long life ...
'Tis a consummation devoutly to be wished. (179)

That's what we laugh at, as we should. Consider, however, that image of
a sow on the run, "squealing most horrible," of a dog running himself
to death. And now think of the nub concealed within the Shakespearean
parody: the Duke and King are debased men, the townspeople are debased,
and debasement in both cases is a metonym for the slave trade. The stray
dog is Jim on the run, or it's Huck *hounded* by civilization. The animal
kingdom is paraded before us as in a deadpan Eden: pigs, dogs, and people
mingling contentedly in mud, and the joke lies in the calamity we humans
make of "so long life." Clearly, this is the world of what scholars have
termed the Late Dark Twain: the world of *The Damned Human Race*, *The
Great Dark*, and the satanic *Letters from the Earth*, where man, the lowest
of all animals, is "first and last and all the time ... a sarcasm"[7]—a world of
Calvinism without God.

Question: What's funny about *Huckleberry Finn*? Answer: the con-man
teller of this tall tale has persuaded us that he's a Comic Writer. I mean to
explore his method of persuasion through three typical jokes, each of them
marking a crucial connective, a major unifying link, in the narrative. The first
joke is Twain's first: his opening "Notice" to readers:

Persons attempting to find a motive in this narrative will be
prosecuted; persons attempting to find a moral in it will be
banished; persons attempting to find a plot in it will be shot.
    BY ORDER OF THE AUTHOR,
    Per G. G., Chief of Ordnance (xxv)

This is a kind of quick preview of the main characters in the story. It introduces the reader to the text and connects Mark Twain ("THE AUTHOR") with Huck Finn, who has authored "this narrative." The deadpan connective, "G. G.," who orders the Notice, links all the above (narrative, reader, author, and protagonist), and the Notice itself is a directive concerning interpretation. Overtly, to be sure, it's a directive against interpretation, but (we must never forget) it's a deadpan directive, which therefore requires interpretation. For obviously the Notice is a form of kidding around, a tall tale of sorts; and then, too, there's a satirical edge to it, a con-man's laughter directed against pompous authority. And then again, there's the violence within the subversive tone—think of the penalties for trespassing (prosecution, banishment, death), and the deadly pun that reinforces them: "ordnance" is not just a colloquial misspelling; technically, it means "cannon or artillery." A "Chief of Ordnance" in this case is a military officer ready to blow you to bits. And to do so, be it noted, for the least of interpretive offenses: not for seeking motive or moral, but just for finding a plot.

All this makes for an especially funny predicament. We're not allowed to interpret (not even on the most elemental level), but the story Huck tells *demands* interpretation, demands it unrelentingly and all the time. We can't get any of its jokes without figuring out motive and plot, and we can't possibly do that without assuming a moral position. Take even the simplest joke: say, the story that Huck tells Jim about Solomon and the disputed child. No reader has failed to laugh cheerfully at the incident and no careful reader can fail to notice that it points satirically to key themes of the novel: the cultural connectives between fatherhood, the Bible, schools, and civil authority. It's perfectly natural, then, for Huck to "slide" from Solomon to kings in general. He tells Jim about European ex-kings who migrate to America and teach French; he then shows off his French ("S'pose a man was to come to you and say *Polly-voo franzy*—what would you think?"), and proceeds to explain why people need to have different languages (humans are different from one another, as dogs are different from pigs, pigs from horses, etc.). Jim's famous rejoinder is that all people are alike (all people, universally, are different from dogs, pigs, etc.). If he's a man, says Jim, "*Well*, den! Dad blame it, why doan he *talk* like a man?" (97–98).

This has key elements of the tall tale, but basically it's a parody of social pretension: Huck, the master of the colloquial style, is bragging in the language of the elite, as French then was. And in turn the parody is a sick joke about southern history: Jim, the victim of chattel slavery (so-called because slave-society rhetoric built on the comparison between blacks and animals)—Jim, the example of man-reduced-to-beast-of-burden, is articulating the self-evident truths of human equality. How can we not interpret? And our interpretation is prodded, if we need prodding, by Huck's concluding response: "You can't learn a nigger to argue. So I quit" (98). Huck doesn't see the fun in all this; he's simply frustrated. We do see the fun because we know we're hearing a comic tale (by Mark Twain, humorist); but in order to take that step we have to interpret. In short, we interpret because Huck doesn't.

I will return to that hermeneutic twist later on. First, let me repeat what's funny about the Notice. Officially, we're prohibited from interpreting on pain of death, but the narrative demands interpretation. So the nub lies in the inversion: far from forbidding interpretation, the Notice is *calling attention to it*. It's reminding us of our *compulsion* to look for plot, moral, and motive, and then the narrative itself does the rest of the work: it *forces* us to interpret. Having recognized that much, we should feel uneasy. There's something funny about this emphasis on interpretation—it's a deadpan artist's emphasis. What's *his* motive? What's the *plot*?

To explore the question I turn to my second example, the last joke in the novel. I refer to what is surely Huck's best-known line—his decision to light out for the territory. The long-standing consensus on its meaning is that Huck leaves because he wants to be free. And no doubt he does; but the text itself tells us something else:

> ... then Tom he talked along and talked along, and says, le's all three slide out of here, one of these nights, and get an outfit, and go for howling adventures amongst the Injuns, over in the Territory, for a couple of weeks or two; and I says, all right, that suits me ... (361)

So Huck decides to light out "ahead of the rest" (362), and the nub is: *he's just kidding around*. He plans to get an "outfit" and leave for a while ("a couple of weeks or two"), which we interpret as a flight to freedom—and then, if we follow critical tradition, we proceed to allegorize it as the freedom of the spirit. Over the past century that allegory has established itself as a cultural icon: Huck Finn, the rebel hero of the open road.

It's a startling flight of interpretation. Just think of the deadpan connection here between African Americans and Native Americans: Jim dressed up for "howling adventures amongst the Injuns"! This joke is akin to (I'd say, sicker than) that of the Duke and King when they dress Jim up as a "*Sick Arab—but harmless when not out of his head*" (203). Huck reports that they used "King Lear's outfit" for the occasion, and, since Jim-in-disguise is a recurrent theme (from the Bewitched World Traveler in the first section to the Romantic Prisoner in the last), it may not be too much to see a link

between Shakespeare's outcast king howling on the heath and Jim "howling
... amongst the Injuns." In any ease, Twain's deadpan play in the novel's
final scene (tall tale and confidence game combined) should alert us to the
intricate narrative pattern he has developed. Huck is about to light out
from the Phelpses for the Territory: this liminal moment joins two crucial
dimensions of Huck's culture, and ours. First, the dimension of space: the
"settlements," as defined emphatically by the N-word, are being linked to the
Territory, as defined explicitly by the I-word, *Injun* territory. Then, there's
the dimension of time: "Injun" is a clue to the cultural connections implicit
in the novel's double time frame. The fictional time, the period of Huck's
adventures, is the antebellum South, the slavery era. The authorial time,
the decade in which Twain wrote the book, was the era of Indian-killing.
What joins both time frames is nothing less than the most sinister line of
continuity in American history, from slavery to genocide—in the pre–Civil
War period, the country's economic growth through slavery; after the Civil
War, the country's territorial growth through Indian Removal, mainly in the
deadly sense of the word "removal"—"skinned alive," as Twain punned in
a satirical tribute to "Plymouth Rock and the Pilgrims" (1881), speaking in
the guise of a solitary survivor ("Where are my ancestors? ... Whom shall I
celebrate? ... My first ancestor, gentlemen, was an Indian.... Your ancestors
skinned him alive").[8] For between the time when *Huckleberry Finn* was begun
and when it was completed, the territories provided the setting for the final
wars against the Native Americans—from Wounded Knee (1876) to Little
Big Horn (1890)—under the notorious banner, "the only good Indian is a
dead Indian."

Huck's "escape to freedom" is a con-man's sinister tall tale which
suggests how much can be excluded in the act of interpretation. And it
suggests further what this kind of exclusion makes room for. I refer to the
cultural commonplace ("lighting out") that draws its force from a powerful
set of national self-definitions: the notion that "the territory" in the United
States means (and always meant) not other peoples' land, but freedom; the
familiar interpretations of "open land" not as expropriation but as promise,
opportunity, and hope. What a sweeping act of mockery is embedded in
this deadpan nub! I spoke earlier of a minstrel show audience being mocked
for laughing along with racist stereotypes. In *Huckleberry Finn* we are being
laughed at for buying into the American belief system.

To put it starkly, the snapper which ends the novel is that interpretation
may be a trap of culture. I mean interpretation now in a special sense—
special but central. We usually think of interpretation as a more or less
independent act, an assertion of what something or someone means to me,
sometimes in opposition to prevailing beliefs. I agree that interpretation

can work this way—that it can lead towards skepticism or revision or disruption—and obviously I hope as much for this essay. But the fact is that interpretation is also, and *far more characteristically*, a cultural institution. And on this institutional level, interpretation is neither skepticism nor revision nor disruption but, on the contrary, a form of acculturation. It is a process carefully nourished by society, from our first Dick and Jane reader to our latest America-is-multicultural handbook. Through this cultural process we learn to confirm, each of us—inwardly, privately—our beliefs in what our culture has taught us to believe. And we do so with deliberation. Scrupulously, voluntarily, step by analytical step—or anxiously, avariciously, and sensuously, like Pecola Breedlove in Toni Morrison's *The Bluest Eye*—we imbibe social aprioris, and so *consent* to the limitations inherent in the culture we inhabit.

Through this process, interpretation directs our deep and abiding need for meaning, towards socialization. It turns our world, imaginatively, into a system; it organizes our fantasies in ways that accommodate us to things as they are; it forges the foundational links between subjectivity and society. And typically in the U.S.A. it does so individualistically, in the manner of the American do-it-yourself kit. Each of us labors self-reliantly to arrive at what turns out to be more or less the same interpretation.

One might go so far as to say that interpretation, so understood, is culture; but that would be to stretch the term beyond its proper limits, or in any case beyond what I intend. Culture is made up of rituals, habits of thought, and networks of meaning that persist (like ideology) as communal apriories, designating the boundaries of our conscious deliberations. It is also made up of disparate traditions, diverse practices, and contradictory beliefs. Those conflicts are mediated—which is to say, defused, deflected, or resolved—by what I just called networks of meaning, whose center and mainstay are society's official institution of interpretation.

Over the past two centuries, the institution of literary interpretation has proved spectacularly effective in this regard. Most remarkably, perhaps, it has served as a pivotal factor in the formation and coherence of national identity, first in Europe and then in America. As an editor of the first major collaborative *History of American Literature* (1917) put it, "In ninety-nine cases out of a hundred [the] astounding transformation of immigrants into citizens ... [as well as] the transformation of ... the native born into Americans ... is very largely accomplished by inculcating American ideals through the language and literature of America.... [We] teachers of American literature are [thus] ... special custodians" of society. His charge was elaborated thirty years later in the next standardized American literary history. "Increasing power and strength are extraordinarily characteristic of [our nation]," declared Robert Spiller and his coeditors. "Never has nature been so rapidly and so extensively altered by the efforts of man in so brief a time. Never has conquest resulted in a more vigorous development of initiative, individualism, self-reliance, and the demands for freedom." Hence the "Americanness of our major authors." Ours has been a literature "profoundly influenced by the ideals and practices developed in democratic living. It has been intensely conscious of the needs of the common man, and equally conscious of the aspirations of the individual.... It has been humanitarian" and made "virile by criticism of the actual in comparison with the ideal."[9]

Huckleberry Finn is a great example of this enterprise in socialization, perhaps the great example. Consider these facts about the state of the novel over the past three decades (our current period of multiculturalism, ideological self-consciousness, critical diversity, and the hermeneutics of suspicion). In 1990, the aggressively revisionist Heath *Anthology of American Literature* gave special prominence to the novel, actually printing it in its entirety. During the 1990s, *Huckleberry Finn* "was taught [in our high schools] more than any other novel, more than any other long work (such as a play by Shakespeare), and more than any other work in American literature." After 1970, the very debate over Twain's racism provided a vehicle for consensus. With "ritual repetition" the authorities of academia defended the book as a model of "integration, and the importance of this cultural work overrode the offense the book generated among many of its newly authorized, but [now] also newly obligated African-American readers." "Even though his society was racist," went the argument, Twain "was not, and so 'we' are not. For African Americans to challenge this view [was] to challenge ... the America he 'quintessentially' represent[ed]."[10]

If we read the novel's last scene closely, those facts come as a violent cut at the funny bone. They indicate how in this country, during one of its most volatile periods, the institution of literary interpretation helped conceal the single most unsavory aspect of our past: the incongruity between national realities (slavery, genocide) and national beliefs (open road, free opportunity). Technically, the tall tale (or con man) frame of *Huckleberry Finn* is, first, the subtitle, *Tom Sawyer's Comrade*, concerning the character we try desperately to dissociate from Tom, and, secondly, the monologue signature, "Yours Truly," by the novel's most conspicuous liar. Within this framework, the joke about Huck's lighting out is funny enough, in the sinister sense, to provide the finale to the greatest deadpan act in the history of American sick humor.

Interpretation may be a trap of culture: it may be well at this point to recall the differences and continuities between the tall tale, the confidence game, and deadpan. The tall tale delineates the bounds of communal interpretation. The confidence game plays upon those common grounds, draws out the need for belief, in order to prey on the community. Deadpan incorporates both forms in ways that make interpretation itself—the very stuff of credulity—the subject of the narrative. So understood, Twain's final snapper is especially striking in context of the current critical scene, with its obsessive search for subversion. The artist, in this perspective, becomes something of an Eternal Disrupter (as Christ had been the Eternal Reconciler in the old New Criticism); his or her methods of reversal, miming, riffing, and inversion constitute a network of escape routes from cultural oppression. And of course that archetype extends by implication to the subversively discerning critic of art.

The impression this conveys of the powers of interpretation is as flattering as it is familiar. Conversely, Twain's joke about Huck's flight to freedom is as discomforting—and as deflating—as it is surprising. The misfit it reveals between the text before us, literally, and the meaning we assign it, spiritually, should remind us once more—but now in an entirely new, genuinely threatening sense—of Twain's opening warning: Beware of Interpretation. As I've been arguing, our official institutions of interpretation, including that of literary interpretation, serve above all as centers of social control. And I would venture that statement as a cross-cultural generalization. Historically, across time and place, the status quo has defended itself precisely at its points of conflict, its potential weak points, by means of interpretation. One need only think of the immense integrative force of the four-fold method of medieval exegesis, with its levels of meaning ascending as in a Jacob's ladder from earth to heaven, from literal and political to moral and mystical. It is hardly too much to say that for a millennium in the Christian West the doctrine of the divine right of kings thus fortified every segment of society, securing the status quo precisely at the intricate, potentially vulnerable intersections of gender, class, and religion, spiritual imperative and civil law, public and private life.

In America, of course (Twain's and ours), the process of official interpretation works differently. Medieval exegesis was instated hierarchically, by the literate elite. Our forms of exegesis work by democratic consent. They are based on doctrines of individualism, contract, pluralism, and the separation of church and state. These are the apriorities of our personal and social lives, the ideological limits of our polity. And insofar as earlier modes of Christian hermeneutics persist in spite of these doctrinal limitations—as indeed they do (that legacy is a main butt of Twain's humor)—they are Protestant modes: basically individualist, grounded in personal conscience rather than papal bull. But the results are no less binding and systemic. Chairman Mao missed the mark when he wrote that power comes out of the barrel of a gun. Guns are not even the most effective instrument of state power. They merely force us to submit; interpretation gets us to consent. And consent—voluntary, self-affirming—is the American basis not only for association (as Alexis de Tocqueville pointed out) but also, *ipso facto*, *by association*, for socialization. Society works through civic and economic mechanisms; culture, through the circulation of alluring artifacts and stories. These constitute the moral lifeblood of the body politic, whose heart is the process of interpretation. The effect of a sound cultural heart in a healthy body politic is that what's most personal—our capacity for independent judgment, our power of consent—becomes a source of social revitalization. The success of society in the fragmented, decentralized body of the United States (the fact that this past one hundred years has proved to be the American century) is due in no small measure to the fact that, well before 1900, the culture had developed a distinctive network of literal-political-moral-spiritual meanings, together with a complex set of interpretative techniques appropriate to a modern, free enterprise, open market way of life.

This elemental, conservative power is what Twain's deadpan compels us to recognize. He himself came to recognize it gradually, and in some measure through psychic stress and personal loss. According to his biographers, the decisive years fall between 1876 and 1885, when his "grievances piled so rapidly upon previous griefs that they surfaced visibly, undeniably." A short list of those griefs and grievances include "a fatal break with [his close friend] Bret Hart, fatal troubles with his publisher, [Elisha] Bliss ... financial troubles, ruinously expensive involvements with the Paige typesetter and other patents; a bitterly disappointing return to the Mississippi River, Hannibal, and boyhood scenes; and the beginnings of chronic ill health for the four [deeply loved] female members of his family"—all this precisely at "the height of his creative powers," through the decade of the stop-and-start making of *Huckleberry Finn*. By the time the novel appeared in 1885, Twain had developed a series of "deterministic principles" that accounted for all values and beliefs as the product of cultural "training." In 1883, in an essay entitled "What Is Happiness?," he declared that "the human machine gets all its inspirations from the outside and is not capable of originating an idea of any kind in its own head"; and two years later, in an essay called "The Character of Man," he added to his definition of "the human machine" a certain agency—an instinctive, inalienable tendency towards "malice, cruelty, servility, and nastiness." He named this tendency the "Moral Sense" and saw in it the "source of man's incorrigible depravity: it enabled man to distinguish right from wrong so as to choose the wrong, which he chose from a vicious predisposition." Thus, Twain concludes jokingly, man "tarries his little day, does his little dirt, commends himself to God, and goes out into the darkness to return no more, and send no messages back—selfish even in death."[11]

In short, man's fate is acculturation, a vicious predisposition, and the exit into darkness: that's the nub of the greatest American "humorous story." The deadpan point of Huck's adventures is that we're ensnared not only in the joints of the social body, but in the movement of history: trapped, that is, within the very cultural transitions—from slavery to Reconstruction, from civilization to the Territory (and back again)—through which we had hoped to escape. As Twain put it four years later, "Training—training is everything; training is all there is *to* a person.... We have no thoughts of our own, no opinions of our own; they are transmitted to us, trained into us."[12] This is Hank Morgan's lament for medieval England in *A Connecticut Yankee in King Arthur's Court*—and by training (his Gilded Age blinders) he cannot see that he is the chief victim of that process. In fact, the crimes of Camelot function much with the con-man effect of the crimes of slavery in *Huckleberry Finn*: representing as they apparently do the evils of a bygone age, they work to lull us past the nubs of the crimes of the present (the feudal baronies of 1889, the nigger-hunts of Reconstruction). In *A Connecticut Yankee* the narrator, Hank Morgan, is the butt of a deadpan joke directed against the myth of progress. In *Huckleberry Finn*, we are the objects of humor and the joke is directed against our faith both in progress and in interpretation. It makes for a very unnerving shock to the funny bone; but we can't stop there. We owe it to ourselves, and to Twain's art, to account for our laughter.

To that end, I turn to my third and main example. The passage comes when Huck lands at the Phelps Plantation, where he meets Sally Phelps, who mistakes him for her nephew Tom Sawyer. Huck reflexively goes along with his new identity, but gets confused in explaining what now turns out to be his late arrival: Tom had been expected by steamboat some time before. Huck at first explains that the boat had been grounded; then can't think of which grounding—but, (resourceful liar that he is),

> I struck an idea, and fetched it out: "It warn't the grounding—that didn't keep us back but a little. We blowed out a cylinder-head."
>
> "Good gracious! anybody hurt?"
>
> "No'm. Killed a nigger."
>
> "Well, it's lucky; because sometimes people do get hurt. Two years ago last Christmas, your uncle Silas was coming up from Newrleans on the old Lally Rook, and she blowed out a cylinder-head and crippled a man. And I think he died, afterwards. He was a Babtist. (279)

Again, we're at a structural crux of the narrative. The arrival at the Phelps Plantation unites all three sections of the novel (Hannibal, the river journey, and the Phelps episode), and it connects all three layers of Trickster fun (cheerful, satirical, and sinister). It also demonstrates Twain's hermeneutic imperative—we must interpret this scene (its humor leaves us no alternative)—while offering a model example of what's funny about our habits of interpretation. I take the joke to lie in the infamous one-liner "No'm. Killed a nigger." Actually it's a one-liner divided into two parts: "No'm [full stop]. Killed a nigger." We are then diverted from its nub by Aunt Sally's story of the Lally Rook. To recall Twain's instruction: when the joke comes, "the listener must be alert, for ... the teller will divert attention from the nub by dropping it in a carefully casual or indifferent way, with the pretense that he does not know it is a nub." The "Babtist" is a decoy; it allows the story to bubble gently along. In fact, to keep it bubbling, just in case the reader doesn't laugh straight off, Twain extends Aunt Sally's ruminations: "Yes, I remember now, he *did* die. Mortification set in and they had to amputate him. But it didn't save him. Yes, it was mortification—that was it. He turned blue all over, and died in the hope of a glorious resurrection. They say he was a sight to look at." A very funny sight, but its nub is encoded in Huck's two-part throwaway line: "No'm. Killed a nigger." In what follows I mean to decode Twain's deadpan by outlining eight points about Huck's response to which we should be alert, if we're courageous enough to want to get the joke.

First, the episode is a model instance of the way Twain combines the tall tale and con game through the sinister aspect of deadpan. Huck's response is a comic-fiction exaggeration, defining the values of a certain social group, which then serves as a successful con job, confirming Huck as Tom. And as such it stands as one of the most vicious jokes in the entire literature of prejudice. Huck's "No'm" reflects back through the narrative, in ways that undermine virtually all of the novel's "good characters," such as the kindly frontierswoman, Judith Loftus, who cuts short Huck's visit to join the "nigger hunt." And it serves as a fit prelude to the long Phelps episode, where Aunt Sally and Uncle Silas are portrayed as warmly hospitable people, the salt of the earth, even as the search for Jim reaches its climax and the "no one" joke is fully enacted, most dramatically, perhaps, when a group of men decide to lynch Jim for all the trouble he has caused—a *"raft* of trouble," is the way Twain humorously has one of them phrase it (352, my italics)—but relent when they realize that, as unclaimed property, Jim is worth more alive than dead.

Second, Huck's use of "nigger" is profoundly racist. We can't argue (as too many critics have) that it's just slang—a poor, ignorant boy's way of saying African American. What Huck means is far worse than what a bigot means by "wop" or "wasp." Huck is saying that a "nigger" is a no one, a nonhuman. It's worth noting in this respect that in 1900 the first professor of American literature at Harvard, Barrett Wendell, focused on this passage in his standardized *Literary History of America*. Huck's "No'm. Killed a nigger," he writes, is a serious statement of relative merit, not only accurate but prescient of what right-minded people believe: not only "an admirably compact expression of [the] temper" of the antebellum South, but "more consonant with New-England temper to-day than it was seventy years ago. Modern ethnology seems to recognise [sic] a pretty marked distinction between human beings in the Stone Age and human beings as developed into the civilization of the nineteenth century."[13] Wendell's case is extreme, an *open* white supremacist, but he was giving an academic stamp to attitudes that were pervasive in Twain's America, North and South. His interpretation suggests the full scope of the joke (from the ebullient Pan in deadpan to his sinister incarnation as *dead*pan) in Huck's response to the straight-man query, "anybody hurt?"

Third, Huck's response is gratuitous, totally unnecessary. That's the joke in the *forced* pause at the center of the line. Huck could just as well have stopped at "No'm." And be it noted that that kind of gratuitous remark, in all its racist implications, is typical of Huck. The casual N-word is fundamental to his vocabulary. As critics over the past three decades have pointed out, the word "nigger" occurs on virtually every page of the novel, and it's worth emphasizing that it took three generations of readers *before them* to take offense. The first debates about *Huckleberry Finn* centered on issues of class, not race. The complaints had to do with Huck's delinquency, bad habits, and poor grammar. The N-word went largely unnoticed until the 1960s, and I believe that the not-noticing was basic to Twain's deadpan. Part of the joke is that the word was woven into the very fabric of Twain's self-proclaimed democratic culture, at once a vicious slur and a ubiquitous, unexamined byword ("catch a nigger by the toe"), ubiquitous because unexamined and unexamined because ubiquitous. Once again, Huck's response is entirely appropriate, to him and his readership alike.

It's also appropriate to the plot of the novel. That's the fourth point to make about Huck's remark. His joke concerns a dead person, or rather a dead nonperson, and death is a main narrative thread—death in the deadpan mode, gilded over by humor, as in the early passages concerning Tom's gang:

> ... Tom got out a sheet of paper that he had wrote the oath on, and read it. It swore every boy to stick to the band, and never tell

any of the secrets; and if anybody done anything to any boy in the band, whichever boy was ordered to kill that person and his family must do it.... And if anybody that belonged to the band told the secrets, he must have his throat cut, and then have his carcass burnt up and the ashes scattered all around, and his name blotted off the list with blood....

Everybody said it was a real beautiful oath ...

Some thought it would be good to kill the *families* of boys that told the secrets. Tom said it was a good idea, so he took a pencil and wrote it in. Then Ben Rogers says:

"Here's Huck Finn, he hain't got no family; what you going to do 'bout him?"

"Well, hain't he got a father?" says Tom Sawyer.

"Yes, he's got a father, but you can't never find him these days ... hain't been seen in these parts for a year or more."

They talked it over, and they was going to rule me out, because they said every boy must have a family or somebody to kill, or else it wouldn't be fair and square.... Well nobody could think of anything to do—everybody was stumped, and set still. I was most ready to cry; but all at once I thought of a way, and so I offered them Miss Watson—they could kill her. Everybody said:

"Oh, she'll do. That's all right. Huck can come in." (9–10)

This is funny, although not to Huck (he's "most ready to cry"). It's Tom who's having fun, along with us.

But Twain has a different point in mind. And (as in the case of Huck's N-word, in response to Aunt Sally) the point is obvious once we're on to his method. Death and violence are writ large throughout the novel, in virtually every scene and episode. The blood bond that Tom invents is a mirror reflection of the world of *Huckleberry Finn*. It foreshadows the death hoax that Huck thinks up when he leaves for the river ("I pulled out some of my hair, and bloodied the ax good" and made a track so that they'd look "to find the robbers that killed me" [41]); and the horrific scene earlier, when his blind-drunk father chases him around the shack with a "clasp knife" (laughing with "*such* a screechy laugh"), cursing and roaring that Huck is the Angel of Death, and that he will now kill him once and for all (36). These sorts of fantasies and facts are the adventures of Huck. They come to life in the Boggs murder, in scenes of lynching and tar and feathering, in the Grangerford-Shepherdson clan massacre, even (and in a way most tellingly) in the wreck of the *Walter Scott* when Huck steals the robbers' skiff, acting as he imagines Tom Sawyer would have—thereby, presumably, leaving the robbers to drown. According to Twain scholars, there are thirty-three corpses in *Huckleberry Finn*, and that does not include either those probably drowned robbers or the ghastly corpse in the section Twain omitted, surely one of the most vivid and morbid he ever wrote, describing Pap's dead body. One early review (and in this single respect a uniquely discerning one) complained that Huck's adventures were simply one "bloodcurdling" adventure after another;[14] and indeed it's not too much to say that dead bodies, real and imagined, are the anatomical links of his story. It's appropriate that G.G., the deadpan link between Twain and Huck, reader and narrative, should be a Chief of Artillery—appropriate, too, that his Notice should warn that anyone seeking a plot would be shot. Getting killed is a key to the novel's plot line.

The fifth point to make about Huck's "joke" concerns the cause of death. On the river he travels, explosions are a common experience. Aunt Sally confirms this in the case of the poor Baptist, and we can find many other examples in the novel (steamboats grounded, blown up, cutting rafts in two). The point is: this river is sinister. Critics have tended to sentimentalize it—T. S. Eliot called it the "River God that gives to Man his dignity"—and to be sure such sentiments are invited by its deadpan author. But if we pay attention Twain makes it all too plain that this "great brown god" is a deadly con man. "Kill, kill, kill," Satan reports in *Letters from the Earth*, Nature "is murder all along the line," and *Huckleberry Finn* might have been his proof-text.[15] The river is the source of storms and water snakes, it calls up the fog that keeps Huck and Jim from reaching Cairo; it is "dangersome" to those on it and those who live near it. One example of many:

> the houses was sticking out over the bank, and they was bowed
> and bent, and about ready to tumble in.... People lived in them
> yet, but it was dangersome, because sometimes a strip of land
> as wide as a house caves in at a time. Sometimes a belt of land a
> quarter of a mile deep will start in and cave along till it all caves
> into the river in one summer ... the river's always gnawing at it.
> (183)

This river affords Huck and Jim some wonderful moments together; and to underscore these, critics like to quote Huck's description of life on the raft: "what you want ... is for everybody to be satisfied, and [to] feel right and kind towards the others" (165). But they have failed to take stock of Huck's far more typical *melancholy* on the raft and his overriding sense of loneliness: "there wouldn't be nothing to hear nor nothing to see," he comments about the river, "—just solid lonesomeness" (157). They have failed, too, to add that Huck's desire to please "everybody" registers Jim as a "nobody" once again: that's how Huck *rationalizes* allowing the King and Duke to have their way ("it warn't no use to tell Jim" [165]). And perhaps most important, critics have never yet to my knowledge noted that for most of the river journey (almost two-thirds of it) life on the raft is controlled and directed by those "rapscallions" (204), as Huck charitably calls them. There are about three pages devoted to the happy idyll of Huck and Jim on the fiver, most of them at the start of chapter 19. Albert Bigelow Paine rightly commented long ago that "[t]his is the Huck we want, and this is the Huck we usually have, and [have] ... been thankful for"; although in the standard edition these three pages—on the basis of which critics have repeatedly asserted (as a claim "not worth arguing") that "life on the raft is idyllic, and *Huckleberry Finn* is a pastoral fiction that looks back nostalgically to an earlier and simpler America"—these three pages occupy less than one percent of the book.[16] And in what might well be viewed as a deadpan joke on Twain's part, they directly precede the Duke and King's invasion of the raft. Huck and Jim may be in flight on the Mississippi, but the Mississippi is the natural habitat of the Duke and King, just as it is naturally the cause of mud slides. *This* river is emphatically not an emblem of Nature's Nation; it belongs to the world of Hobbes, not Emerson. Nothing is more natural about Huck, nothing more clearly shows how *close* he is to the river, how well he knows it, than does his spontaneous invention of the exploding cylinder that (only) "Killed a nigger."

Not that Huck needs the river to prompt his invention; he always thinks in terms of death and disaster. That's the sixth point to note about his casual response. It alerts us to the fact that he's a death-haunted young boy. I'm referring now to the way he thinks and imagines rather than to what he experiences. Twain provides two clues to Huck's inner world: the lies Huck tells and the images he conjures up when he's alone—in other words, the reality that Huck himself makes up, for others and for himself. In both cases, it's the reality of the grotesque. Huck talks not so much "gravely" (deadpan-style) as grave-ly. The stories he invents for strangers are a series of horror tales: families dead, dying, or diseased. And he thinks grave-ly too—except that in his solitary musings the dead return as ghosts. Consider his arrival at the Phelpses' plantation:

> When I got there it was all still and Sunday-like, and hot and sunshiny—the hands was gone to the fields; and there was them kind of faint dronings of bugs and flies in the air that makes it seem so lonesome and like everybody's dead and gone; and if a breeze fans along and quivers the leaves, it makes you feel mournful, because you feel like it's spirits whispering—spirits

that's been dead ever so many years—and you always think
they're talking about you. As a general thing, it makes a body
wish he was dead, too, and done with it all. (276)

Or consider Huck's first long meditation, sitting alone in his room at Miss
Watson's:

> I set down in a chair by the window and tried to think of
> something cheerful, but it warn't no use. I felt so lonesome I most
> wished I was dead. The stars were shining and the leaves rustled
> in the woods ever so mournful; and I heard an owl away off,
> who-whooing about somebody that was dead; and a dog crying
> about someone that was going to die; and the wind was trying to
> whisper something to me, and I couldn't make out what it was,
> and so it made the cold shivers run over me. Then away out in
> the woods that kind of sound a ghost makes when it wants to tell
> something that's on its mind and can't make itself understood,
> and so can't rest easy in its grave, and has to go about that way
> every night grieving. (4)

What's funny about these descriptions is that actually, to all appearances, it's
a lovely Sunday morning, a starry summer night. There's no reason for Huck
to think this way, except that that's the way he thinks.

But of course he's not alone when he invents the cylinder explosion; on
the contrary, he's trying hard to please someone else. He's being led on by
Aunt Sally, who prods him about the grounding. He knows what she'd like to
hear, and he knows she'll think a "nigger" is "no one," just as he knows she'd
like him to be Tom. And naturally he complies. That's the seventh point
to note about his response. Huck wants to conform. More precisely, he's a
conformist who can't make it. Huck would like to please everyone, including
Miss Watson. He would even like to live with Pap, if Pap would let him live;
he tries as best he can to "satisfy" the Duke and King; he tells us he'd gladly
join the Grangerfords (at the expense of abandoning Jim); and he'd love to
be Tom Sawyer—but he can't. Huck Finn is Woody Allen's Zelig in reverse:
a deadpan artist's Zelig. Zelig may not want to be a Chinese chef or a Nazi,
but he can't help becoming just like whomever he's with. Huck's dilemma is
just the opposite: he can't help being different. Certainly we sympathize with
his difference, we applaud it, but the nub remains. Huck's desire to fit in is
underscored by his inability to do so. That's because he so totally believes in
society. He *believes* in racism, class hierarchy, Southern aristocracy, Sunday
school religion. Why else would he be so disappointed, towards the end of

his adventures, in Tom's plan to "steal" Jim? "Well, one thing was dead sure," he says, crestfallen, after trying to persuade Tom otherwise,

> one thing was dead sure, and that was that Tom Sawyer was in earnest, and was actuly going to help steal that nigger out of slavery. That was the thing that was too many for me. Here was a boy that was respectable, and well brung up; and had a character to lose; and folks at home that had characters; and he was bright and not leather headed; and knowing, and not ignorant; and not mean, but kind; and yet here he was, without any more pride, or rightness, or feeling, than to stoop to this business, and make himself a shame, and his family a shame, before everybody. I couldn't understand it no way at all. It was outrageous.... (292–93)

If this were a children's book called *Tom Sawyer*, we could read this passage ironically, as a salutary bit of social satire. The white-trash boy is at once denouncing (when he shouldn't) and looking up to (when he needn't) the respectable head-of-the-gang. But *Adventures of Huckleberry Finn* is something else altogether. It's a complex, sophisticated narrative about a black–white relationship. To recall Twain's phrase, it's a work "of high and delicate art ... [as] only an artist can tell it"—one in which an African American takes on extraordinary human force. Jim, we learn, is the noblest person in Huck's life; virtually the novel's hero, if we could get beyond the minstrel-show humor to which (in one of the most vicious cuts of Twain's deadpan) Jim himself is subject; the father we feel Huck deserves and never had; and by any measure the novel's most sympathetic adult figure. Can it be funny that Huck thinks like *this* after his long experience with Jim on the river? After all he has seen of Jim—having acknowledged, however reluctantly, Jim's goodness, intelligence, and caring; having felt so ashamed of his behavior towards Jim, on one singular occasion, that he actually apologizes for it (though "it was fifteen minutes before I could work myself up to go and humble myself to a nigger" [105])—after all this can Huck believe that it would be "leather headed" for Tom to "stoop to this business"?

In order to explain this nub we need to rehearse its context. The last narrative section, occupying almost a third of the novel, has become a familiar critical crux. Twain scholars have debated its merits ever since Hemingway advised readers to skip it altogether. Evidently Tom's tricks at the Phelpses' did amuse the Reconstructionist audience of the time, and in the decades following (the world of Barrett Wendell, of the minstrel show, and of D. W. Griffith's epic celebration of the Ku Klux Klan, *The Birth of a Nation*, filmed in the decade after Twain wrote "The United States of Lyncherdom"): Jim shackled in a wood-shack (into which Tom and Huck "smuggle" rats, spiders, and snakes), rolling a grindstone uphill with a chain "wrapt ... round and round his neck," writing messages "with his blood," biting into a corn pone with a candlestick hidden in it. "It most mashed all his teeth out," Huck reports, and then explains, straight-faced: "Jim he couldn't make no sense it but he allowed we was white folks and knowed better; so he was satisfied" (329, 323, 309–10). Tom's higher knowledge comes from the romances of Alexander Dumas (whose African ancestry, if Twain knew of it, would add another dimension to the satire); he names his scheme the Great Evasion; and the joke, it turns out, is that Jim has already been freed. If we carry the logic of the joke to its absurd end, we could say Jim was *lucky* he didn't get to Cairo and the North, since he would then never have known that he was a free man.

To their credit, critics over the past half century have roundly denounced the hoax and all it implies. We can now safely say that it's a grand sarcasm on Twain's part directed against Tom Sawyer. The usual critical term here has been irony. But in the ironic situation, classically defined (from Sophocles through Jane Austen), the readers know, or gradually learn, what's actually going on; they are the author's accomplice. In the deadpan situation, they are the author's victims. That's precisely the case in the Great Evasion. The irony of the Good Bad Boy, whose mischief-by-the-book we see through and scorn, deflects us from the snapper. It's as though our eagerness to interpret Tom as reader (applying the rules of Dumas's *Count of Monte Cristo* to Jim in bondage) preempts a view of ourselves as readers of Huck's complicity. For what's really funny about Tom's hoax is that the Bad Bad Boy, *our* Huck, goes along. Fundamentally, he's no different at the end from the racist, death-haunted, would-be conformist he was before he set out on his adventures. That's what makes it appropriate for him to respond to Aunt Sally as he does, in spite of all he has learned about Jim. Or rather, *because* of all he has *not* learned, for (as his gratuitous "Killed a nigger" should shock us into recognizing) Huck never develops. Far from being a moral and aesthetic collapse, as critics have lamented, the novel's third and last section is perfectly in keeping with Twain's design—although for reasons antithetical to those usually proffered by his apologists. Huck's final adventures are substantively no different from all his others, as far as he himself is concerned, just as his attitude towards Tom Sawyer remains constant throughout, and just as his subservience here to Tom resembles his subservience to the Duke and King on the raft. Huck speaks and thinks and feels at the Phelpses' pretty much as he does at Miss Watson's or at the Grangerfords'. The great middle part of the novel, the so-called journey to freedom, is the deadpan center piece of a triptych—Tom Sawyer's gang, a precarious raft on a treacherous river, and a wood-shack prison at the Phelps plantation—whose three panels are variations on a nub.

Now, there's a technical reason for this: *Adventures of Huckleberry Finn* is Huck's personal retrospective, specifically intended to set the record straight. He wants to retrieve the true story, he tells us, from Mr. Mark Twain's stretchers. If he had realized what we'd like him to have realized, he would have written an entirely different book. He would have felt different not only about Jim but about Tom and all others, including himself at that time. The boy who might have emerged from his adventures chastened and humbled, as critics have told us he did, would never have said, not even early in his river journey, that "you can't learn a nigger to argue," or later, after one of his particularly horrific experiences, "Well, if I ever struck anything like it, I'm a nigger" (210); he would have felt obliged to explain why he abandoned Jim to live with the Grangerfords (and he would at least modified the values which he tells us here and elsewhere he learned from his father about the importance of social class); he would have expressed regret for not having confided to Jim what he knew about the Duke and King—or to put this another way, he would have applied to this situation something of what he learned at the Wilkeses, where he does report that the Duke and King are frauds, and feels better for it ("I'm blest if it don't look to me like the truth is better, and actually safer, than a lie" [239])—and surely he would not have expected Jim, this grown man eager to free his wife and children, to join him and Tom in the territory. That is to say, if Huck Finn had really grown morally, Twain the deadpan artist could not gull us into thinking that he does. There would be no snapper to the story. Humorously speaking, his tale would be un-American.

Huck doesn't develop so that we can be conned into believing he does: this eighth aspect of the snapper reminds us that what we believe in ultimately is Huck's integrity. He has the same poignant purity from start to finish. He's always the lovable boy with the "sound heart"; from the outset his innate decency is set in contrast to society's "deformed conscience." And to draw out this con game, it's precisely that admirable aspect of him, the potential we discern within Huck's innocence, which invites us to interpret his narrative. That much-discussed, much-celebrated innocence—that *echt*-American innocence which links United States popular culture, high culture, and global politics—lies at the very heart of the con game. For Huck is emphatically not innocent of the world around him. Quite the contrary: he has been thoroughly socialized into it, as his reply to Aunt Sally demonstrates. He is not innocent, for example, of the abolitionist cause, which he roundly denounces. Nor is he innocent of the values of the Southern class system, as he demonstrates by his awestruck admiration for the pseudo-sentimental, phony-aristocratic, meretricious life at the Grangerfords. Nor of course is he innocent (or critical) of how those he respects will judge him. What will the people of Hannibal "think of *me*!," he trembles, when it gets "around that Huck Finn helped a nigger to get to his freedom[?] ... if I was to see anybody from that town again I'd be ready to get down and lick his boots for shame" (268). We may say, however, that Huck is innocent insofar as innocence means ineducability. Huck is innocent of alternatives to the way things are. Therefore (to repeat) he doesn't develop, and *therefore* we do it for him. We know him better than he knows himself. Indeed, we know him as he *cannot* know himself, since his naïveté, his forever-unrealized potential, is what we know about him, and what we cherish.

The con game this involves posits two contrary responses on our part: first, our superiority to Huck; and second, our identification with him. The deadpan link in this opposition lies in Twain's directive for interpretation. I said earlier that the deadpan Notice *goads* us into seeking moral, motive, and plot. I would now add that the snapper is then meant to guide us into a *certain* mode of interpretation—one that *compels* us to miss the nub, so as to keep the humor bubbling gently along. Just how this works is well illustrated by the scene that critics have rendered the locus classicus of Huck's moral progress. It is perhaps the most frequently cited passage in the novel, along with the river passage at the start of chapter 19, and always with the same heartening interpretation. Huck learns that the Duke and King have disclosed Jim's whereabouts, and he decides that rather than see Jim sold to "strangers," he should return him to Miss Watson, "his true and proper owner." Then he succumbs, conscience-stricken, to memories of how he himself helped this "runaway nigger" so that now "people would [rightly] call me a low down Abolitionist" (52; cf. 124):

> I tried the best I could to kinder soften it up somehow for myself, by saying I was brung up wicked, and so I warn't so much to blame; but something inside of me kept saying, "There was the Sunday school, you could a gone to it; and if you'd a done it they'd a learnt you there that people that acts as I'd been acting about that nigger goes to everlasting fire.
>
> It made me shiver. And I about made up my mind to pray; and see if I couldn't try to quit being the kind of a boy I was, and be better. So I kneeled down. But the words wouldn't come.... You can't pray a lie—I found that out.... At last I had an idea; and I says, I'll go and write the letter—and then see if I can pray.... So I got a piece of paper and a pencil, all glad and excited, and set down and wrote:

Miss Watson, your runaway Nigger Jim is down here two mile below Pikesville and Mr. Phelps has got him and he will give him up for the reward if you send. HUCK FINN.

I felt good and all washed clean of sin for the first time I had ever felt so in my life, and I knowed I could pray now. But I didn't do it straight off, but laid the paper down and set there thinking ... [and went on thinking] and then I happened to look around and see that paper.

It was a close place. I took it up, and held it in my hand. I was a-trembling.... I studied a minute, ... and then says to myself:

"All right then, I'll go to hell"—and tore it up.

It was awful thoughts and awful words, but they was said. And I let them stay said and never thought no more about reforming ... (269–71)

What's funny about this scene is: (1) cheerful—it's a mock-conversion that turns into a Devil's Pact; (2) satirical—it's a sweeping indictment of the ravages of Southern Evangelical Calvinism; and (3) odd, curious, and sinister—it's a mockery of our relation to the text. For in order to get the joke we *have* to interpret, and yet we feel sure that our interpretation is voluntary. This comes straight out of the American con-man's interpretation-by-consent bag of tricks. The meaning we find seems purely subjective, a meaning from the heart, and yet it's entirely predictable, a meaning directed step by step by Twain's deadpan. For notice that we are led to interpret in a perfectly consistent—a suspiciously consistent—pattern of inversions. Huck says "conscience" meaning the Right Thing to Do, and we think "source of evil"; he says "wicked" and we think "kind"; Huck laments that he was "brung up wrong" and we're glad that he has held fast to his virtues; he tells us he shivered with fear and we think he's brave and independent; he says, trembling, "I'll go to hell" and we think "he's saved!"

Is this a tall tale on Twain's part, or a con game? In either case his deadpan point is that our pattern of inversion is an act of protection. Whether or not we're aware of it, we're reaching between the lines to save Huck from everyone around him, from Tom and Miss Watson and the Grangerfords and the Phelpses. And our act of protection is in turn a claim to ownership. It makes Huck *ours*. The opening gang-oath is worth recalling in this regard. The question that Tom raises about family hostages opens into a much larger question: to whom does Huck belong? The narrative plays out a series of options—Pap, Miss Watson, Tom's gang, Jim, the river, the Territory—until it becomes obvious that Huck belongs *only to us*. We adopt him; we take him into our hearts; we interpret him in our likeness; we rewrite his text, figuratively (and sometimes literally, as in the novels of John Seelye and Richard Slotkin or in the many filmic adaptations of the novel, direct and indirect, from children's movies to *Shawshank Redemption*); we appropriate Huck as the child-in-us. The interpretive plot, then—that is, the process of interpretation carefully elicited from us, with all the sly diversions of deadpan art—leads inexorably from inversion to protection to adoption to, triumphantly, appropriation.

Let me name the snappers. First, there's the issue of style. Huck Finn is a great writer; his grammar and spelling are faulty, but that simply accentuates the beauty of his expression, which is extraordinarily simple, spontaneous, and vivid. And yet we have to protect him all the time from his own text. We have to explain away his words, to redefine the emotions he records, to reverse the convictions he sets out. Huck is a master of the literal statement; he writes with unfailing lucidity and directness; he's the prime example, as Hemingway declared, of the American plain style. And yet we have to save Huck at every turn from his own plain meanings. (Think of what fun it would be to read Hemingway this way!) We have no choice, as it were, but to recast "shiver," when Huck says "it made me shiver," into *something* positive, to deny the import *for Huck* (the stated effect) of his decision to choose hell, to white out his numerous N-words. Once we've done all that, we can laugh along with Huck, *our* Huck, the uncorrupted child in us who (we're certain) does not believe, would never really think, that a nigger is a no one. To paraphrase Jim: we're sophisticated folks, and so we know better, and can smile contentedly, and be satisfied.

Still, we should be very uneasy by this point about the process we're engaged in. Our act of appropriation ends with the child-in-us—who is *us*? As Huck tells the story we come to feel that his conscience is the object of Twain's exposé. It's conscience that makes Huck a racist, conscience that keeps leading him astray, and we interpret his conscience, properly, as an indictment of the values of the antebellum Southwest. But there was no need in 1885 to indict slave society. Primarily Twain's deadpan is directed against his readership, then and later, even unto our own time—against, that is, the conscience-driven forms of liberal interpretation. To a certain extent, his project here reflects the frontier sources of tall-tale humor that I quoted at the start of this essay: the storyteller's "pleasure in dethroning the condescension of gentility at the thickly settled Eastern core, while at the same time reproducing the radical discrepancies and incongruities at the root of all American experience," Eastern-intellectual as well as roughneck-Southwest. What better, and more cutting, way to accomplish these ends than to get the Eastern gentility to identify condescendingly with this con-man's outcast-redneck hero?

And it's precisely in this sense, I submit, that a distinct liberal theme permeates the discourse about the novel, a critical main current that runs through virtually all sides of the argument (provided that the critic does not dogmatically, *foolishly*, condemn the book for being racist). To judge from a century of Twain experts, Huck is "self-reliant," "an Adamic innocent," "exemplifying the ... strong and wholesome [individual that] ... springs from ... the great common stock," exemplifying too the heroics of "the private man ... [for whom] the highest form of freedom [resides in] ... each man's and each woman's consciousness of what is right," and thereby, in its absolute "liberation," "ultimately transcending even anarchy as confinement"—in sum, an independent spirit," "the affirmation of adventure," "enterprise," and "movement," the soul of "tolerance, and common sense." More than that: Huck and Jim on the raft have been taken as an emblem of the ideal society. In contrast to the settlements, they represent the "spiritual values" of "individualism compatible with community"—not just the proof of "Twain's commitment to black civil rights" (and his appeal to "compensate" the blacks on "the national level" for "injuries" done them during the slavery era), but his summons to the "cause of freedom" in general. Huck and Jim together forecast "a redeeming hope for the future health of society"; they stand for the very "pinnacle of human community"; they provide "a utopian pattern of all human relationships." Critics have reiterated these "great redemptive fact[s] about the book" over and again, with what can only be called reflexive adoration. As Jonathan Arac observes, "it is as if 'we' uttered in self-congratulation: 'Americans have spiritually solved any problems involved in blacks and whites living together as free human beings and we had already done so by the 1880s'."[17] I would add that, beyond smugness, what this attests to is the process of interpretation as self-acculturation—a striking example of what I called the literary enterprise of socialization, in compliance with the charge bequeathed to "teachers of American literature" (society's "special custodians"), to inculcate the values of "enterprise, individualism, self-reliance, and the demand for freedom."

More interesting still, this process of interpretation reveals just how socialization works. The abstractions I've just rehearsed are admittedly "American ideals" but they are applied as universals, as though Huck represented not just what America but what all humanity ought to be. Thus a particular cultural vision—individualism, initiative, enterprise, and above all personal freedom ("What *Huckleberry Finn* is about is the process ... of setting a man free")—becomes a sweeping moral imperative. And as moral imperative it is then reinstated, restored as it were from heaven to earth, from utopian "alternative world" to actual geographical space, as a definition of the quintessential American. As Norman Podhoretz, editor of the conservative journal *Commentary*, has written: "Sooner or later, all discussions of *Huckleberry Finn* turn into discussions of America." Or in the words of the late Irving Howe, writing in his left-wing journal *Dissent*: "Huck is not only the most American boy in our own literature, he is also the character with whom most American readers have most deeply identified." Or once again, according to the centrist Americanist scholar Eric Sundquist, *Huckleberry Finn* is "an autobiographical journey into the past" that tells the great "story of a nation." Harold Bloom accurately summarizes the tone of his collection of "best critical essays" on the novel when he remarks that the "book tells a story which most Americans need to believe is a true representation of the way things were, are, and yet might be."[18]

That "need to believe," is the core of the "American humor" of *Huckleberry Finn*. It may be true that in its magnificent colloquialism the novel marks "America's literary declaration of independence ... a model of how one breaks free from the colonizers culture." But as a deadpan declaration the model it presents is, mockingly, the illusion of independence. It reveals our imprisonment *within* what Lewis Hyde, in his sweeping overview of the Trickster figure, calls the "joints" of culture. For Hyde, this concept involves a heroic view of the possibilities of interpretation. He pictures the Trickster's cultural work in physiological terms, as an assault upon the vulnerable parts of the social body, most tellingly its "*flexible* or *movable*" joints, where variant spheres of society (home, school, church, job) intersect.[19] At these anatomical weak points, he writes, Tricksters come most vividly to life, unsettling the system, transgressing boundaries, exposing conflicts and contradictions—thus freeing us, he contends, as sympathetic interpreters of their subversion, from social constraints. If so, Mark Twain is a kind of laughing anti-trickster. It's not just that he's mocking the tricksters in the novel: Tom, the Duke and King, Huck himself. It's that he's mocking our would-be capacities for Trickster criticism. What's funny about our interpretation of the novel—both of the narrative and of its autobiographical hero—is that what begins as our independent assessment, and often our oppositional perspective, leads us happily, of our own free will, into the institutions of *our* colonizing culture.

Thus it was all but inevitable that in our multicultural era, Huck should be discovered to be (in addition to everything else that's positively American) multicultural. This is not the place to discuss Huck's blackness—or for that matter the possibility of his ethnic Irish-Americanness—but it's pertinent here as elsewhere to recall Twain's warning that interpretation may be a trap of culture. He speaks abundantly of the nature of that trap in his later writings—in letters to friends, for example, reprimanding them for presuming that "there is still dignity in man," whereas the plain fact is that

"Man is ... an April-fool joke played by a malicious Creator with nothing better to waste his time upon"; and in essays protesting that he has "no race prejudices ... [nor] color prejudices, nor creed prejudices ... I can stand any society. All that I need to know is that a man is a human being; that is enough for me; he can't be any worse"; and in journals documenting how "history, in all climes, all ages, and all circumstances, furnishes oceans and continents of proof that of all creatures that were made he [man] is the most detestable ... below the rats, the grubs, the trichinae.... There are certain sweet-smelling, sugarcoated lies current in the world.... One of these ... is that there is heroism in human life: that he is not mainly made up of malice and treachery; that he is sometimes not a coward; that there is something about him that ought to be perpetuated." In his posthumously published novel, *The Mysterious Stranger*, Twain exposes the nub itself—lays bare the mechanism of the trap of hope. Here his stand-in deadpan artist, Satan, pairs up with a poor-white, innocent, sound-hearted little boy, a boy not unlike Huck—befriends him and conjures up for him a variety of alluring spectacles and promises, only to reveal, at the end, the absurdity of each one of them. "You perceive now," Satan declares, that it "is all a Dream, a grotesque and foolish dream." And then the boy's epiphany: "He vanished, and left me appalled: for I knew, and realized, that all that he had said was true."[20]

That's the humorous point of *Huckleberry Finn*, if we're alert. The novel's underlying moral and motive, its deadpan plot, is that this grand flight to freedom—black and white together, the individual regenerated by nature—was all a dream. Not a grotesque dream, to be sure, but a foolish one because it is a dream that befools. Recall the image of the novel with which critical tradition has left us. The plot is a river story, the style is a flow of humor, and our interpretation is a raft that promises protection (from conscience, from civilization, from all the slings and arrows of outrageous adulthood). Now consider the facts. The river keeps returning us again and again and yet again to the settlements, the raft proves to be a con-man haven, and on this "raft of trouble," on this river that betrays and kills, we're left with two mock-symbolic figures. One is Huck Finn, bond-slave to society, mostly scared to death, speaking a language we don't trust, and (as Pap puts it, in a drunken flash of insight) an Angel of Death. The other is Jim, the fugitive black who need never have run off, and who leads Huck into what Jim himself, early in the novel, calls the Black Angel's hell's-pact. So the nub is: the Angel of Death and the Black Angel, on a deadpan raft-to-freedom, drifting deeper and deeper into slave territory. It makes for a savagely funny obituary to the American dream.

* * *

Before, however, we confront the full import of that dead-end humor, we should account for an abiding paradox in our response to *Huckleberry Finn*. I have in mind the odd, curious fact that even after we get Twain's devastating nub—after we've struck through the comic mask and seen the deadpan leer behind it—even then our *experience* of the novel is exhilarating. From this perspective, what's funny is that the novel leaves us in good humor, as in some uncanny return of the cheerful and satiric layers of "funny" which the deadpan had sought to repress. For all our powers of recognition, in some sense the narrative resists that sinister ultimum—resists, that is, its own deadpan moral, motive, and plot.

Let me try to set that resistance in a larger literary perspective. The bleakness of *Huckleberry Finn* is not a unique instance in the history of American humor. There's a great line of the sinister deadpan mode, one that runs from (say) *The Confidence-Man*—Melville's absurdist-apocalyptic caricature of a world where, as the "waning light [of the last lamp] expired," "truth comes in with darkness"—through the Depression-era novels of Nathanael West, the self-styled "laughing mortician" of America's consumerist "dream dump," and the postmodern novels of Thomas Pynchon, all of them obsessed with "the legacy America," and all lamenting (laughingly) that the one way "to be at all relevant to [the legacy, is] as an alien, unfurrowed, assumed circle into some paranoia."[21] Within this persistent tradition—embracing the tall tale and the con game under the aegis of deadpan—Mark Twain is *the* American Funnyman. His vision and method are related to Melville's, West's, and Pynchon's, but he differs from them in the quality of his humor. That difference lies in what I called at the start his strategy of inversion (reversal, concealment). Twain plays out his deadpan while wearing the Mask of Comedy, but because he succeeds the Mask comes to life, as it were. His novel is genuinely *funny*. The other humorists in this tradition make us shudder, wince, or squirm even as we laugh. Twain makes us laugh outright, with an almost childlike delight. Somehow the novel does cheer us up, in the manner of the tall tale; it even manages at times to reinforce normative ideals, in the manner of con-game satire—as *Pierre* and *The Confidence-Man*, *Miss Lonelyhearts* and *The Day of the Locust*, *The Crying of Lot 49* and *Gravity's Rainbow* emphatically do not.

Perhaps the best way to describe that paradox of exhilaration is through the affective sense as distinct from the analytical. I refer to the fragile, brittle link between authorial intention and textual intentionality. Think of the disjunction between what Twain meant to do and what he wrought—between the terrible story he tells and the radiance of Huck's monologue—and now recall D. H. Lawrence's famous dictum, "Never trust the artist. Trust the tale." That's surely *the* anti-deadpan principle of interpretation, and it may legitimately be objected that it's out of place here as being inimical to Twain's art. But we might recall the allegations of Twain's "inadequate control over his materials" and his inelegant manipulations of plot.[22] And even if we simply discount these charges, as I believe we should, we must take account of the complexity of Twain's strategy, which requires us to focus not just on his (the author's) tricks, but, equally, on the dynamics of humor that Huck (the narrator) sets loose. Thus *up to a point* we have a critical obligation to attend to Lawrence's injunction. An important distinction between Twain and his contemporaries may help clarify that obligation. Twain's is a humor of extremes, in the manner of Southwestern humor; but the extremes in other tall tales and con games highlight discrepancies *within* the culture: they build upon the gap in frontier experience between civilized language and "the language of sweat." *Huckleberry Finn* speaks at once from inside and outside the culture: inside it, because it pivots on the *conjunction* of Huck's vernacular and our civilized interpretation; outside it, because the deadpan nihilistically makes fun of *both sides of that conjunction*. On one hand, there's an extraordinarily daring con game at work: we're being sold on the American dream-works, all of it, lock, stock, and barrel. On the other hand, there's a correspondingly daring tall tale in process: we're being asked to fall in love with Huck. And one game depends on the other. We must buy into the dream-works if we are to preserve our love for Huck, *and the other way around*: we must preserve our love for Huck in order for Twain's design upon us to work.

The result is a simultaneity of contrary effects, hence a constant volatility of perspective. And—here's the Lawrencian snapper, if I may call it so—that volatility undermines the deadpan mode, since deadpan is basically systemic. It depends on a comprehensive, bottom-line meaning: the nub, the realization, that explains (even as it undoes) everything that has come before. In other words, deadpan humor, incorporating as it does both the tall tale and the con game, implies a hierarchy of levels of meaning, leading to an ultimate meaning, not unlike the medieval four-fold method or Renaissance Protestant allegory. Ultimately, Dante's Jerusalem is anagogical; ultimately Bunyan's Pilgrim represents the Redeemed Christian. By contrast, the term I have used throughout, *layers* of meaning, signifies meanings that are mobile, shift-shape, like a kaleidoscope. It depends on which way you turn them; and by definition they are always subject to another turn, or series of turns.

Twain's art entwines both strategies. His humor, as I've been arguing, builds simultaneously on hierarchical levels *and* volatile layers of meaning. It thus translates into a bifurcated language that for all its cunning works at cross purposes. By Twain's design, the novel's levels of meaning depend on cause and effect: first there's the joke we laugh at, then the shocking recognition. But Twain's design also demands that we bubble merrily along, moving from sick joke to tall tale, from the imaginary nigger to the Baptist on the Lally Rook. Thus the layers of meaning within (and inseparable from) what I called the analytic process involve a pattern of affective inversions. As we read and reread, conscious of the humorous nubs and yet flowing happily with the currents of comedy, our response keeps shifting from cheerful to satirical to sinister, sinister to satirical to cheerful, back and forth, and (in mood) up and down, down and up. So although the plot leads deterministically downward—affectively, down in hope; geographically, "down the river"—the strategy behind it requires an anti-deterministic flow of aesthetic give-and-take. As the stakes are raised in the narrative snappers (that is, the sinister mental game directed against us), they must be raised proportionately, for the trick to work, in the love-game (that is, the effervescent monologue through which Huck becomes ours). In other words, the very process by which Twain the deadpan artist controls both satire and exaggeration, con game and tall tale alike, keeps Huck alive and well—within his own world (*his* monologue), alive, buoyant, on the go.

I mean linguistically on the go. In fact, Huck had nowhere to go, as Twain's dismal attempts at continuity (such as "Huck and Tom among the Indians") demonstrate, and as his notes for a "true sequel" make plain: "Huck comes back, 60 years old, from nobody knows where—& crazy."[23] In this sense we may speak of an excess of language in *Huckleberry Finn*, an overabundant (or even indeterminate) humor that, up to a point, allows Huck to slip out of Twain's control. We might then proceed to posit a Derridean monologue: a Huck Finn who deconstructs in the very process of storytelling. Or (my own preference) we might posit a Levinassian presence: a protagonist whom we can never fix or label, a Huck Finn who is neither merely what he says he is (poor white trash), nor merely a version of the American ideals we project upon him, nor (again) merely the laughing stock of a humorous story, but towards whom we cannot help feeling protective in some way. That protective feeling is the result neither of superiority nor of identification. Quite the contrary: it comes from our recognition of *difference*. We might even argue that on some unarticulated (because culturally inaccessible) level a similar protective relation, a felt mutuality based on respect for otherness, springs up between Huck and Jim. In any event, we are compelled by Huck in this version because he's not like us; and we come to appreciate him best precisely when we *laugh at our urge to appropriate him*. Such laughter is directed at ourselves, it's self-incriminating; but what's funny about it is that it enlarges our capacity for love. It helps us see in Huck what Emanuel Levinas calls a "height of the good" that transcends categories of logic—the logic of critical analysis no less than deadpan logic and the logic of culture—so that the novel provides a kind of lifebuoy (a coffin-lifebuoy) to the ethical like.

We might call this the serious alternative—normative, satirical, universalist—as distinct from the cheerful alternative I outlined earlier, involving the sheer-fun volatility of language-play. But here as before, alas, we can follow the prospect only up to a point. The problem in both cases is that the alternative entails a comic resolution, and any such resolution, however we frame it, diminishes Twain's fantastic achievement: the high and delicate art by which he takes us in, and through which he offers us the opportunity to have a good laugh at ourselves, good enough (in the sinister sense) to do the job he believed all laughter should do, which is to "blow [history] to rags and atoms at a blast."[24] More important: to indulge in those dreams of transcendence, formalist or philosophical—those flights from textual-historical meaning into some free territory elsewhere—is to return in a metaphysical or aesthetic (or anesthetic) fog to the Humorist's raft once again, drifting into precisely the traps of culture which the novel works to expose and explode. Nor will it do to seek a political resolution in that act of exposé as in the neo-Marxist forms of ideological critique advanced by Louis Althusser, Antonio Gramci, and Raymond Williams. In this perspective, the fact that Twain's snappers distance us from Huck (and the American belief system he represents) attests to the radical potential of interpretation. Although we cannot transcend ideology, we have critical resources within the culture at large which allow for resistance, which indeed prod us toward alternatives to the dominant culture. Again, a happy prospect, perhaps; and again, *Huckleberry Finn* is meant to disabuse us of precisely such visionary or utopian expectations. What's positive for Twain is our capacity for humor in clear-sighted despair—which is to say, for the laughter of realism, in all its bleakness, as against the illusions of progress.

Freud offers a helpful insight into the contrast I'm suggesting. As a rule, he observes, the comic serves to distance us from the "distressing effects" of humor—the kind of humor that "does damage" and "causes pain"—to the point where we are entirely disengaged from the painful situation. "The victim of the injury," he writes, "might obtain *humorous* pleasure, while the unconcerned person laughs from *comic* pleasure."[25] That's the core of the difference between Twain and those who would find ways out of the predicament he describes. To disengage from the injury is to slight both form and content in Twain's art. *Huckleberry Finn* exploits the pleasure principle in order to shock us, painfully, into self-recognition.

In effect, Twain's inversion of traditional deadpan is a general disavowal of comic modes. I said at the start that my concern was with his concept of humor rather than with theories of the comic; but as I've indicated by my references to Althusser and Freud, Derrida and Levinas, I believe that his concept can be sharpened by contrast with certain theories of our time. The most relevant of these involves the current interest in the *skaz*, the Russian vernacular monologue, where the humor lies partly in the vernacular itself, as in *Huckleberry Finn*. According to Mikhail Bakhtin, the *skaz* is characterized by irony, satire, and parody, all of which either advance social norms or else offer spiritual or intellectual alternatives—a prospect, in either case, which is precisely the object of Twain's ridicule. That ridicule applies, too, to the sort of "liberating magic" which Walter Benjamin attributes to the folktales of Nikolai Leskov: tales told in a vernacular which evokes "the earliest arrangements that mankind made to shake off the nightmare of which the myth had placed on its chest."[26] Twain, on the contrary, exposes liberation (as in Jim's last-minute emancipation by Miss Watson) as con-game magic, or as one of those mirage-like points of light (such as Huck's apology to Jim, or the river idyll, or the respite on Jackson's Island) that flicker briefly from time to time in the ever-darkening journey back into slave country. Twain's deadpan foregrounds the unshakable burden of history—the nightmare into which we are forever locked by training and human predisposition.

More telling still (considering the novel's slavery-era context) is the laughter-through-despair mode of Jewish humor. I think particularly of Holocaust humor and its related forms in the Yiddish *skaz*—notably the monologues of Sholem Aleichem—describing the besieged *shtetl*. To begin with, *Huckleberry Finn* pointedly refuses what David Roskies claims for pogrom jokes: to fortify us against "the trauma of history" by "laughing [them] off," hence providing a sort of enclosed communal garden "against the apocalypse." Concerning Sholem Aleichem (with whom Mark Twain has been compared), Roskies argues that his monologue technique "gives us the laughter that results from the clash between languages and life ... [and the] greater the discrepancy, the funnier it is, and the funnier it is, the more fortifying"—a technique which is the target of Twain's snappers. Secondly, *Huckleberry Finn* ridicules the notion that humor can "embrace" so as to "diffuse hostility," as Terrence Des Pres says of "Holocaust laughter." In fact, Twain's deadpan does just the opposite: it turns our laughter into hostility—at society, at ideals, and at ourselves for wanting to embrace either one or the other. His snappers (as the humor bubbles along) do not save; they annihilate. Finally, Twain's deadpan reverses the effect of what Henri Bergson calls the "bisociated contexts" of comedy. Peter Berger applies that theory to the general "tragedy of man," claiming that, by highlighting discrepancies in context, humor "relativizes" the tragic, and so "provides yet another signal of transcendence." Arthur Koestler speaks in this vein directly about gulag and concentration camp jokes. The subversive writer, he argues, manipulates events that are "capable of being interpreted in two entirely different meanings at the same time" so as to ridicule authority. Twain too manipulates the bisociated contexts of comic meaning (including the contextual parallels between the slavery and Reconstructionist periods); but he does so in ways that reject signals of transcendence and make us the objects of ridicule.[27]

In an important recent essay that builds on most of these Holocaust commentators, Sidra Ezrahi defends Holocaust humor (as in Roberto Benigni's film *Life Is Beautiful*) as an "aesthetics of deferral" developed by Jews over the course of their long diaspora, one that balances recurrent disasters against scriptural promises of millennial redemption. Twain's case is very different. He has been said, accurately, to invoke the American redemptive dream—the river idyll as "an anticipation of the Messianic time (which is called the time of the 'continuous Sabbath') of ... peace and harmony"—but it's a deadpan millennium. And the nub this involves points to one of the darkest aspects of Twain's humor. I refer to the fact that the American promise is precariously open-ended, forever provisional, and therefore potentially an anticipation of its opposite, doomsday. That's the potentiality which American dark humorists have traditionally seized upon. The Jewish "theodicy [of] ... the happy end" is guaranteed, absolute, inscribed from eternity in the Bible.[28] For the Late Twain, the vision of a New World paradise is the last and greatest of history's con jobs. To recall the first recorded definition of deadpan (someone "holding four aces in his hand and you wouldn't know it"), the game being trumped by this card-shark—his poker face lit up in a broad and cheerful (or is it satiric?) smile, setting out one shocking snapper after another—is the American millennium.

Holocaust laughter is thus the obverse of Twain's. It may be that all laughter, even Satanic laughter, is a sign of hope, since it implies continuity; and continuity, even within the bounds of culture, testifies to human agency and will. But there's a world of difference between the Jewish context and that of *Huckleberry Finn*. Indeed, if we can allow the analogy, a Holocaust Huck would be a derelict, sound-hearted German boy—call him Heinz Pfin—running away from home and teaming up accidentally with an adult Jew just escaped from a concentration camp, an empathetic, loving, extremely capable, and enormously grateful man, desperate to reunite one day with his family. In spite of himself, Heinz sometimes treats the escapee as an equal (though far more often as his "benign superior"[29]), all the while feeling ashamed for doing so (how will he explain all this back in his Bavarian hometown? he keeps thinking). And he feels ashamed because *fundamentally he believes that the Jew is what his Nazi culture has taught him* (a "nobody," a nonperson). Accordingly, he refers repeatedly to "Jew-vermin" ("you can't learn a kike to argue"; "if I ever struck anything like it, I'm an *Ungezeifer*"), or, in his most generous gesture, directly after the escapee has saved his best friend's life, at the risk of his own, "I knowed he was aryan inside." Imagine reading a genuinely funny book of this kind and concluding that this boy is not just forgivable (for his sound heart and ostensible innocence), but a moral hero, the very model of what boyhood should be. That would be deadpan on the author's part. And to follow Twain to the bitter end, the book would have to be addressed to a German readership that was still very much anti-Semitic, as Twain's Reconstructionist readership was still very much racist. So imagine, further, members of that readership laughing at themselves for having been taken in by the deadpan, but, according to the author, having no alternative—no way out of the process of acculturation (and an inherently vicious predisposition) that made them admire the boy in the first place.

What to do, then, with that paradox of exhilaration? We must leave it simply as paradox, I believe, and find the courage to confront the import of Twain's deadpan. Those who have hitherto evaded it betray a certain desperation, well expressed some forty years ago in Perry Miller's rhetorical question: "Can Americans imagine what they would take themselves to be if ... *Huckleberry Finn* were expunged from the national recollection? How, without that book, would even those of us who had never seen the Mississippi River know who we are?" How indeed, except by somehow meeting the challenge of Twain's devastating American humor? Other writers found a way out of despair—Wordsworth, for example, who recalled his "utter loss of hope itself/And things to hope for" with the tranquillity of faith restored. Twain never recovered; on the contrary, he made contempt for hope his ground of creativity. To the last, he maintained that an optimist was a "Day dreamer more elegantly spelled"; to the last, he claimed that there were no thoughts, no opinions, except those that were "transmitted to us," so that (as he lamented in his final autobiographical dictations) there "was no escape from [our social and] natural environment, not even for someone [like himself] who recognized it."[30] Miller's question entails a comic view of *Huckleberry Finn*. But at the very least the comic mode calls for a celebratory reunion at the end, if only as a fiction to accommodate audience desire. By contrast, the proposed reunion that ends *Huckleberry Finn* is a snapper directed against the convention of happy endings, and the laughter it provokes is designed to change desire to distress. In Freud's terms, it turns our protective "*comic* pleasure" into a self-ridiculing "*humorous* pleasure." Twain seeks to demonstrate *through* our laughter the process of our victimization.

The laughter of the victim: a bleak prospect, none bleaker. It's like imagining Job laughing at his misfortunes, before (or rather without) the author's cosmic resolution. Perhaps even that grim comparison is inadequate. "Though He slay me," says Job (13:15) in his darkest hour, "yet I will maintain my integrity." In the deadpan version, we would be invited to laugh at Job's belief not only in God's concern but in his own integrity. No comfort here; but then, there are always plenty of comforters at hand, secular and religious, nationalist and universalist, left and right. We owe it to Twain's art to attend to his disconcerting nubs and snappers. Could we not find in them something enabling after all? Enabling, not ennobling: a wisdom without consolation, a strategy for survival in a world bereft of comic resolutions. We don't have to endorse this stance in order to acknowledge its insight, even its heroic quality—which involves the integrity to confront dilemmas *as dilemmas*, no end in sight, the fortitude to laugh at the traps that beset us, without seeking refuge in our laughter. So understood, what's funny about *Huckleberry Finn* is that its most positive feature—the one aspect of the novel that may be said to promote interpretation, rather than mock it—lies in its denial of comic relief.

NOTES

1. Mark Twain, "How to Tell a Story," in *Mark Twain: Collected Tales, Sketches, Speeches, and Essays, 1891–1910*, ed. Louis J. Budd (New York: Library of America, 1992) 201–02. This essay incorporates materials from a talk delivered at an American Literature Association Conference on the Trickster, and published as "The American Humor of *Huckleberry Finn*," in *Trickster Lives: Culture and Myth in American Fiction*, ed. Jeanne Campbell Reesman (Athens, GA: Georgia UP, 2001) 53–83. A shorter version of that talk appeared as "What's Funny about *Huckleberry Finn*?" in *New England Review*, xx (1999) 8–28. Here I take issue with both of these earlier (wholly inadequate, as I now think) efforts on my part to explain the humor of Twain's novel. I would like to express my gratitude to Lewis Hyde for his astute editorial guidance, and to Susan L. Mizruchi for her brilliant and generous critical insight. For important bibliographical references, my thanks to Louis J. Budd of Duke University and to Joe Lockart and Victor Fisher of the University of California at Berkeley.

2. *The Cassell Dictionary of Slang* (New York: Jonathan Green, 1994).

3. Walter Winchell, "A Primer of Broadway Slang," *Vanity Fair* November 1927: 68; *Oxford English Dictionary* (Oxford: Clarendon Press, 1989).

4. Henry B. Wonham, *Mark Twain and the Art of the Tall Tale* (Oxford: Oxford UP, 1993) 20–21.

5. Hilton Mantled Obenzinger, *American Palestine: Melville, Twain, and the Holy Land Mania* (Princeton: Princeton UP, 1999) 166.

6. Mark Twain, *Adventures of Huckleberry Finn*, ed. Walter Blair and Victor Fischer (Berkeley: U of California P, 1988) 2; see also 7, 77, 84, 125, 141, 167, 174, 233, 234, 334. The parenthetical page numbers for *Huckleberry Finn* within the text are from this edition.

7. Mark Twain, *Letters from the Earth*, in *Collected Tales, Sketches, Speeches, and Essays, 1891–1910*, ed. Louis J. Budd (New York: Library of America, 1994) 884.

8. Mark Twain, "Plymouth Rock and the Pilgrims" in *Collected Tales ... 1852–1890*, ed. Budd, 782.

9. Stuart P. Sherman, "American and Allied Ideals: An Appeal to Those Who Are Neither Hot Nor Cold," *War Information News*, no. 12 (Washington, D.C.: Committee on Public Education, 1917) 6. (This is a succinct, if crude, summary of the Introduction to the *History*); the editors' "Address" to *The Literary History of the United States*, ed. Robert Spiller et al. (New York: Macmillan, 1948) xx–xxi.

10. Jonathan Arac, *Huckleberry Finn as Idol and Target: The Functions of Criticism in Our Time* (Madison: University of Wisconsin Press, 1997) 8, 11, 13, 21.

11. Jay Martin, "The Genie in the Bottle: Mark Twain in *Huckleberry Finn*," in *One Hundred Years of Huckleberry Finn; The Boy, the Book, and American Culture*, ed. Robert Sattelmeyer and J. Donald Crowley (Columbia: U of Mississippi P) 56–57 (Hart and Bliss are the appropriate deadpan names in this context); Paul Baender, *Introduction to What Is Man and Other Philosophical Writings*, ed. Baender (Berkeley: U of California P, 1973) 4–5, 9, quoting Twain's essays; Mark Twain, "The Character of Man," in *Collected Tales ... and Essays, 1852–1890*, ed. Budd 858. The precise dates of Twain's Dark Period have been a matter of contention, and even during this period Twain continued to write and speak (for money) in the lighter satirical or tall tale vein but even biographers who date his full despair only after 1890 concede that it begins in the early 1880s.

12. Mark Twain, *A Connecticut Yankee in King Arthur's Court*, in *Mark Twain: Historical Romances*, ed. Susan K. Harris (New York: Library of America, 1994) 326.

13. Barrett Wendell, A Literary History of America (New York: Charles Scribner's Sons, 1900) 342. Wendell later calls *Huckleberry Finn* a "masterpiece" (477). I am uncomfortably aware of my own position in the descent of Harvard professors of American literature, all of whom have contributed significantly to the consecration of Huck Finn as the quintessential American. The line runs from Wendell through Perry Miller and his students, such as Henry Nash Smith and Leo Marx; and in all its variations, from Wendell's praise of Huck's racism to Marx's denunciation of what he considered to be Twain's betrayal of Huck's cause of freedom. My own iconoclasm in this respect is not consciously prompted by an anxiety of influence, but I should note that I first elaborated my views in my first class on *Huckleberry Finn* at Harvard in 1983. My sense then was that my (indignantly received) interpretation was prompted by my relative innocence—my lack of acculturation—as an immigrant in the United States of Huckdom. In retrospect, I feel that my interpretation also registered an era in academia marked by a suspicion of all rhetorics of nationalism and a globalist deconstruction of traditional forms of Americanism. Ironically, this was also the beginnings of what may be called the Americanization of the world; and I venture to predict (since the process of Americanization has long since come to incorporate literary studies as well) that the mythic-liberal-heroic Huck will prevail, in one form or another—not just in the U.S.A., but, in due time, and with due training, globally.

14. [Robert Bridges], "Mark Twain's Blood-Curdling Humor," *Life*, v (26 Feb. 1885): 119.

15. T. S. Eliot, "Introduction" to *Adventures of Huckleberry Finn*, in *Adventures of Huckleberry Finn: A Case Study in Critical Controversy*, ed. Gerald Graft and James Phelan [Boston and New York: Bedford Books, 1995] 288; Lionel Trilling, "Introduction" to *Adventures of Huckleberry Finn*, in *Huck Finn and His Critics*, ed. Richard Letis, William E. Morris, and Robert F. McDonnell (New York: MacMillan, 1962) 328 (quoting T. S. Eliot); Mark Twain, *Letters from the Earth*, in *Collected Tales ... 1890–1910*, ed. Budd 882.

16. Albert Bigelow Paine, *Mark Twain: A Biography* (New York: Harper and Brothers, 1912), II, 795; Richard Chase, *The American Novel and Its Traditions* (New York: Doubleday, 1957) 148.

17. Richard P. Adams, "Unity and Coherence in *Huckleberry Finn*," and Carmen Bellamy Gladys, "Roads to Freedom," in *Twentieth Century Interpretations of Huckleberry Finn*, ed. Claude M. Simpson (Englewood Cliffs: Prentice Hall, 1968) 18, 22; Harold Beaver, *Huckleberry Finn* (London: Allen and Unwin, 1987) 196; Lawrence Howe, *Mark Twain and the Novel: The Double-Cross of Authority* (Cambridge: Cambridge UP, 1998) 116; Bruce Michelson, *Mark Twain on the Loose: A Comic Writer and the American Self* (Amherst: U of Massachusetts P, 1995) 138; Paul Taylor, "Huck Finn: The Education of a Young Capitalist," Robert Shulman, "Fathers, Brothers, and the 'Diseased': The Family, Individualism, and American Society in *Huck Finn*," Stanley Brodwin, "Mark Twain in the Pulpit: The Theological Comedy of *Huckleberry Finn*," Roy Harvey Pearce, "'Yours Truly, Huck Finn'," and James M. Cox, "A Hard Book to Read," in *One Hundred Years*, ed. Sattelmeyer and Crowley, 317, 337, 353, 385, 401; Leo Marx, "Mr. Eliot, Mr. Trilling, and *Huckleberry Finn*," in *Huckleberry Finn: A Case Study*, ed. Graff and Phelan, 293; Bernard De Voto, "Mark Twain's America," and Vernon L. Parrington, "The Real Mark Twain," in *Huck Finn and His Critics*, ed. Lettis, Morris, and McDonnell, 306, 308, 315; Stacey Margolis, "Huckleberry Finn; or, Consequences," PMLA (2001) 331, 340; Jocelyn Chadwick-Joshua, *The Jim Dilemma: Reading Race in Huckleberry Finn* (Jackson: UP of Mississippi, 1998) 7; David E. E. Sloan, *Mark Twain, as a Literary Comedian* (Baton Rouge: Louisiana State UP, 1979) 144; Arac, *Huckleberry Finn as Idol and Target*, 8. See also the essays collected in James S. Leonard, Thomas A. Tenney, and Thadious M. Davis, ed. *Satire or Evasion? Black Perspectives on Huckleberry Finn* (Durham: Duke UP, 1992).

18. Lawrence B. Holland, "A 'Raft of Trouble': Word and Deed in *Huckleberry Finn*," in *American Realism: New Essays*, ed. Eric J. Sundquist (Baltimore: Johns Hopkins UP) 66; Arac, *Huckleberry Finn as Idol and Target*, 8, 3 (quoting Podhoretz, Howe, and Sundquist); Harold Bloom, Introduction to *Mark Twain's Adventures of Huckleberry Finn*, ed. Harold Bloom (New York: Chelsea House, 1986) 1.

19. Shelley Fisher Fishkin, *Lighting Out for the Territory: Reflections on Mark Twain and American Culture* (New York and Oxford: Oxford UP, 1997) 184–85; Lewis Hyde, *Trickster Makes This World* (New York: Farrar, Straus, and Giroux, 1998) 256.

20. Mark Twain, letter to William Dean Howells, quoted in Warwick Waddlington, *The Confidence Game in American Literature* (Princeton: Princeton UP, 1975) 284; "Concerning the Jews" in *Collected Tales ... 1890–1910*, ed. Budd, 359, 854–55; "The Character of Man," in *Collected Tales ... 1852–1890*, ed. Budd, 854–55; *No. 44, The Mysterious Stranger*, ed. William M. Gibson (Berkeley: U of California P) 187.

21. Herman Melville, *The Confidence-Man: His Masquerade* and "The Piazza," in *Herman Melville; Pierre, or the Ambiguities, Israel Potter, The Piazza Tales, The Confidence-Man, Uncollected Prose, Billy Budd*, ed. Harrison Hayford (New York: Library of America, 1984) 634, 1112; Nathanael West, "Editorial," *Americana* (November, 1932), front page cover, and *The Day of the Locust*, in *Nathanael West: Novels and Other Writings*, ed. Sacvan Bercovitch (New York: Library of America, 1997) 326; Thomas Pynchon, *The Crying of Lot 49* (New York: Harper & Row, 1965) 182.

22. D. H. Lawrence, *Studies in Classic American Literature* (Garden City, NY: Doubleday, 1951) 13; Jeffrey Steinbrink, "Who Wrote *Huckleberry Finn*? Mark Twain's Control of the Early Manuscript," and Victor Doyno, *Adventures of Huckleberry Finn: The Growth from Manuscript to Novel*" in *One Hundred Years*, 89–95. These sorts of

objections reflect mainly the critic's view of what he or she thinks the text ought to be, as when Doyno criticizes Twain for the "loopy logic" of Pap's diatribes (95).

23. *Mark Twain's Notebooks and Journals, Volume III (1883–1891)*, ed. Robert Pack Browning, Michael B. Frank, and Lin Salamo (Berkeley: U of California P, 1979) 606. I theorize this view of layers vis-à-vis levels of meaning in "Games of Chess: A Model of Literary and Cultural Studies," in *Centuries' Ends, Narrative Means*, ed. Robert Newman (Stanford: Stanford UP, 1996) 15–58, 319–28.

24. Mark Twain, "Chronicles of Young Satan," in *Letters from the Earth* manuscripts (Mark Twain papers, University of California at Berkeley. The reference to Levinas (above) is from Richard A. Cohen, *Elevations: The Height of the Good* in Rosenzweig and Levinas (Chicago: U of Chicago P, 1994) 123.

25. Sigmund Freud, *Jokes and Their Relation to the Unconscious* (1905), trans. James Strachey (London: Routledge and Kegan Paul, 1960) 228. Interestingly, Freud's distinction here between humor and the comic builds on examples from Mark Twain's writings.

26. Walter Benjamin, "The Storyteller," in *Illuminations: Essays and Reflections*, ed. Hannah Arendt, trans. Harry Zohn (New York: Schocken, 1969) 102.

27. David Roskies, *Against the Apocalypse: Responses to Catastrophe in Modern Jewish Culture* (Cambridge, MA: Harvard UP, 1984) 163, 177, 182; Terrence Des Pres, "Holocaust Laughter?", in *Writing and the Holocaust*, ed. Berel Lang (New York: Holmes & Meir, 1988) 216, 232–33; Henri Bergson, *Laughter: An Essay on the Meaning of the Comic*, trans. Bloudesley Bereton and Fred Rothwell (Los Angeles: Green Integer, 1999) 90; Peter Berger, *A Rumor of Angels: Modern Society and the Rediscovery of the Supernatural* (New York: Anchor Books, Doubleday, 1990) 79; Arthur Koestler, "Comedy," in *Insight and Outlook* (New York: Macmillan, 1949) 16.

28. Tony Tanner, *The Reign of Wonder* (Cambridge: Cambridge UP, 1965) 162; Sidra DeKoven Ezrahi, "After Such Knowledge, What Laughter?" *Yale Journal of Criticism*, xviv (2001) 306–07. This point warrants a brief elaboration. Twain's deadpan, I am arguing, invokes a broad nationalist rhetoric of all or nothing: millennium or doomsday; America either as humanity's "last, best hope" or else as its "last best hope." Thus in two antithetical yet complementary surveys of classroom experience, Eric Solomon sees the novel as a composite dream-image of ultimate "hope in America" while Hamlin Hill discusses it as a "nightmare" vision of cosmic collapse ("My *Huckleberry Finn*: Thirty Years in the Classroom with Huck and Jim," and "Huck Finn's Humor Today," in *One Hundred Years*, ed. Sattelmeyer and Crowley, 254, 306). This choice is something of a ritual refrain throughout our literature and as such it constitutes a bipolar symbolic strategy (dream/nightmare) through which the culture has sustained itself, in effect foreclosing any alternative to national ideals—which is to say, keeping all interpretative options locked within the basic premises of the dominant culture. (See my discussion of the "anti-jeremiad" in *The American Jeremiad* [Madison: U of Wisconsin P, 1978] 191–97). Does Twain himself fall into this hermeneutic trap? I suggested above that he seeks to avoid it through the opposition between interpretation as illusion and what he might call the realism of the nub. Of course, Twain's realism is itself an interpretation but this does not discredit the claims he makes, or the challenge they pose to our own sanguine views of the powers of interpretation.

29. Waddlington, *Confidence Game*, 267. Together with James Cox and Hamlin Hill (in the essays quoted above), and Alan Trachtenberg, "The Form of Freedom in *Adventures of Huckleberry Finn*," *Southern Review*, VI (1970) 954–71. Waddlington comes closest to recognizing the nature of Twain's nubs, but he too sees in them a "quintessentially comic vision" (250), or as Trachtenberg puts it, a "negativity [that] implies an ideal" (971).

30. Perry Miller, "An American Language" (1958), in *Nature's Nation* (Cambridge, MA: Harvard UP, 1967) 229; William Wordsworth, *The Prelude* (1805), IX, 6–7, ed. J. Wordsworth, H. H. Abrams, and S. Gill (New York: Norton, 1979); Mark Twain, "More Maxims of Mark," in *Collected Tales ... 1891–1910*, ed. Budd, 945, and *Autobiographical Dictations* (sometime after 1906), as paraphrased in Baender, Introduction to *What Is Man*, ed. Baender, 4–5.

JEFFREY STEINBRINK

Who Shot Tom Sawyer?

Mark Twain did. He saw to it that bullets flew pretty freely throughout *Adventures of Huckleberry Finn*, and of course ultimately he was responsible for all of them, but the particular bullet that fells Tom Sawyer bears evidence of deliberate authorial meddling as indelibly as Huck and Jim do when, a little earlier in the story, they are made to find their way to the Arkansas farm of Sally and Silas Phelps, who happen to be Tom's aunt and uncle. Mark Twain was doubtless a realist, but when a story needed invigorating he was not above causing a boy or a bullet to take a lucky turn. The bullet in question, after all, could have behaved like the myriad bullets around it and simply contributed to a general sense of urgency and danger during the final crisis in Tom's elaborate "evasion" scheme. Or it could have struck Huck or Jim, making for a different story in either case. Or it could have killed Tom, making for still another. Mark Twain was not a man to spend bullets thoughtlessly, his early experience with a profligate "Allen" revolver in *Roughing It* notwithstanding. In *Huck Finn* he had used them with particular economy in the poignant deaths of Boggs and Buck Grangerford and in ridding the world of Pap Finn. In his way he was as handy with a gun as James Fenimore Cooper, whose Natty Bumppo, he claimed, could have hunted flies with a rifle.

From *American Literary Realism, 1870–1910* 35, no. 1 (Fall 2002): 29–38. © 2002 by the University of Illinois Press.

119

Mark Twain shot Tom Sawyer, but he was not without accomplices—the actual trigger-man in the story, certainly, an impatient reader here or there, perhaps—and not without motive. Even some critics, peaceable generally, have implied that Tom deserved a good shooting. The following meditation assembles this medley of suspects, discussing each in turn, its intention being to show how our response to the shooting reveals something important about our reading of *Huck Finn*, the book, and Tom Sawyer, the boy.

We can begin by reminding ourselves of the circumstances in the story that precipitate the bullet that catches Tom Sawyer: Tom, too has made his way to the Phelps farm and has astonished Huck by pledging to help free Jim from captivity. In doing so he concocts and carries out the elaborate escape sequence with which the novel ends and with which critics have been contending for generations.[1] On the night of the escape the demands of Tom's hyper-romantic imagination have caused him to stir up what Huck calls "a thundering hornet's nest" of agitation among the Phelpses and their neighbors, many of whom are on guard at the farm, with their rifles.[2] At about midnight Jim, Huck, and Tom slip out of Jim's prison-hut and make for the river, the hornets at their heels. The three do evade capture, only to discover that in the scramble Tom has been shot in the calf.

The real shooter, the literal shooter, is one of the hornets. In the world of the novel, that is, one of the Phelpses' Arkansas neighbors puts a bullet in Tom Sawyer, believing him to be either the escaping runaway slave or one of the slave's accomplices. The shooter might even be kindly uncle Silas Phelps. But in the world of the novel it doesn't matter who does the shooting, which is after all the consequence of a fairly random volley from an entirely undifferentiated pack of riflemen; it only matters that Tom is shot. The novel pays no attention at all to Tom's assailant. Tom's injury, though, is made to galvanize our interest and profoundly affects the course of the story.

That no one could be more pleased with this outcome than Tom himself suggests Tom himself as a suspect. We might, with only a little ingenuity, declare his a self-inflicted wound. Did Tom Sawyer shoot Tom Sawyer? Consider the facts: we know, or we come to know, that the entire evasion episode is a needless contrivance of Tom's to *set free* a man he knows already to *be free*. We know that Tom has spared no effort to complicate this needless process, compounding the degree of difficulty of the escape in his quest for romantic glory.[3] We know that in service to this superheated romanticism he insists not simply on "stealing" Jim away from the Phelpses, but on warning them that he is about to do so. He writes what Huck calls "nonnamous" letters that alarm the neighborhood about "a desprate gang of cutthroats" and even specify when the gang will strike (333–34). Then he places himself, together with Huck and Jim, in the center of the bulls-eye he has drawn by carrying out the evasion at the appointed hour. When it dawns on Huck that he is about to step into the wrong end of a shooting arcade, he is sensibly terrified:

> I couldn't hardly get my words out, I was so anxious; but I told Tom as quick as I could, we must jump for it, now, and now a minute to lose—the house was full of men, yonder, with guns!
> His eyes just blazed; and he says:
> "No!—is that so? Ain't it bully! Why, Huck, if it was to do over again, I bet I could fetch two hundred!" (338)

As an index of the contrast between Tom's imagination and Huck's experience, this one is pretty well calibrated: Huck, who has seen, for instance, Buck Grangerford shot and killed, is appalled by the fifteen armed farmers in the Phelps parlor who may shortly be training their guns on *him*. At the sight of them he says, "I was most powerful sick, and slunk to a chair and set down" (336).[4] Tom, whose books have led him to believe that gun barrels disgorge not death but glory, wishes only that those fifteen could be two hundred. A thousand would be better still—and if it were possible to do so with honor, Tom would happily shoot himself. The evasion enables him to do the next best thing.

This is not to say that Tom Sawyer is suicidal. He is about as far from suicidal as a fatuous mortal can be. He can't conceive of his own death except in terms of the silly, melancholic narcissism that he practices in his own book, a book in which, moreover, he is allowed to enact his immortality by surviving to prevail at his own funeral.[5] If Tom takes a bullet—and I think the phrase is well chosen—it will serve not to slay but to ornament him. And in this attitude, or in this conviction, he is the soul-mate not of Becky Thatcher but of W. D. Howells' Editha Balcom, who is so dreadfully inconvenienced when her insufficiently romantic fiancé is shot stone-cold dead in a war she fully expected to ennoble them both.

If Tom's Byronic code won't quite allow him to shoot himself, the general impatience of this essay in dealing with him betrays another suspect: *I* could have shot him. It no doubt puts me at the lethal extreme of reader-response critics to confess a brotherly enthusiasm for the Arkansas farmer who actually does hobble Tom. But after the rats, the spiders, the snakes; after that millstone; after the rope-ladder pie, the journal-writ-in-blood, the coat of arms; after those "nonnamous" letters and the bloody graffiti he scrawls on the Phelpses' doors; after making *Jim* wear a *dress*—after all that, given means and opportunity, I'm not sure I could throttle back the temptation to do Tom harm. I am not alone in these unhandsome sentiments. Down through the decades since *Huck Finn*'s publication, angry critics have gathered, like the thundering hornets in the Phelps' parlor, to rue the day that Tom set foot on Phelps property and at least figuratively to take their best shot at him.[6] I suspect that the ranks of the disenchanted have grown recently, as controversies over Jim's treatment in the novel have heightened readers' awareness of Tom's role in causing him to suffer.

This brings us back to Mark Twain, who *did* have a shot at Tom Sawyer and who was, with whatever motivation, guiding the bullet that found Tom a lot more attentively than the Arkansas farmer who fired into the darkness after the fugitives. Contemporary readers of *Huck Finn* are by many accounts considerably quicker than their predecessors to grow impatient with Tom's behavior. Given their particular attentiveness to Twain's social consciousness, they are more likely to suppose that he shares their frustrations and further to suppose, therefore, that shooting Tom Sawyer amounts to a comeuppance or pay-back, a form of rough authorial justice. We imagine, that is, that he too gets so fed up with Tom's selfish, bookish, derivative, sentimental, demeaning damned foolishness that he is anxious to repay Tom for some of the pain he has caused Huck and especially Jim. Indeed the record is clear that Samuel Clemens saw this sort of estrangement coming. "If I went on, now, & took him into manhood," he wrote of Tom to Howells just as he was finishing Tom's own book, "he would just be like all the one-horse men in literature & the reader would conceive a hearty contempt for him."[7] Many critics have observed that Tom may already have crossed the line into one-horse manhood by the time that book ends: the Bad Boy has become a respected, even a revered, figure in St. Petersburg.[8] He leads Huck not out for a smoke on Jackson's Island but off the streets and back into the Widow Douglas' protective custody. Judge Thatcher imagines him in a military academy and then law school. Twain could hardly have damned Tom more roundly if he had appointed him to a seat in Congress.

So there is reason to think that Mark Twain had had his fill of Tom Sawyer by the time he finished Tom's book and believed that to go any further with him would be a mistake.[9] And yet there Tom is at the beginning and especially at the end of Huck's book, making himself available to our hearty contempt. Twain seems to be getting Tom in his cross-hairs, making a target of him. Consider Tom's initial encounter with Huck after the two of them find themselves together again at the Phelps farm. Huck is there to try to free Jim, whom the king and duke have sold out for forty dirty dollars. Huck almost learns Jim's whereabouts from the duke himself, before the duke thinks better of it and lies. "'I'll tell you where to find him,'" the duke says.

"A farmer by the name of Silas Ph—" and then he stopped. You
see, he started to tell me the truth; but when he stopped, that way,
and begun to study and think, again, I reckoned he was changing
his mind. And so he was. (274)

Twain orchestrates Tom's first exchange with Huck at the farm in such a way
that Tom precisely mimics the duke. When Huck tells him that he means to
set Jim free, Tom says,

"What! Why Jim is—"
He stopped and went to studying. (284)

Like the duke, Tom is changing his mind. Like the duke, he starts to tell
the truth: "'What! Why Jim is *free as any cretur that walks this earth!*'" (356).
Like the duke, he stops, studies, and lies; nine chapters will pass before he
finishes this sentence honestly. Tom seems, like the duke, to be a con-man
accustomed to furthering his own interests at the expense of others.

To the extent that Mark Twain regards and treats Tom as an object of
contempt—as he surely does the duke, and as he seems prepared to do in this
scene—he is likely to be driving the bullet that catches Tom, and he is likely
to mean for it to sting. But the general tenor of the evasion chapters toward
Tom shows that that is not the case. Our dudgeon over Tom's treatment of
Huck and especially of Jim during the evasion is more a reflection of our
contemporary sensibility than a response to authorial signals that Twain
sends, despite this early instance linking Tom's behavior to the duke's. We
have been especially willing lately to overread the broad humanity and
decency for which Mark Twain spoke in his day to the point of recasting him
along a paradigm of social values established in our own. As I've admitted, *my*
indignation and resentment at the torments and belittlings that Tom inflicts
on Jim—on Jim!—are savage enough to make me wish for the chance to
join those Arkansas farmers at the shooting arcade. But as I read the ending
of *Huckleberry Finn*, Mark Twain comes across as entirely tolerant of Tom's
outrageousness—appreciative of it, even.[10]

Downright grateful for it, in fact. Twain's first concern in this novel, as
in everything he wrote, was in making it go, in getting it somehow to *move*
along. Tom's romantic excessiveness is a powerful—and familiar—engine in
this struggle, and the writer's discovery, or invention, of the notion that Tom
could be enlisted in the novel's final action, Jim's escape, must have seemed no
less incandescent to him than it does to Huck.[11] When Tom appalls and pleases
Huck by promising to help steal Jim from the Phelps farm, something like
foreshadowing happens: "I let go all holts," Huck says, "like I was shot" (284).

Tom's book-fired imagination remains a target for Twain's satire in the later stages of *Huck Finn*, as it was in Tom's book. But from the author's point of view it is also, again, a rich source of humor and of movement in the novel. Tom makes things happen—funny things, from Twain's perspective, even if (or perhaps especially because) they are manifestations of a particularly virulent case of the Sir Walter Disease. Huck is far more conflicted about Tom's obnoxious plans than Twain seems to be; very little of the book's ironic energy is directed against Tom, who is treated simply as a boy by all the story's grown-ups, including its author. When Huck details for Aunt Sally the misdemeanors he and Tom have committed in freeing Jim—the petty thefts, the household upsets, the dire warnings—she responds that the "little rapscallions" deserve a good spanking (356). And when Aunt Polly arrives on the scene she is not at all surprised to find "such a scamp as my Tom" in hot water (358). Twain's treatment of Tom is entirely consistent with Howells' characterization of Tom in his review of *Tom Sawyer*:

> He is mischievous, but not vicious.... He is cruel, as all children
> are, but chiefly because he is ignorant; he is not mean, but there
> are very definite bounds to his generosity.... In a word, he is a boy,
> and merely and exactly an ordinary boy on the moral side.[12]

Having nearly reached maturity by the end of his own book, Tom is in fact reincarnated as a boy when he reappears in Huck's. Away from St. Petersburg and the celebrity he has earned there, Tom returns to a sleepy, summertime world where he is free to operate just outside the field of vision of obtuse, unsuspecting adults. While critics have made much of Huck's saying that "it was like being born again" to be mistaken by the Phelpses for Tom (282), it is really Tom who is reborn, or at least rejuvenated, in *Huckleberry Finn*. Tom may indeed be headed for a contemptible, one-horse manhood, but he is further removed from it at the end of Huck's book than at the end of his own.[13]

The excesses, even the romantic excesses, of a boy characteristically occasion Mark Twain's tolerant bemusement; he reserves his vituperations, and his gun-play, for older, more accountable targets. The bullet that fells Tom Sawyer is I think best understood as a token of the writer's appreciation, not his vitriol. Tom gets not what he deserves, according to our latter-day sensibilities, but what he wants—a lead badge of courage. Having filled the Phelpses' yard with riflemen, Tom insists that Jim and Huck precede him in breaking for the fence and the fields beyond. As he is clearing that fence, either Tom or Twain contrives to make Tom an even likelier target by catching the seat of his pants on a splinter. Only when the three have made their way to what seems like safety does Tom reveal—triumphantly, of course—that he's been hit. "We was all as glad as we could be," Huck says of their narrow escape, "but Tom was the gladdest of all, because he had a bullet in the calf of his leg" (340).

Mark Twain gets good service from that bullet, as he does from Tom. The bullet necessitates Huck's recruiting a doctor to treat Tom, which in turn offers Twain the chance to resurrect Jim's humanity by having him forfeit his freedom for the sake of Tom's well-being. The fever that the bullet wound induces in Tom lasts just long enough to reestablish and even to deepen the terms of Jim's servitude before Tom returns to consciousness with the remarkable news that Jim is and has been free. In the book's last paragraph the bullet ends up around Tom's neck, which the contemporary reader may fervently wish to wring with his own two hands. But not Mark Twain. He allows Tom simply to talk right along, blocking out the plot for "howling adventures amongst the Indians, over in the Territory" (361). Just the sort of place where, with any luck at all, someone else might take a shot at Tom Sawyer.

NOTES

1. This is no time to rehearse, let alone to lengthen, this venerable debate, which turns fundamentally on the question whether the "evasion" sequence amounts to a fitting conclusion to Huck's story or a major falling off. For an engagingly polemical recapitulation and commentary, see Richard Hill, "Overreaching: Critical Agendas and the Ending of *Adventures of Huckleberry Finn*," *Texas Studies in Literature and Language*, 33 (Winter 1991), 492–513.

2. Mark Twain, *Adventures of Huckleberry Finn*, ed. Walter Blair and Victor Fischer (Berkeley, Los Angeles, London: Univ. of California Press, 1985), p. 336. Subsequent citations are noted parenthetically.

3. More than three decades after its publication James M. Cox's delineation of the motivation and context of Tom's behavior remains the most comprehensive. "Tom simply has to shine if he can," Cox says, "and he utilizes every resource at his command to do so." What makes Tom's own book stand apart, according to Cox, are "its commitment to the pleasure principle" and Tom's agency in enacting that commitment (*Mark Twain: The Fate of Humor* [Princeton: Princeton Univ. Press, 1966], pp. 137, 146). Cox is nicely answered and supplemented by Forrest G. Robinson, who elaborates the social consequences of "Tom's unwavering commitment to a dream of himself as hero in a world of play" ("Social Play and Bad Faith in *The Adventures of Tom Sawyer*," *Nineteenth-Century Fiction*, 39 [June 1984], 3).

4. Huck's response to the actual violence of Shepherdsons slaughtering Grangerfords is much the same. "It made me so sick I most fell out of the tree," he says. "I ain't agoing to tell *all* that happened—it would make me sick again if I was to do that" (153).

5. An important difference between *Tom Sawyer* and *Huckleberry Finn* hinges on the transformative power of play. The former, according to Cox, witnesses "the conversion of all 'serious' community activity—all duty, pain, grief, and work—into pleasure and

play." It offers "a world of boyhood in which play was the central reality, the defining value" (146–47). This is nowhere more evident than in the funeral episode, where even death capitulates to play. There is no such capitulation in *Huck Finn*, although Tom's surviving—prevailing in—the evasion scene with a non-lethal wound echoes his role and power in the earlier book.

6. Some critics find in Tom's performance at the Phelps farm not just a bratty heedlessness but something substantially, even archetypally, more corrupt. Observing, for example, that Tom "is capable of terrible selfishness and cruelty," Georg Meri-Akri Gaston says, "There are many villains in [*Huck Finn*], but Tom is the most sinister" ("The Function of Tom Sawyer in *Huckleberry Finn*," *Mississippi Quarterly*, 27 [1973], 33, 36). While Huck embodies a Dickensian innocence that reflects a romantic reverence for childhood, according to John Seelye, "in the shape of Tom Sawyer there is centered a darker, yet more vital force, the demonic power ... that mingles love and hatred, creativity and destruction" ("What's in a Name: Sounding the Depths of *Tom Sawyer*," *Sewanee Review*, 90 [Summer 1982], 410). Cox maintains that Tom exhibits "a unique cruelty in a book which depicts so much cruelty," and gauges the impact of that cruelty on a contemporary sensibility. "Having felt Huck's slow discovery of Jim's humanity," he says, "the reader perforce deplores Tom's casual ignorance and unawareness" (175).

7. *Mark Twain–Howells Letters: The Correspondence of Samuel L. Clemens and William D. Howells, 1872–1910*, ed. Henry Nash Smith and William M. Gibson (Cambridge: Harvard Univ. Press, 1960), I, 91.

8. William C. Spengemann, for instance, made the case early and succinctly: "Tom has gone over to the other side; he has sold out his freedom and innocence for acceptance and security. Earlier in the book Tom was the bad boy, but by the end the townspeople treat him as one of themselves" (*Mark Twain and the Backwoods Angel: The Matter of Innocence in the Works of Samuel L. Clemens* [Kent: Kent State Univ. Press, 1966], p. 46).

9. "By & by," he wrote Howells, "I shall take a boy of twelve & run him on through life (in the first person) but not Tom Sawyer—he would not be a good character for it" (*Mark Twain–Howells Letters*, I, 92). Victor Doyno is among those critics who believe that the ending of *Huck Finn* validates Clemens' judgment. "The reintroduction of Tom Sawyer and his behavior in the last section of the novel," Doyno says, "compellingly demonstrate Twain's artistic intuition that Tom was the wrong sort of boy to trace to maturity. Instead Tom dramatizes a particular kind of moral corruption, a combination of subservience to his authorities and absolute, arrogant disregard for his companions" (*Writing Huck Finn: Mark Twain's Creative Process* [Philadelphia: Univ. of Pennsylvania Press, 1991], p. 164).

10. Here I may differ with Doyno, the best of *Huck*'s recent readers, who says that "the attitude toward Tom becomes contemptuous at the end of Huck's book" (225). The ambiguity of the line invites a distinction: I agree that readers bringing a turn-of-the-twenty-first-century sensibility to the book are very likely to regard Tom with contempt, but 1 see little evidence in the text to suggest that Twain shared or sought to elicit this response. For a sharply contrasting view, see Michael Oriard: "Although Huck is incapable of articulating any judgment against Tom, behind Huck's narration lies an implicit authorial voice that registers scorn upon the discovery that Tom's game has had no meaning at all" ("From *Tom Sawyer* to *Huckleberry Finn*: Toward Godly Play," *Studies in American Fiction*, 8 [1980], 197).

11. After an affecting discussion of Huck's "depression" toward the end of the novel, Henry Nash Smith reaches a similar conclusion about Tom's strategic value, but puts it more somberly. "Mark Twain," he says, "has found out who he must be in order to end his

book: he must be Tom" (*Mark Twain: The Development of a Writer* [Cambridge: Harvard Univ. Press. 1960], p. 133).

12. Howells, *My Mark Twain: Reminiscences and Criticisms*, ed. Marilyn Austin Baldwin (Baton Rouge: Louisiana Univ. Press, 1967), p. 106.

13. I am in some ways here reversing the polarity of Seelye's argument, which maintains that in his own book "Tom Sawyer remains forever a boy, ... unregenerate, forever committed to the world of play," and that only in *Huck Finn* "does Tom become a victim of his illusions" (423–28).

MARY P. NICHOLS

Huckleberry Finn *and*
Twain's Democratic Art of Writing

Well, we can't help it; we've got to do the best with the material we've got.
—Tom Sawyer, in *The Adventures of Huckleberry Finn*

All the principal characters in *The Adventures of Huckleberry Finn* are
storytellers. Huck himself is a weaver of tales, adopting one disguise after
another as he makes his way down the Mississippi with runaway slave Jim.
Most importantly, Twain presents Huck as the narrator, even the author,
of *The Adventures of Huckleberry Finn*. Thus Huck tells the story of his own
storytelling. It is Tom Sawyer, however, who is the master whom Huck
emulates. "I did wish Tom Sawyer were there" Huck tells us more than
once (33, 188),[1] for Tom would have thrown in the "fancy" touches and
the "gaudy" details (see e.g., 33, 188, 230, 250, 254). Not only is Tom "the
unchallenged scholarly authority on the [romantic adventure] literature the
boys enjoy," in the words of Twain scholar Robert Hill, but "as a practitioner
of the imaginative hoax, ... he is also the village's premier artiste."[2] But as
the premier artiste, Tom is also the contriver of the rescue of Jim at the end
of the novel that critics find so troubling—a rescue in terms of medieval
romances that they believe is demeaning to Jim, loses sight of the novel's
moral thrust, and turns satire into burlesque.[3] And because Jim has already
been freed by Miss Watson's will due to her pangs of conscience, Twain is

From *Seers and Judges: American Literature as Political Philosophy*, edited by Christine Dunn
Henderson: 17–32. © 2002 by Lexington Books.

129

accused of a lapse of moral vision, "a failure of nerve" that abandons his critique of respectable society that gives the novel meaning.[4]

Twain of course is well aware of how ridiculous the "rescue" of Jim appears, if only because he registers Aunt Sally's and the neighbors' reactions to it. It is possible that Twain's purpose is not simply the criticism of social conventions which critics look for in novels,[5] but a criticism of the effects of story telling, and even an exploration of how democratic societies are susceptible to "imaginative hoaxes," whether in the form of Tom's absurd pranks or of the even more harmful schemes of the duke and the king, the novels' two con-men who join Huck and Jim in their travels. It would be somewhat paradoxical, however, for a storyteller himself to write a story that criticizes storytelling. Does *The Adventures of Huckleberry Finn* itself escape its own criticism of the harmful effect of books and, more generally, of the imagination, on human life?

My examination of these issues will discuss the different kinds of storytelling we find in Twain's novel, especially the differences between Tom, and the books he reads, and his comrade Huck, and the book he writes. I shall argue that in spite of Huck's attraction to Tom, the differences between the two boys are crucial for understanding the novel. Huck is a thoroughly democratic character, distinguished by the simple pleasures he derives from nature, his compassion, and his common sense and practicality, all of which qualify him more than Tom as a model for democratic society. But Twain shows us that these qualities in Huck must be refined or educated. His experience of nature's goodness must be expanded into an experience of human goodness. Huck's natural compassion or sympathy underlying the latter must in turn be moderated by an appreciation for admirable human qualities and the human beings who manifest them. Finally, Huck's common sense must move beyond experience to understanding, while resisting Tom's romanticism. In short, Huck's naive goodness must yield to self-reflection. Twain documents Huck's development or education in the course of his "adventures" on the river, including both Huck's experiences and his reflections on them. Huck's relationship with Jim is the most important, but not the only, factor in Huck's development. After discussing Huck's education in the first part of this essay, I shall argue in the second part that it is his capacity for reflection and self-knowledge that qualifies Huck more than Tom to narrate his *Adventures*.[6] By his portrayal of Huck's development, Twain suggests an education appropriate to democratic man, one more consistent with responsible citizenship than the playful and selfish romanticism of Tom. Twain thus demonstrates democracy's need for an art of writing that elevates its noble propensities while warning against romantic attempts to transcend the limits of democratic life.

In offering such a reading of this novel, I recognize, I seem to go against the authority of Mark Twain himself, who gives notice at the outset that any attempt to find a motive or a moral in his novel will be prosecuted by law (2). But as Huck reveals on the very first page of his book, Mr. Twain like most everyone he knows tells a few stretchers from time to time (3). And if we were to simply follow the authorities in books, we would run the risk of being as ridiculous as Tom Sawyer himself.

HUCK'S EDUCATION

As Huck escapes from Pap's confinement, he finds "a good rest and a smoke out of his pipe." Lying in the bottom of his canoe, he enjoys the evening, for "the sky looks ever so deep when you lay down on your back in the moonshine" (35). Later when Jim joins him, and they float down the Mississippi, Huck finds "It's lovely to live on a raft," with "the sky up there, all speckled with stars" (115). In contrast to Tom, whose pleasures derive in large part from elaborate imitations of the romances he has read (see, e.g., 239), the pleasures Huck seeks are simple, and hence accessible to anyone who looks up at the stars at night, or takes the time to light his corncob pipe.

To some extent Twain is mocking Huck's experiences of the goodness of nature, for the boy forgets the floods and life-threatening storms on the river (64–65; 81). Moreover, "living on a raft is lovely" due to the watchfulness and care of Jim, who repairs the raft and makes it sea-worthy.[7] But there is more than mockery here, and more to Huck's simple experience of nature than first appears. As he enjoys his pipe and the moonlight from his canoe, he hears the voices of "people talking at the ferry-landing," and their laughter (35). Later when he tells of viewing the stars with Jim, he reports, "we used to ... discuss about whether they was made or only just happened." While Huck at first supposes the latter, as "it would have took too long to *make* so many," he finds support for Jim's speculation that the moon could have laid them from his experience of frogs who lay almost as many eggs (115). Huck appeals to nature to understand nature, even the wondrous things of nature, but his pleasures in nature are shared, and they lead to discussion. In all these ways, Huck's experiences of nature are *human* experiences.

Most important about Huck's experiences of the goodness of nature, however, is that they are an imperfect manifestation of another experience of goodness, at first simply a natural compassion for suffering human beings, and then an admiration for human excellence. Twain shows us that Huck's sympathy for the suffering of others can act as a restraint on his own desires and as a force that prevents him from hurting them. "Laws, knows," Huck admits, "I *wanted* to go bad enough" to join Tom, but every time he sneaks down the lightning-rod he sees Aunt Sally's tears, and goes back up to his room, "swearing that I wouldn't never do nothing to grieve her anymore" (271).[8]

Similarly, Huck's sympathy with Jim's suffering leads him to recognize Jim's humanity. Jim "was often moaning and mourning that way nights [for his wife and children whom he had left in slavery], when he judged I was asleep." Huck has to admit that Jim "cared just as much for his people as white folks does for their'n" (150). Huck's experience of Jim's pain at his separation from his family no doubt prepares his own reaction to "the sight of them poor miserable girls [the Wilks' sisters] and niggers hanging around each other's necks and crying," when the duke and the king separate the families of the Wilks' slaves to sell them down the river. Even later when Huck tells the reader of his adventures, he admits, "I can't ever get [this scene] out of my memory" (176). Huck's natural compassion serves as a better guide than his "conscience," which takes its bearings from the precepts of society and its condonation of slavery.

Twain nevertheless suggests the inadequacy of compassion when it leads Huck to sympathize with the plight of the murderers and even to risk Jim's freedom in order to save them, thinking "how dreadful it was, even for murderers to be in such a fix" (70). Huck's compassion for the murderers becomes comic as he observes that the kind Widow Douglas, who had tried to teach Huck to help others when he was under her care (12), would be proud of him, for "rapscallions and dead-beats is the kind that the widow and good people takes the most interest in" (73). It was the good judge's "sympathy" for Pap, after all, that led him to give Huck back to his father, and try to help Pap lead a new life (22). It was a sympathy, however, that he was soon to regret.[9]

Thus while Huck sympathizes with the victims of the duke and the king (it made "[his] heart ache to see them getting fooled and lied to so" [176]), Huck is pained as well by the sufferings of the two con-men when they are discovered and punished. "It was a dreadful thing to see," he admits. "Humans can be awful cruel to one another" (222; see also 119). Natural compassion is indiscriminate, focusing on suffering, and not on whether the suffering (for example, the punishment) is deserved.[10] It is only when Huck comes to know Mary Jane and to appreciate her excellence—especially her generosity toward others and her insisting to her sisters that they act in kind (168)—that he is moved to action: "I says to myself, this is a girl that I'm letting that old reptile rob of her money" (169). And so Huck determines to help her and to betray the duke and the king. Compassion must be qualified by an admiration for character.

As Huck remarks of Mary Jane, "there warn't no back-down to her, I judge.... [S]he had more sand in her than any girl I ever see ... and when it comes to beauty—and goodness, too—she lays over them all." Although he never saw Mary Jane again, "I reckon I've thought of her a many and a many a million times" (184–185).[11] Twain prepares us for Huck's ability to distinguish character from the outset when confronted by the religious teachings of the Widow Douglas and her sister Miss Watson he judges "there was two Providences," and "reckoned [I] would belong to the Widow's if he wanted me" (13).[12] And with Mary Jane, Huck chooses to protect her and her sisters from the con-men. He now acts on his perception of her goodness.

Huck undergoes a similar development in his relationship with Jim. Huck sympathizes with Jim's suffering, as we have seen, but he also feels for Jim's owner, "poor Miss Watson," who would suffer if her slave got away (85). It is when Huck sees that he himself is responsible for hurting Jim that he recognizes the obligations of close human relationships. Twice Huck attempts to play a joke on Jim, "thinking there'd be some fun" at Jim's expense (52)—much along the lines of Tom's desire "to tie Jim to the tree just for fun" (7). But Huck's "fun" leads to unintended and harmful consequences. When Huck inadvertently attracts a rattlesnake to Jim's bed by placing its dead mate there, Jim is laid up for days from its bite (52). Huck is nevertheless not deterred from having more fun at Jim's expense, when he makes Jim believe that the rough storm that separated them during the night was only a dream. Jim interprets his "dream," "painting it up considerable," until Huck points to the leaves and rubbish on the raft and broken oar. The hurt Jim describes his work during the storm to find Huck, his heart "mos' broke bekaze you wuz los'," and his joy in seeing him alive again, "en all you wuz thinkin; 'bout wuz how you could make a fool uv ole Jim wid a lie," Jim "interprets" the signs of the storm, as "trash"—"which is what people is dat puts dirt on de head er dey fren's en makes 'em ashamed" (84).

Jim's moving reply is not lost on Huck. The episode is clearly a turning-point in his education. Huck is moved not only by Jim's pain but also by his claims about friendship and about Huck's betrayal of it. When Huck "humbles [him]self to a nigger," he "warn't ever sorry for it afterward, neither," and does "no more mean tricks," just as he "wouldn't done that one if I'd 'a' knowed it would make him feel that way" (84). Although Huck does not infer that slavery is wrong, he finds it impossible to betray Jim back into slavery, and even determines to rescue Jim when the duke and the king do so. Indeed, it is because he does not question the morality of the institution of slavery that his determination is so heroic: "all right, then, I'll *go* to hell" (206). His decision is made not simply or even primarily because of his compassion for Jim's suffering, but because of his recognition of Jim's good qualities that he has grown to appreciate and even to love during their voyage on the river: as he remembers Jim's care for him and the good times they have shared, "I couldn't seem to find no places to harden me against him, but only the other kind" (206).

But does Huck's conceding to Tom's plan to free Jim, once he is held on the Phelps's farm, not amount to a betrayal of Jim, just the sort of "mean trick" Huck promises never to play again? So the critics have argued, as I have mentioned, who find that Tom's "antics" for Jim's escape "divest Jim, as well as Huck, of much of his dignity and individuality," and "diminish [the] importance and uniqueness of Huck's victory [over his 'conscience']."[13] As Leo Marx, for example, asks, "if [Huck] cannot accept Tom's harmless fantasies about the A-rabs [who Tom claims were transformed by magicians into a Sunday school picnic], how are we to believe that a year later Huck is capable of awe-struck submission to the far more extravagant fantasies with which Tom invests the mock rescue of Jim?"[14]

But Marx does not give Huck credit where credit is due. In the first place, Huck does not know that the rescue is a "mock" rescue as does Tom, who knows enough about Huck to stop himself from revealing to him that Miss Watson has freed Jim in her will (217). Tom, in other words, recognizes a difference between himself and Huck that Marx does not, for Tom is aware that he cannot count on Huck for a "pretend" rescue if Jim is already a free man. Tom is rescuing Jim for the fun of it. Tom "was in high spirits," Huck reports: "He said it was the best fun he ever had in his life, and the most intellectural; and said if he only could see his way to it we would keep it up all the rest of our lives and leave Jim to our children to get out" (239). And because Tom wants the rescue to be so grand that it will be "celebrated" (239), it must be done in style, following nothing but "the best authorities" (224, 230). But Huck simply wants the result, and therefore the quickest way to the desired result:

> When I start in to steal a nigger, ... I ain't no ways particular how it's done so it's done. What I want is my nigger; ... and if a pick's the handiest thing, that's the thing I'm a-going to dig that nigger ... out with; and I don't give a rat what the authorities thinks about it nuther. (237)

Huck may from time to time note and regret Tom's absence in his adventures, but it is always because "he would 'a' throwed more style into it." As for the adventures themselves, Huck once "reckoned Tom Sawyer couldn't 'a' done it no neater himself" (188).

In the rescue of Jim, Huck does not simply accept all the devices Tom contrives, and consistently tries and sometimes succeeds in moderating his friend (e.g., 238). He questions Tom's plans all the way through, and constantly suggests quicker and more practical ways of handling the problems at hand (224 ff.).[15] Huck even expresses some sarcasm as he recounts Tom's plans.[16] Indeed, the introduction of Tom Sawyer into the last fifth of the novel shows not that Huck has lost his moral stature in submitting to the authority of Tom, but that the differences between the two boys have been accentuated by Huck's adventures with Jim on the river.

This is most clear when Tom has been shot in the escape with Jim, and his wound has become infected by the time they arrive at the island where the raft is hidden. When Huck and Jim determine that Huck will go for a doctor, in spite of Tom's "considerable row" that they ignore the wound and proceed on, "me and Jim stuck to it and wouldn't budge" (264). When it is a matter of Tom's life, Huck does not yield to Tom's authority. Nor does he show any enthusiasm for Tom's advice to blindfold the doctor, swear him to silence, give him a purse of gold, or lead him all around the back alleys and in a roundabout way in the canoe. Huck simply agrees, and does none of it.

Huck thus yields to Tom's romanticism at the end no more than he does at the beginning, when he tests Tom's book-learned wisdom about the power of old tin lamps to produce genies by finding one and trying it for himself (15–16). Huck rejects Tom's interpretation of reality and trusts his senses—a Sunday school picnic is not a band of Arabs and Spaniards transformed by magicians, with diamonds for the taking by Tom Sawyer's Gang (13–16), and the farm shed where Jim is being held is not a castle with a moat around it (230). So too does Huck's common sense serve as a corrective to Jim's superstitions: even though Huck like Tom and the other boys in St. Petersburg worries about ill luck from turning over the salt shaker (16), he nevertheless puts Jim's mind to rest about the voices they hear on the river, for he knows that "spirits wouldn't say, 'dern the dern fog'" (115). That such voices are those of spirits is no more reasonable than Tom's "imaginative" understanding of things.[17] In rejecting authority of various kinds and relying on himself, Huck resembles the Americans whom Tocqueville observed, who follow the precepts of Descartes without studying them.[18]

There is one way, however, in which Twain suggests that Huck's common sense understanding of things might be expanded—beyond the empirical world although not to an unintelligible one. We have seen Jim's attempt to "'terpret" what he thought was his dream as warnings, and Huck's "refutation" of Jim by pointing to the visible evidence on the raft from the storm. What do the leaves and rubbage and broken oar "stand for," he asked Jim (83). The effects of the storm are obviously signs that the storm occurred.

But Jim's different kind of interpretation of what "dey stan' for"—the trash who mistreat their friends—points Huck beyond the simply empirical to the truths that characterize human relationships, and that Huck's own feelings immediately confirm (84). Jim's interpretation of the events is tested, and if genies do not come forth as a result, Huck does humble himself to Jim and resolve never to play any more mean tricks on him.

When Huck arrives in search of Jim at the Phelps' farm and is taken for someone else, he is all joy when he discovers that he is supposed to be Tom Sawyer: "for it was like being born again, I was so glad to find out who I was" (215). But Twain does not show that Huck's final disguise in the novel is not a disguise at all. Rather, Aunt Polly's later revelation that Huck is not Tom (see 278, where she calls Huck to come out from under the bed) speaks for Twain himself. That is, Huck is finally and clearly revealed not to be Tom Sawyer. Tom embodies democracy's attempt to be more than it is, even to see itself in terms of a more colorful and adventurous past that it imagines to have existed. Tom is democracy escaping from the mundane, and trying to gain glory for doing so. Tom tries to find a beauty and excitement through romances that does not arise readily in times of equality. So, too, do the people at the camp meeting quickly believe the king's story that he is a converted pirate, and join their resources to his cause. Huck, in contrast to Tom, offers Twain more appealing democratic material. If Huck's "adventures" are possible, we have less need of Tom's more outlandish, and even cruel, ones, or of the "entertainment" that the con-men provide. However much Huck remains Tom's comrade, as Twain suggests in the novel's subtitle, Tom turns out to be less a model than a foil.

TELLING STORIES

One of the most obvious differences between Huck and Tom is seldom discussed,[19] but it is one to which Twain immediately calls our attention. Huck introduces himself with reference to *The Adventures of Tom Sawyer*, a book "made by Mr. Mark Twain," in which we might have met him (3). *The Adventures of Huckleberry Finn* will take up where that previous novel left off—with Tom and Huck having found robbers' money in a cave and Huck living with the Widow Douglas. That is, Huck Finn will take over where Mark Twain leaves off. Huck is not only narrating *The Adventures of Huckleberry Finn*, but he is also its author, even if by the time he reaches its conclusion he is "rotten glad" that "there is nothing more to write about" given how much "trouble it was to make a book" (281). Tom Sawyer is neither the narrator nor the author of *The Adventures of Tom Sawyer*.

At first glance, however, it seems that avid reader Tom Sawyer is a more likely storyteller than Huck. Not only is he better read, but he also delights in telling his adventures, and embellishing them. It is Tom rather than Huck, for example, who wants the rescue of Jim to be done with such style as to gain glory (251). Huck's plan, Tom tells him in disgust, will work but it's "too blame simple.... it wouldn't make no more talk than breaking into a soap factory" (224). But what could bring greater glory than writing a book about his adventures, and who could do it better than the well-read Tom Sawyer?

Moreover, while Tom seems a likely author, Huck seems an unlikely one. The first several chapters that Huck writes, in fact, serve as an implied criticism of books. In the first chapter, the widow "got out her book and learned me about Moses and the Bulrushes" (4). Huck is interested until he finds out that Moses "had been dead a considerable long time," and then he doesn't "care no more about him, because I don't take no stock in dead people." He is perplexed by the widow's "a bothering about Moses, which was no kin to her, and no use to anybody being gone" (4). When Tom Sawyer and his friends sneak to the cave at night to form Tom Sawyer's Gang in chapter 2, Tom follows the "authorities" and the ways of highwaymen that he has read "in books" even if he does not always know what they mean, such as ransoms (11–12). In chapter 3 Tom Sawyer's Gang goes into operation, but they rob no one, kill no one, Huck reports, "only just pretended." When they charge hog-drivers and women taking stuff to market, Tom calls the hogs "ingots," and the turnips "julery" (13). And as to the band of Arabs and Spaniards, and their elephants, that Tom claims were turned into a Sunday school picnic by magicians, Huck reckons that Tom really "believes in A-rabs and the elephants, but as for me I think different. It had all the marks of a Sunday school" (16). Twain shows that some books at least distort reality, give us inappropriate models for action, and lead us to care about what is no kin to ourselves.

If Huck takes "no stock in dead people," should he not also take no stock in books? Or is Huck's authorship a way in which Twain attempts to avoid his own criticism of books? We know immediately that the narrator is not speaking with the authority of Twain, and we soon learn that its narrator is a fabricator of tales. That is, Twain gives us fair warning. But Huck is not simply a deceiver. When Tom tells Huck about the magicians who transformed the Spaniards and Arabs, Huck wants to go after the magicians, and even get their own genies to help them (14–15). Huck wants a magic that counters magic, or that allows the appearances of things to reveal their truth. And if the adventures of Huckleberry Finn reveal anything it is that the appearances are not sufficient without interpretation.

Huck may know that the vegetables on their way to market are not "julery" because they do not appear to be, but he is fooled by the circus people, "the splendidest sight that ever was," and "every lady with a lovely complexion, and perfectly beautiful, and looking just like a gang of real sure-enough queens, and dressed in clothes that cost millions of dollars, and just littered with diamonds" (142–143). "Tom Sawyer's lies" may be easy to detect because they are so far removed from the appearances of things, but other deceivers know they must make their deceptions appear real. If this were not true, the circus would not entertain. Nor would deceptions persuade. When Huck escapes from Pap, he contrives appearances so that they will be interpreted to mean his own death at the hand of robbers. No one will try to track him down.

The greatest deceivers of the novel, however, are the two con artists who join Jim and Huck on the raft, and who pretend to be an English duke and the exiled dauphin of France. Posing as nobility, they expect Huck and Jim to call them "your Majesty" and "your Grace," to bow down on one knee to speak to them, wait on them, and not sit down in their presence until asked to do so (119–121). Just as he detects Tom Sawyer's lies, Huck knows that these men who pretend to be better than others are frauds and rapscallions, but then "all kings is mostly rapscallions," Huck informs Jim (148–149). His democratic criticism of nobility applies to the institution of slavery itself, although Huck does not go so far as to do so. Nor does Jim question the claims of the con-men as he had questioned the conventions of language: if Frenchmen are men, why do they not talk like men? (77–78). And if slaves are men, we might ask, why are they enslaved?

The con-men do not simply play a duke and a king, however, they play a duke and a king who have become con-men (as Jim observes, it is difficult for royalty to find positions in this country, [77]). And as con-men they play a variety of roles. There is the king's role at an evangelical camp meeting of a pirate converted to Christianity and desirous of becoming a missionary to other pirates, but of course he needs money to finance his voyage (128). The king and the duke also pretend that they are Shakespearean actors from London, David Garrick the Younger and Edmund Kean the elder, who play such royalty as Hamlet and Richard III (133–134). But their greatest performance is as the Wilks from England, who come to claim the inheritance from their just-deceased brother. Although the town has a few skeptics, most, including Mary Jane Wilks and her sisters, accept the duke and the king as those they claim to be. Mary Jane's own simple honesty ill prepares her to detect the deceptions of others. As Huck tells her, "I don't want no better book than what your face is. A body can set down and read it off like coarse print" (183). When the real brothers appear, the townspeople must choose which pair of claimants are the brothers of the dead man. Most choose incorrectly, and even Mary Jane requires Huck's help to identify the frauds (180). Democracy has no wise Solomon to test the claimants (see 76). The devices contrived by its leading citizens to reveal which are the real brothers prove ineffective, for the elder Wilks' signature does not disprove his authorship of the letters he wrote to his brother, for his illegible script forced him to dictate them to another (192–193). Only when the king and duke escape do the townspeople know for sure which pair of brothers is the true one.

When Twain introduces the duke and the king into the story, he offers us less attractive versions of Tom. Just as the "duke" claims to be the Duke of Bilgewater, Tom likes to think of himself as "old Northumberland," staging a rescue from a castle. Just as the "king" pretends to be "the pore disappeared Dauphin" (120), Tom pretends that Jim is the lost dauphin to make his rescue more romantic (249). To discourage would-be slave hunters, the duke dresses Jim in "a long curtain-calico gown, and a white horse-hair wig," just as Tom later costumes Jim in a calico dress as worn by "prisoner[s] of style" for the sake of the escape (152, 258, 272).[20] The duke, like Tom, may be "uncommon bright" (152; see also 223), but he also like Tom has no understanding of true nobility. He plays Shakespeare to the crowd, but so confuses the lines and the plays that the speeches make no sense. His rendition makes Shakespeare inaccessible.

Special effort is needed to understand not merely because of such frauds as the duke and the king, or gangs of robbers who enslave others without knowing what ransom means, but because meanings are not always on the surface. Huck knows that the turnips of the woman going to market are not "julery," but not that the fake diamonds of the circus performers are not real.[21] Trusting one's sense is not enough. Human beings see without understanding the significance of what they see. It is Tom who figures out where Jim is being held as prisoner on the Phelps farm: the food the slaves are carrying to the hut must be for Jim, and not for dogs. Dogs don't eat watermelon. Huck is impressed, because he never thought about dogs not eating watermelons. "It shows how a body can see and don't see at the same time," he muses (223). Nevertheless it is not Tom who immediately sees the meaning, but Huck who knows that he didn't see all there was to see. It is Huck who understands that appearances must be interpreted and who therefore might become a successful teller of tales. Indeed, throughout his adventures Huck develops his capacity for storytelling. He is prepared to be an author of his story.

Sometimes Huck's stories serve simply to protect himself, as when he explains to Pap that he has his gun because he was guarding against intruders

(30). The truth is that he feared his drunken father who chased him with a knife, threatening to kill him and calling him the Angel of Death. Huck's story to his father is much more prosaic than the truth he reports to us. With Pap, Huck has an easy audience, and an easily believed tale.

Once on Jackson Island, and teamed up with Jim, Huck sneaks ashore disguised as a girl to gather information. His story to the astute Mrs. Loftus about his distressed family becomes suspect when he doesn't know how to thread a needle, throws a piece of lead at a rat with the swing of a boy, and catches something in his lap by clapping his knees together (60). When the duke and the king disguise themselves as Englishmen and take Huck along as their "valley," even the youngest of the Wilks' sisters spots the "stretchers" Huck tells (168). Just as Huck cannot play a girl, he cannot play an Englishman, but then there is no kind Mrs. Loftus to give him lessons in playing the part (60). When he is called upon to tell about Sheffield, his life there, and the English Wilkses, he provokes the laughter of the town's doctor, and the comments of its lawyer that "I reckon you ain't use to lying, it doesn't seem to come handy; what you want is practice. You do it pretty awkward." Huck admits to us that he "didn't care nothing for the compliment" (192).

The lawyer notwithstanding, Huck doesn't "want practice" telling tales. He is only unconvincing when he tells stories about people and places of which he has no experience. He can't play a girl, or an English boy. But he has no difficulty persuading the Grangerfords that he is George Jackson from an Arkansas farm, whose family died off in one misfortune after another (96). Even if he has trouble remembering his name, he knows the character he has invented, as he does Buck Grangerford whom he prods into revealing his name by prompting him to prove that he can spell it (96). When Huck is playing a boy from a farm or town just down the road, he always succeeds. And when he is trying to help someone, Huck is particularly good at fabricating stories, as when he persuades the ferryboat watchman to go to the rescue of the shipwrecked *Walter Scott* (71–73), or when he keeps two men looking for fugitive slaves away from Jim by tricking them into thinking that his family is on the raft suffering from smallpox (87–88).

Huck's final role in the novel is Tom Sawyer, whom he knows well. "Being Tom Sawyer was easy and comfortable," and Huck tells the Phelps so much about his family his "chin was so tired it couldn't hardly go anymore" (215). The one way in which Huck cannot play Tom Sawyer, however, is his talk of medieval castles, moats, and coats of arms, for he has not read the books Tom has. But such talk does not impress, whether it be the neighbors of the Phelps or the countless readers of *Huckleberry Finn* who think that by the end of the novel Twain's art failed him. When Tom is carried back to the farm, once the bullet has been removed from his leg, he waxes about how they set Jim free to Aunt Sally:

> what work it was to make the saws, and pens, and inscriptions, and one thing or another, and ... the pictures of coffins and things, and nonnamous letters from the robbers, and get up and down the lightning-rod, and dig the hole into the cabin, and made the rope ladder and send it in cooked up in a pie, ... and load up the cabin with rats and snakes and so on, for company for Jim. (276)

But while Tom supposes he is describing something "elegant" (275), Huck tells us that Tom and Aunt Sally were "both going it at once, like a cat convention" (276). Tom was "so proud and joyful," Huck relates, that he "just *couldn't* hold in" (276). But then Huck has been present when Tom wasn't—for the neighbors' talk about the event that Tom imagined would bring them all glory—and saw that Jim's carvings on the grindstone were taken only for "everlast'n rubbage" and Jim to be crazy (267). The "talk" may indicate astonishment but hardly the admiration that Tom expects. Tom's tales are too disconnected from any reality to be effective. If Huck was not aware before, he is now, of how mistaken Tom was, and he will have a better understanding than Tom of the audience for his stories. And in contrast to Tom, Huck will have a better sense of when to speak and not to speak, when to "hold in."

An important part of the story of Jim's "rescue"—in that it affects how Jim is viewed and treated—is told by the kind doctor concerning Jim's help during the operation on Tom's leg: the doctor reports never to have seen "a nigger that was a better nuss or faithfuller, and yet he was risking his freedom to do it, and was all tired out, too" (273). Tom doesn't mention this, although he may have been too out of his mind with the infection from the bullet wound to notice. Huck, however, is "mighty thankful to the old doctor for doing Jim that good turn" (274), and of course includes the doctor's story in his book.

It is not simply that Tom's tales of nobility—of Lady Jane Grey, of Gilford Dudley, of old Northumberland (247–248)—are too removed to be effective, it is that Tom does not recognize nobility when he sees it. He may be well read, but he does not read well. When Huck asks Tom why they can't see the Arabs and elephants, Tom replies that "if I warn't so ignorant, but had read a book called Don Quixote, I would know without asking. He said it was all done by enchantment" (14). Tom is as deluded as Don Quixote, and while enchantment appeals to him he does not understand what really enchants. While Huck may learn the need for enchantment from Tom, he must look elsewhere for what truly enchants—the human characters whom Huck most admires, especially Mary Jane.

Throughout the adventures Huck recounts, he has been practicing and observing storytelling, discovering what works and what doesn't work, for others as well as himself. He sees the duke's confused rendition of *Romeo and Juliet* fail (132–134, 145), but he watches the young lovers Sophia and Harney escape the tragic feud between their families, Twain's version of the Montagues and Capulets (111–112). Sophia's deceased sister Emmeline is the occasion of Huck's first—but aborted—attempt to write poetry. "Poor Emmeline," "made poetry about all the dead people when she was alive,"—even getting to the corpse to "scratch" out her verse before the undertaker arrived (100)—and "it didn't seem right [to Huck] that there warn't nobody to make some about her now she was gone." Emmeline "could write about anything you choose to give her just so it was sad" (100), but when Huck "tries to sweat out a verse or two" about her, he "couldn't seem to make it go somehow" (101). Just as Huck does not appreciate Tom's romanticization of life, his writing skills are not suited to a romanticization of death, Emmeline-style. That Huck is an Angel of Death is only his father's drunken misconception. Huck can, however, capture Emmeline in mocking prose: "with her disposition she was having a better time in the grave" (99). His "poetry" comes closer to Twain's sarcasm. And while he tells as much as he can of the sad end of the feud and its awful effect on him (112), he also writes of Emmeline's sister Sophia, who escapes the deathly atmosphere of her family by eloping with Harney Shepherdson. That is, he does not forget the happy ending for the lovers, incorporating an element of Shakespearean comedy into horrible outcome of the feud. And by delivering Harney's message to Sophia he inadvertently assumes a role in the play (112).

Huck discovers that in helping Mary Jane Wilks avoid being conned by the duke and king "the truth is better and actly safer than a lie," even if he is so surprised that he "must lay it by in [his] mind, and think it over some time or other" (180). Huck does not treat us to his later reflections about the relationship between storytelling and truth. That he undertook such reflections is plausible, for we often see him thinking over other matters in the course of his adventures. There is his attempt to ascertain whether prayers will be answered, as Miss Watson says. At first he "sets down ... in the woods, and had a long think about [what Miss Watson said]" (12). But after praying three or four times for a fishhook with no result, he concludes "there ain't nothing in it" (12). Besides, why can't the widow get back what was stolen by praying for it? Or the deacon recover the money he lost? But Huck's conclusion does not prevent his taking the matter up with the widow, who tells him that he must pray for "spiritual gifts" and must look out for other people. Again, Huck goes "out in the woods and turn[s] it over in [his] mind long time," but saw "no advantage about it—except for other people." And so he will not "worry about it any more, but just let it go" (12).

Yet we should not suppose that this is the end of Huck's reflections on prayer, or the end of the widow's influence. After escaping Pap, Huck arrives rather hungry on Jackson Island. While a cooking fire would be seen by the people on the ferryboat looking for his corpse, Huck remembers that "they always put quicksilver in loaves of bread and float them off, because they always go right to the drownded carcass and stop there." Well content with the "baker's bread" that floats by, the thought strikes him that "the widow or the parson or somebody prayed that this bread would find [him], and here it has gone and done it." And so the boy modifies his conclusions about prayer—"there is something in [it]," although it doesn't work for him, but "for only just the right kind" (37). If the widow's prayer is answered, however, it is not for what she literally prayed for, but only in a metaphorical sense, and in a way that she would have wished had she thought it possible. Huck's capacity for metaphor frees him from the literal, or the sensible. He is satisfied not only by the bread but by its significance, as he senses the good that good people ("the right kind") can accomplish beyond anything science or the empirical can explain. Science may account for quicksilver's finding his corpse, but it cannot account for the bread's finding him hiding in the bushes. Huck thus demonstrates a potential for telling stories that find in the ordinary occurrences of life a goodness that elevates and gives them meaning.[22]

Of course it may not be the Widow's or the parson's prayer, but only good luck that the bread finds him, and even that it happens to be baker's bread—"what the quality eat; none of your low-down corn-pone" (37). But it is good luck, which therefore reminds Huck of the widow's kindness. Huck also imagines the possibility that if the people on the ferry were using real bullets when they fired cannon over the water trying to make his corpse rise, "they'd 'a' got the corpse they was after" (38). But they are not firing bullets, and no one finds him, corpse or otherwise.

Huck's speculations about the widow's prayer differ from Jim's superstitions, which have more to do with devils and witches than with providence (cf. 8 and 13). As Huck points out, Jim's explanation of "signs" have more to do with bad luck than good (45). At the beginning of the novel, Jim finds a sign that he has been abused by witches,[23] but at the end he comes to remember the signs that boded good luck rather than bad (280). And if Jim is freed in the end by Miss Watson's conscience, surely we may suppose it was due in part to the influence of the good widow, who told her sister right off that she shouldn't sell Jim down the river (43).

While Huck's speculations about the widow's prayer clearly move him, the duke's amalgam of several of Shakespeare's tragedies, moves him no more than it does the handful of people who attend the performance. The duke has greater success on stage with the "low comedy" that he himself invents. Huck sees that the Royal Nonesuch performance works, but only twice, and hence that people can admit their own folly if others do so as well (146–147). In *The Adventures of Huckleberry Finn*, which is neither tragedy nor low comedy, Huck does not hide his own folly, or his own mistakes and failures. He describes the ridiculous figure he made before all the Phelps' neighbors as the butter concealed under his cap begins to melt and roll down his face (261). He tells how the townspeople laughed at his expense when he tries to tell tales of England (191–192). He admits to the reader when he does something he later comes to understand is wrong (84). And because he describes his choice to help Jim become free as one for which he will go to hell, he takes no pride in it. After all, he reckons that he is "so ignorant, and low-down and ornery" that Providence would not want him (13). Because he does not hog center stage as does Tom (see, e.g., 218, where Huck notes that having an audience "was always nuts for Tom Sawyer"), we are pleased to join him on his voyages down the Mississippi. As Twain well knows, a converted pirate is more likely to travel among pirates than others would be. So, too, a humble democrat would be a more effective speaker in a democracy.[24]

At the end of the novel, Huck does not merely reflect on his completed book but he tells us that Aunt Sally is now planning to adopt and "civilize" him, but he's "been there before" (281). He has certainly "been there before"—long enough and "civilized" enough to write a book that was such a heap of trouble that had he known "he wouldn't 'a' tackled it" (281). In the face of Aunt Sally's "civilizing," Huck "reckons [he] got to light for the territory" (281). Huck's lighting out should not come as a surprise; not only has he gone on the adventures he has just recounted, but when living with the Widow Douglas he often went to the woods to think about the civilizing precepts she and Miss Watson tried to instill in him. In Huck's time, a territory was not a pure state of nature, but possessed the rudiments of political and civil organization as it prepared for possible statehood. In between nature and civilized life, a territory offers distance and an opportunity for choice. When Huck says at the end he will light out for the territory, perhaps then he is speaking metaphorically of that space for freedom and reflection that has already made possible his writing *The Adventures of Huckleberry Finn*. And perhaps that is why Huck thinks of lighting out for the territory "ahead of the rest." That is, Huck Finn knows that others will come along. He is not simply private or solitary; others will follow his lead. In whatever way Huck—and Twain—have followers, however, it is not the way in which Tom has followers. Huck and Tom are not the same. Huck Finn could not be the leader of a gang.

NOTES

1. I am quoting from *The Adventures of Huckleberry Finn* (New York: Bantam Books, 1981). References in parentheses are to this edition.

2. Richard Hill, "Overreaching: Critical Agenda and the Ending of *The Adventures of Huckleberry Finn*," in *Adventures of Huckleberry Finn: A Case Study of Critical Controversy*, ed. Gerald Graff and James Phelan (Boston: Bedford/St. Martin's, 1995), 319.

3. See Gerald Graff and James Phelan's discussion of "The Controversy over the Ending; Did Mark Twain Sell Jim Down the River?" in their edited volume, *Adventures of Huckleberry Finn: A Case Study of Critical Controversy*, 279–283, especially 281. Their edited volume includes essays from both sides of the controversy over the ending of *Huckleberry Finn*.

4. Leo Marx, "Mr. Eliot, Mr. Trilling, and *Huckleberry Finn*," in *Adventures of Huckleberry Finn: A Case Study of Critical Controversy*, 305. Marx's essay was first published in 1953 in *The American Scholar*.

5. See Richard Hill's description of literary critics who turn *Huckleberry Finn* into "modern social-agenda fiction" and then criticize Twain for not living up the agenda, "Overreaching: Critical Agenda and the Ending of *The Adventures of Huckleberry Finn*," 320. Hill attempts to "rehabilitate [Huck's] reputation after all the slander" (321). For a different defense of the coherence and moral purpose of the novel, see Catherine H. Zuckert's "Twain's Comic Critique," chapter 6 of *Natural Right and the American Imagination* (Lanham, Md., Maryland: Rowman and Littlefield, 1990), 131–159. Zuckert does not, like Hill, defend Twain by defending Huck, but defends Twain on the grounds that he is ultimately critical of Huck. By showing that Huck "meekly follows Tom once he has returned to civil society," Zuckert argues, Twain demonstrates how little Huck's adventures have changed him (148). What in particular Huck does not learn, especially because he accepts Tom's romantic visions, she argues, is the need for law and convention, which Twain demonstrates by Jim's becoming free only through religion (Miss Watson's conscience) and law (her will)—"two forces that Huck despises" (132). Thus what critics see as a "moral lapse" Zuckert argues is part of Twain's moral purpose (151).

6. I am indebted to Jeffrey Poelvoorde for his inspiring presentation of Huckleberry Finn as a democratic hero, and especially his reflections on the relation between Twain's art and democracy, at the Institute on "Literature and American Democracy," Hatch Lake, New York, August 2000.

7. See, for example, 109. Even when Huck and Jim are on the island, Jim insists they move their supplies into a cavern to protect them and themselves from a summer storm they foresee. When Huck admits that "this is nice," and that he "wouldn't want to be nowhere else but here," Jim comments, "Well, you wouldn't a ben here 'f it hadn't a ben for Jim. You'd a ben down dah in de woods widout any dinner, en gittn' mos' drownded, too" (48).

8. All emphases in quotations from *The Adventures of Huckleberry Finn* are Twain's.

9. The judge comes to realize that "a body could reform the old man with a shotgun, maybe, but he didn't know no other way" (23).

10. Zuckert, "Twain's Comic Critique," 145.

11. Nancy A. Walker also notes that his decision with Mary Jane marks an important step in Huck's "moral development that culminates in his decision to risk his soul to help Jim," "Reformers and Young Maidens: Women and Virtue in *Adventures of Huckleberry Finn*," in *Adventures of Huckleberry Finn: A Case Study of Critical Controversy*, 501–502.

12. That Huck does not view the widow and her sister as interchangeable is also clear when he needs a relative to offer for Tom Sawyer's gang to kill should he reveal the gang's

secret. He offers them Miss Watson (10). For an excellent discussion of the ways in which Twain modified the popular conception of widowhood in the nineteenth century in his creation of the Widow Douglas so as to create a kinder influence on Huck, see Walker, "Reformers and Young Maidens: Women and Virtue in *Adventures of Huckleberry Finn*," 494–496.

13. Leo Marx, "Mr. Eliot, Mr. Trilling, and *Huckleberry Finn*." See also Harold R Simonson, "Huckleberry Finn as Tragedy," *Yale Review* 59 (summer 1970), 532–548.

14. Leo Marx, "Mr. Eliot, Mr. Trilling, and *Huckleberry Finn*," 300.

15. For a good refutation of Marx's thesis, see Richard Hill, "Overreaching: Critical Agenda and the Ending of *The Adventures of Huckleberry Finn*," in *Adventures of Huckleberry Finn: A Case Study of Critical Controversy*, ed. Gerald Graff and James Phelan, 312–334. See also Alan Gribben, "'I Did Wish Tom Sawyer Was There': Boy-Book Elements in *Tom Sawyer* and *Huckleberry Finn*," in *One Hundred Years of Huckleberry Finn: The Boy, His Book, and American Culture*, ed. Robert Sattelmeyer and J. Donald Crowley (Columbia: University of Missouri Press, 1985), 169.

16. When Huck tells us that his plan was rejected for Tom's, for example, he admits that he "could see in a minute it was worth fifteen of mine for style, and would make Jim just as free a man as mine would, and maybe get us all killed besides. So I was satisfied" (224). He shows his awareness of Tom's flaws when he reports that his sneaking in the house by the back door "weren't romantical enough for Tom Sawyer" (226), and even to the doctor whom he fetches to deal with Tom's gunshot wound, "He had a dream.... and it shot him" (265).

17. Huck must insist to both Jim and Tom when they first see him after his supposed "murder" that he is not a ghost (41, 216).

18. Tocqueville argued that in America "the precepts of Descartes are least studied and best followed." Where there are equal social conditions and all are compelled to make their own way, individuals have little time or inclination for philosophic study and learn to trust their own judgment rather than the authority of others (*Democracy in America*, vol. 2, pt. 1, chapt. 1).

19. But see Zuckert, "Twain's Comic Critique," 134–135.

20. The Duke also paints Jim blue, and attaches a sign to the raft, "Sick Arab—but harmless when not out of his head" (152). Tom's imagination, we remember, dressed the Sunday school picnic as a band of Spaniards and Arabs (14). Like Tom, the Duke converts the ordinary into the exotic. Twain's connections between Tom Sawyer and the con-men go even beyond the *Adventures of Huckleberry Finn*. When the king pretends that he is a reformed pirate, we might recall Tom's aspirations to be a pirate in *The Adventures of Tom Sawyer*. Twain, *The Adventures of Tom Sawyer* (New York: Washington Square Press, 1972), 70–71. It is in part democracy's attraction to the romantic or exotic, in part democracy's trust, that leads the camp meeting to accept the king's tall tale. After all, the promise of democracy, at least in America, is to escape the corruption of Old-World aristocracy.

21. Huck claims that the circus was "the splendidest sight that ever was," "every lady with a lovely complexion, and perfectly beautiful, ... and dressed in clothes that cost millions of dollars, and just littered with diamonds" (142–143).

22. The one example Huck gives of providence's benevolence toward him is help in creating stories, for he "just trust[s] to Providence to put the right words in my mouth when the time come; for I'd noticed that Providence always did put the right words in my mouth if I left it alone" (211).

23. But even then, by telling stories about his experience, and "spreading them more and more," Jim is able to convert misfortune into good: "niggers would come miles to hear

Jim tell about it, and he was more looked up to than any nigger in that country." Jim was "monstrous proud" (8).

24. Colonel Sherburn, who addresses and disperses a crowd bent on lynching him, in effect speaks to democracy. But he merely controls democracy at its worst; and his rhetoric debases rather than elevates (141–142). As a cold-blooded murderer, Sherburn cannot be considered morally superior to the mob he contemns. Twain, in contrast, demonstrates the virtues of democracy through his presentation of Huck. I am indebted to Jeffrey Poelvoorde for the contrast between Sherburn and Twain.

PETER SCHMIDT

The "Raftsmen's Passage," Huck's Crisis of Whiteness, and Huckleberry Finn *in U.S. Literary History*

"tell me some mo' histry, Huck."
—Mark Twain, working notes for *Huckleberry Finn*, C-14

Commentary on the "raftsmen's passage" section of Mark Twain's *Adventures of Huckleberry Finn* (1885) usually centers on the conundrum of whether or not to include it as part of the text of the novel's chapter 16. Twain scholarship has reached no consensus on how the passage should be handled editorially, much less on the meaning of the passage for the novel as a whole. In many ways, the raftsmen's passage is a bit like Huck Finn himself, a kind of outcast child of the parental body of the book.[1]

The relative neglect of the raftsmen's passage in *Huckleberry Finn* commentary is surprising when we consider the traumatic heart of the episode. After the raftsmen's boasts and story-telling are finished, Huck is accidentally found hiding in a woodpile at the far edge of the raft at the edge of the firelight; he is roughly pulled from his hiding place and, while naked, interrogated and threatened. He begins crying, though it is questionable whether Huck's tears are involuntary or a ploy for sympathy, and when made to identify himself he chooses the name of the murdered child in a ghost story that he has just overheard. The best interpreter of the passage, Peter G. Beidler, long ago suggested that Huck here is "unconsciously identifying with the dead child," part of a pattern throughout the novel that shows an

From *Arizona Quarterly* 59, no. 2 (Summer 2003): 35–58. © 2003 by the Arizona Board of Regents, University of Arizona.

attraction to death "as a release from the cruelty and suffering that is life—at least 'sivilized' life" (248). Readers may argue with equal plausibility, however, that Huck chooses the name strategically, hoping to get a laugh—which he does (273).

What has not been emphasized about the raftsmen's passage is that it brings to a climax Huck's crisis of racial identity caused by his identification with Jim's escape. Questioned by the raftsmen, Huck uses a phrase that appears to be black English, one he has just heard Jim use. Huck's retrospective narrative itself in this passage also appears to go out of its way to "color" Huck as either blue or black. In addition, Twain's scene echoes wording he used in his short story, "A True Story," published two years earlier, in 1874. That tale was narrated by a black character, "Aunt Rachel," based on a story from her own life told to the Clemenses in Elmira, New York, by their cook, Mary Ann Cord; Twain claimed that the words of the story were entirely hers, not his. Crucial elements of Cord's tale are, in the raftsmen's passage, transposed into Huck's voice—an intertextual confluence that has also so far gone unanalyzed. Of course, chapter 16 is perhaps most well known not for the raftsmen's episode but because in it Huck for the first time decides not just to trick or insult Jim but to betray him back to slavery, prompted in part because Jim articulates for the first time how much freedom means to him. But only by adding the raftsmen's passage back to its original place in chapter 16 (between the second and third paragraphs) can we make an important observation: Huck decides to turn Jim in immediately *after* those moments with the white raftsmen when—for the first time in the novel—Huck understands his own racial identity to be ambiguous.

In general, when the issue of "race" in *Huckleberry Finn* is discussed the debate has focused on Twain's representation of Jim, or whites' racist language and behavior toward blacks, especially Huck's. But what if we were to argue that "race" in the novel cannot properly be discussed without considering how a crisis in *whiteness* is at its center, embodied in a boy who occupies a precarious space on the boundaries of white identity? Toni Morrison suggested as much in *Playing in the Dark: Whiteness and the Literary Imagination* (1992), when she said that

> there is no way, given the confines of the novel, for Huck to mature into a moral human being in America without Jim.... It is not what Jim seems that warrants inquiry, but what Mark Twain, Huck, and especially Tom need from him that should solicit our attention. In that sense the book may indeed be "great" because in its structure, in the hell it puts its readers through at the

end, the frontal debate it forces, it simulates and describes the parasitical nature of white freedom. (56–57)

Morrison's book has had a salutary effect on Twain criticism over the last decade by energizing some of the best of Twain's recent readers—Shelley Fisher Fishkin, Eric Lott, Jonathan Arac, Jocelyn Chadwick-Joshua, Elaine and Harry Mensh, and Carl F. Wieck, among others—into disagreement. Nonetheless, there remain unexplored ways to test Morrison's key generalizations about *Huckleberry Finn*. Morrison's account of the "parasitical" nature of Huck's "freedom" cast a more skeptical eye upon Jim's role as surrogate than any Twain commentator had yet done, but in other ways it followed the majority by suggesting that the early scenes with Huck and Jim may essentially be read as a narrative of Huck's maturation. Yet there is an unexplored tension in Morrison's statement between her phrases "mature into a moral human being" and "white freedom." Although white "civilization" assumes these two terms to be synonymous, the book's narrative keeps putting them in tension, by making Huck's maturation dependent not just upon Jim's aid but also upon *Huck's* aiding black freedom and Jim's quest. Jim explicitly makes such a connection between reconstructed whiteness and black freedom in chapter 16, when he praises Huck as a "white genlman"—the only time in the novel he stresses Huck's race and rewrites his social status, perhaps as a way to encourage Huck to honor his promises to him (83). Huck's discovery that his freedom is dependent upon Jim's, however, causes a crisis in Huck's sense of identity in the early scenes of the book, including the raftsmen's passage, not just the later ones.[2]

It was this developing incoherence in Huck's identity—not just Twain's problem of explaining why his two fugitives would flee further south—that may have caused Twain's writing in 1876 to lose its forward momentum and break off, in the middle of the first extended on-shore episode following Huck without Jim in chapter 18. Indeed, we may think of the developments in chapter 16, including the raftsmen's passage, as a roiling or eruption within Twain's narrative that is a linguistic version (so to speak) of the steamboat that smashes Huck and Jim's raft; it wreaks havoc on any reading we might try to put together of the raft as an Eden-like safe space free from racism or other ills of civilization, in which an autonomous and non-coerced self may be created (these terms are Lionel Trilling's and Henry Nash Smith's, two of the novel's most influential commentators, whose readings Morrison challenges). I present first a brief overview of developments in *Huckleberry Finn* leading up to chapter 16, followed by a more detailed discussion of Huck's racial masquerade in the raftsmen's passage. I then use the textual trouble of chapter 16 as a way of casting new light on recent attempts to place the novel's notorious ending in the context of the post-Reconstruction legal and social history of the U.S.

I

Although chapters 8–16 chronicle Huck's growing bond with Jim, they provide us with a counter-pattern too. At every stage in which Huck affirms how he values Jim he also (often immediately) engages in behavior that does precisely the opposite, as if to reaffirm Huck's sense of distance and superiority. Chapter 14, for example, may begin in fellowship, but it ends with the famous argument between Jim and Huck about King Solomon and the French language. Fine recent readings of these scenes are done by Emory Elliott and Jocelyn Chadwick-Joshua, who stress that these scenes reveal Jim's intelligence and Huck's petulance when he loses arguments (Elliott xxvii; Chadwick-Joshua 50–54). Or consider the scene in which Huck lies to Jim about their being separated in the fog (chapter 15). Eric Lott has it right: Huck "denies his vulnerability by projecting it onto the slave." What Twain has done in chapter 15 is give us a new insight into why Huck periodically needs to reassert his illusion of superiority: he is rebelling not just against his dependency on Jim, for which he feels ashamed as well as grateful, but also against Jim's refusal to "learn" his place when Huck feels he needs to assert his superiority. Each time Huck uses words like *fool* or *nigger*, it is Huck's need for whiteness that is really being reasserted. In Lott's words, Huck is "reerecting racial barriers" ("Mr. Clemens" 139).

The climax of this pattern of white racial panic in the 1876 portion of the novel is chapter 16. The chapter opens with Jim articulating more clearly than ever before that *freedom* is his goal, for himself and for all his family. This causes Huck to have his most violent attack of principles yet; his unease with Jim's behavior (and with his own tie to Jim) is now expressed by Huck's most sinister trick: for the first time in the novel Huck plots to re-enslave Jim. Suddenly the physical and spiritual symptoms that Huck had previously associated with the loss of Jim's presence or with his shame at his violation of their friendship—"I got to feeling so mean and miserable I most wished I was dead" (82), for instance—are now understood by Huck to be signs of his sin against whiteness, or at least (for Huck never generalizes as I have just done) his sin against Miss Watson's property rights. Even more devastatingly, the very term that Huck had once used to describe the times when he was most comfortable hiding out with Jim—"home" (48; chapter 9)—is now at the beginning of chapter 16 used by Huck, to refer to his supposed responsibilities as a white person: "It hadn't ever come *home* to me before, what this thing was [helping Jim to freedom] that I was doing" (82; emphasis added).

Huck's decision in chapter 16 to turn in Jim—and then, at the last moment, his refusal to act on this decision—is of course a rehearsal for Huck's famous spiritual crisis in chapter 31. But it is equally important to see the incident with the slave-hunters as a kind of climax to chapters 1–16, in which Huck's identity undergoes a gradual split. Inspired by his experience of what it feels like to be treated as a social contagion, Huck makes that contagion literal, fooling the bounty-seekers into thinking he is contaminated with smallpox. As with all scenes in which Huck interacts with others, it is possible to interpret his answers not as reflective of some inner state but of how Huck has read his interrogators and improvised a response. In many such cases, Huck appears to play by another's rules. But at other times, as with the slave-catchers, Huck's masquerade challenges the expectations of others, deflecting them from their course. As readers we cannot definitively assign a motive to Huck's actions as either inner crisis or canny improvisation. What is certain is that Huck's interpretation of his actions is decidedly negative, using the language of spiritual crisis and failed white manliness. "I tried to brace up and out with it [to turn Jim in], but I warn't man enough—hadn't the spunk of a rabbit" (83). Huck's self-portrait here is tragically more traumatic than Mark Twain's simple opposition between health and corruption, Huck's "sound heart" vs. his "deformed conscience." In Twain's formula, which aided the novel's canonization as an icon of American literature in the 1950s, Huck's conscience definitively "suffers defeat" and the "good" Huck wins out, though where this moral Gettysburg in the novel occurs Twain did not say.[3]

After his smallpox trick works, despite Huck's bouts of self-loathing, Huck resolves in the future to "do whichever come handiest" (85). Huck's commitment to Jim seems at least temporarily settled through the rest of chapter 16: Huck speaks of Jim's plans to escape to freedom using the first-personal plural unselfconsciously and repeatedly. Perhaps because Huck has given up making a "show" for himself as a white person, he can temporarily be at peace with aligning his freedom-quest with Jim's. If we have any doubts, we should consider Huck's description of the steamboat that knocks them overboard—ironically, a steamboat heading upriver just like the one on which they had hoped to buy deck passage. The boat suggests not only the mouth of Hell as it usually appeared in illustrated Bibles such as Huck might have seen, but also as an all-devouring industrial machine: "all of a sudden she bulged out, big and scary, with a long row of wide-open furnace doors shining like red-hot teeth, and her monstrous bows and guards hanging right over us" (87; cf. Robinson 197–98). There is no stronger image in *Huckleberry*

Finn for the nightmarish world Huck fears will swallow him when his bond with Jim is broken. The Hell that actually engulfs Huck, though, comes from another, unexpected direction.

II

What if something happens to Huck on the men's raft that gives us a crucial piece of the puzzle of Huck's changes, as described above? Let us approach the deleted raftsmen's passage with new eyes, keeping the focus on Huck rather than on what appears to be the primary purpose of this episode, allowing Twain to display his mastery of the modes of frontier oral culture (including boasting and insult contests, balladry, and ghost-tales) with which he first made a name for himself as an author.

Of all the tales that Huck overhears while hiding on the large raft, the most important for interpreting Huck's state of mind is the ghost story about how a murdered child named Charles William Allbright haunts his father. A classic ghost story about guilt and the return of the repressed, the tale has several features of particular interest. The boy haunts his father by following his father's raft hidden in a barrel, drawing closer to the raft every night and crippling one raftsmen after another, until one of their mates begins acting so strangely that they suspect him of causing them all to be haunted. The murderer is forced to confess when one of his mates courageously brings the barrel on board and a "stark naked baby" is revealed inside. After telling his tale, the father jumps overboard with the child in his arms, an act of contrition and suicide that is also described as the man's first act of tenderness toward the child: he "jumped overboard with it hugged up to his breast and shedding tears, and we never see him again in this life ..." (272).

The ghost story becomes even more fascinating when placed in the context of Huck's own troubled relationship with parental figures, especially Pap. When Huck is violently pulled out from hiding and questioned by the raftsmen, the boy who staged his own murder to escape his father's beatings answers that his name is "Charles William Allbright, sir." Of those who know Huck, only Jim is aware he is still alive. Huck also has spent many nights in a "hogshead" barrel as his only home, as mentioned in *Tom Sawyer* and the first chapter of its sequel. After the men finish laughing at Huck's answer, they treat him noticeably better. But they are still dictatorial; they still force him to tell one story after another about who he is until Huck gets a version that *they* find plausible. ("Come, now, tell me a straight story, and nobody'll hurt you" [273].) They use the same threat of rawhide whippings Huck associates with Pap. Huck's identification with the murdered child makes psychological sense, and strategic sense as well, but what else can we make of this crossing of identities?

Shelley Fisher Fishkin has pointed out that there are many elements in Huck's writing that Twain strongly associated with black story-tellers whom he admired, and black American speech patterns in general. The majority of her examples, understandably, come from Huck's narration, not his rendering of his own conversation. But no moment in Huck's conversation in the novel sounds more like the black English that Twain knew than the reply Huck gives the raftsmen's hectoring advice: "'Deed I will, boss. You try me" (274). "Boss" is used in such a way only rarely in *Huckleberry Finn*. Obviously the word signifies someone with power and authority; Pap uses it early in the novel several times when his right to abuse Huck is questioned; as Huck renders Pap's thinking, "he said he was boss of his son" (21, chapter 5). Huck (before he meets Jim) also boasts that "I was boss of" Jackson's Island; and the King praises one of the Duke's scams as a "boss dodge" (152, chapter 25). But it is Jim's use of the word that most influences Huck's choice of it. Jim employs the word only twice, all in the same scene: when he is speaking defensively after Huck has lied to him about being lost in the fog. ("[L]ooky here, boss, dey's something wrong.... Is I *me*, or who is I? ... En did't I ... have a turrible time en mos' git drownded? Now ain' dat so, boss—ain't it so?" [78]). Jim says the word with an inflection that I hear in part as both pleading and commanding. But Jim surely also has an edge of scathing criticism in the word's tone; he is signifyin', marking the ways in which Huck is trying to reassert his superiority and his whiteness—for "boss" was very much expected to be used by blacks to show deference to whites.

In calling the raftsman "boss," Huck may express deference, perhaps even abasement, guessing that these are his expected roles. We might claim, though, that Huck's performance cannot be interpreted so simply. The raftsmen may no longer be expecting a "straight" story from Huck at this point. Is Huck's response taken by the raftsmen to be heartfelt genuflection? Or is Huck understood to be engaging in a *parody* of sincerity, a performance he guesses the rogues will enjoy because they will recognize the familiar blackface mask of the "harmless," shuffling, incorrigible liar? Minstrel performance routines, as Eric Lott and others have emphasized, are similarly complex to interpret.

The coded "racial" language of the raftsmen's passage gets even stranger. Black and white references figure significantly in both the ghost story and its aftermath. The barrel that holds Charles William Allbright, it is emphasized, was "a black something" that kept following the raft, and its revenge on the raftsmen takes place during a thunderstorm in which the world seems to turn into black and white. Blue is also significant. The barrel has "blue lights winking around it"; when the raftsmen first discover Huck one of them threatens to "get out the paint-pot and paint him a sky blue all over from head to heel"; and a raftsman's parting words to Huck are, "Blast it, boy, some raftsmen would rawhide you till you were black and blue" (270–73). Huck is never so painted in the novel, of course—but *Jim* is, in a later scene that invokes the face-painting and spectacle that were central elements in minstrel shows. That episode is the one beginning chapter 24, in which the Duke proposes to paint Jim "a dead dull solid blue, like a man that's drownded nine days," and advise him to "fetch a howl or two like a wild beast" to keep intruders away (143). Only Tom is able to top the King and the Duke in abusing Jim while claiming to do him favors. Such a "painting" of Jim is a form of dehumanization quite akin to slavery itself, including nineteenth-century theories justifying slavery that emphasized Negroes' supposedly animal-like qualities, with some writers even arguing that they were a subhuman species.[4]

By adding so many markers not just of color but of the behavior Negroes were expected to endure, Twain's novel makes it impossible to interpret the raftsmen's threat to "paint" Huck simply as a random threat. It is a form of humiliation and dehumanization that carries deep overtones of being marked with the broad brush of the color-line. Huck is, literally, threatened with being made "black and blue," with losing even his lowly status as a poor white boy. In response, Huck replies in kind, employing black English he has just heard from Jim and the mask of abasement daily demanded of Negroes. That the men enjoy his performance in no way erases the fact that their power over Huck precisely parallels the complex power dynamic between performers and audience in blackface's racial masquerade.

One other black voice is twined into the raftsmen's passage, this time not Jim's but the voice of an actual person Twain knew well—Mary Ann Cord, his cook in Elmira, New York, and the storyteller whose account of some of her experiences in slavery and the war, Cord inspired Twain's short story "A True Story, Repeated Word for Word as I Heard It" as told by an "Aunt Rachel," published in *The Atlantic Monthly*, November 1874. This tale has received prominent attention recently from Shelley Fisher Fishkin (*Lighting Out* 85–90, 223–24), primarily as one of several publications in which Twain paid tribute to the verbal skills and historical memory of particular black story-tellers and acknowledged their influence on his own art. For Fishkin, "[s]tories like Mary Ann Cord's were central to the genesis of *Huckleberry Finn*" (89). What has not been noticed, however, is how the climax of the raftsmen's passage directly echoes language used by Mary Ann Cord.

Mary Ann Cord told Twain of being torn from her family on a slave auction block. She particularly emphasized the trauma of the loss of her youngest son:

> dey begin to sell my chil'en an' take *dem* away, an' I begin to cry; an' de man say, "Shet up yo' dam blubberin'," an' hit me on de mouf wid his han'. An' when de las' one was gone but my little Henry, I grab' *him* clost up to my breas' so, an' I ris up an' says, 'You shan't take him away,' I says; 'I'll kill de man dat teches him!'" I says ... (*Writings of Mark Twain, Definitive Edition*, Vol. VII, 242–43)

Henry is sold, but later escapes slavery, journeys North to freedom, and after the war is reunited with his mother. Twain said his published story is an exact "copy" of the tale Cord told him in the summer of 1874, two years before Twain began *Huckleberry Finn*; what he published in a national magazine was "not in my words but her own," testimony to "a shameful tale of wrong & hardship" and also "a curiously strong piece of literary work" (Fishkin, *Lighting Out* 85, 224).

In discussing this tale, Fishkin stresses its general influence on *Huckleberry Finn*. That is, she sees it as one of the stimulants for Twain's own new perspective in that novel on the world of his Missouri childhood—a world where Jim's love of his family, the pain of slavery, and his determination to seek freedom now came to play a central role. Fishkin sees a more direct textual connection to another work, *A Connecticut Yankee*, chapter 21, which depicts a slave auction and slave mother losing her family and being beaten (*Lighting Out* 87–88). Fishkin is persuasive about these general and particular links between "A True Story" and the rest of Twain's oeuvre. But there is one scene in *Huckleberry Finn* that draws more closely than any other narrative of Twain's on Cord's, though it transposes its referents. It too features crying, a parent grabbing a child to the breast, the threat of beating, and the cry "I'll paint [vs. kill] the man that teches him!" This scene, of course, is the raftsmen's passage. Certainly there are differences between the two passages: it's a raft, not a slave auction; a "white" boy (actually two—Charles William and Huck), not a black child, etc. Perhaps most crucially, the tale features not a slave mother but two white father figures—the repentant murderer who grabs the ghost-child to his breast and the raftsmen named Davy who protects Huck. For Twain it is as if the power of Cord's story has returned, transposed, in a dream. The scene arguably has much more profound emotional resonance than his more literal and self-conscious transcription of the auction scene in *A Connecticut Yankee*, which contains little of Mary Ann

Cord's words or eloquence. Twain turned to the power of Cord's language when he needed to portray Huck at his most vulnerable. He also created his own version of the happy ending in Cord's story, by imagining two different male protector figures for Charles William and Huck.

In the deepest level of Twain's imagination, then, Huckleberry Finn in trouble in the raftsmen's passage has become part *black*—not just in appearance and speech, but because in imagining Huck's most desperate circumstances Twain drew upon narrative elements of a powerful slave narrative that he had heard only two years before. Furthermore, when the raftsmen's passage is re-integrated into its original place within Chapter 16, we can see that Chapter 16 represents the climax of the portrait Twain wrote in the summer of 1876 of the developing split in Huck's identity caused by his aligning himself with Jim's quest for freedom. Part of Huck convinces himself that he has become a traitor to the white race, while another part of Huck not only uses the first person plural to describe his union with Jim, but uses terms to describe himself that may not be definitely "black" but certainly make his racial status liminal and ambiguous. A number of commentators have valuably discussed certain generic parallels between *Huckleberry Finn* and slave narratives, but reading the "Raftsmen's Passage" as an involuntary racial masquerade brings a new dimension to our developing understanding of Twain's indebtedness to black narrative traditions.[5]

Reading the raftsmen's passage as a crisis of whiteness means that we cannot wholly subscribe to the most prevalent interpretation of Huck's development in the first 16 chapters of the novel, the one emphasized by Lionel Trilling, Henry Nash Smith, Emory Elliott, Ken Burrs, and many others—who all (to varying degrees) stress Huck's magnificent moral development away from racism, with the raft as a privileged site for the recovery (or perhaps the improvised invention) of American innocence. I would argue instead that Twain's first draft of the novel dramatized not a narrative of progressive development but the story of Huck's gradual disintegration as a coherent self; chapters 14–16 in particular detail increasingly more violent struggles within Huck, with each moral "advance" toward treating Jim as an equal followed by an equally violent regression. This pattern accelerates exponentially after Huck undergoes his experience on the raftsmen's raft. In a fit of shame, Huck plots to betray Jim, then turns upon himself when he can't go through with it. Huck had been self-critical before, but it is only after his encounter with the raftsmen that he castigates himself for not acting white enough.[6]

Twain's writing momentum in the summer of 1876 broke down, as we now know, in Chapter 18, in the middle of Huck's involuntary immersion in the Grangerford/Shepherdson feud across the Kentucky/Tennessee border.

Underwritten by sentimental pieties, this slaughter is also Twain's brilliant allegory for the American Civil War itself—a war whose very name is an oxymoron combining violence and euphemism. Twain stopped writing at the line in Chapter 18 when Huck asks Buck to "tell me about it [the feud]" (99)—that is, just at the moment when his hero is about to hear the story of a civil war. Ironically, despite Huck's moral nausea at the violence of the feud, he continues to think of the Grangerford house as his "home" now that he believes the raft and Jim are lost (92; chapter 17). Furthermore, the fight into which he has stumbled is really no less violent than the one that Huck has been undergoing internally.

The disintegration of Huck's identity into warring factions in chapters 1–18 can be read in another way. Barbara Ladd has made the invaluable observation that late in Twain's career his narratives tended to break apart precisely at the moment when "'white' and 'American' or 'nationalist' voices" were displaced by "black and extra-national, or pre-national ones." Ladd's insight is worth quoting more fully:

> Many readers have ... observed both the displacements of geographical and temporal settings in Mark Twain's late works as well as the apparent loss of authorial control, the fragmentation of narrative, the fragmentation of character, and the disturbing recapitulations of character or plot or motif in different geographical and temporal contexts. I am thinking in particular of stories that begin, break off, begin again, to remain either unfinished or seemingly forced to premature or otherwise unsatisfactory conclusion (as the end of *Pudd'nhead Wilson*, for example); of characters or figures duplicated and reduplicated in ways that seem to defy reason....
>
> Although traditional literary criticism has taken these features of the late texts as little more than signs of the originating author's loss of creative power and discipline, there is more to it. What is so apparent when one looks at these texts from a New Historicist perspective is that the fragmentation of narrative seems to accompany the displacement of "white" and "American" and "nationalist" voices by black and extra-national or pre-national ones..... Of all Twain's late works, *Pudd'nhead Wilson and Those Extraordinary Twins* might be the most complex—and most successful—example of the use of "black" and "foreign" voices (or voicings) to explore and explode the myth of the racially "pure" or determinate and culturally innocent American.... It is a complex example of the use of black and white, foreign and

domestic, northern and southern social bodies to examine the
myths of racial purity, national unity, and individual autonomy,
upon which the ideal of authorship was constructed in Victorian
America.... All this [in *Pudd'nhead Wilson*] ... is hitched to a story
of child switching and race mixing among the locals. (130)

The depiction of Huck in chapters 14–16 of *Huckleberry Finn*, particularly
with the raftsmen's passage added, however, suggests that what Ladd calls
Twain's explosion of conventions of character coherence, racial purity, and
national unity began far earlier than *Pudd'nhead Wilson* or other late texts,
though it is inescapable in those. It may be that on the raft Huck is growing
so forcefully under Jim's tutelage that his "white" identity splits apart as if
it were an outdated casque or shell. The raft is only rarely (and briefly) a
sanctuary from conflict, a "raft of hope" in Ralph Ellison's words (483). For
most of the time in the novel the raft is the primary locus of the civil war in
Huck's soul, and the violence he encounters on other rafts or onshore seems
only a shadow of the trouble in Huck's own heart. What Twain's magnificent
opening portion of his novel makes indelible—especially if the raftsmen's
passage is included—is that Huck's conflict over his bond with Jim is really
a conflict over who he understands himself to be. And Huck's conflicts and
his mask-wearing are also the nation's: they are continually denied and
misunderstood yet are always there, shadowing the nation like that barrel in
the ghost story.

III

I turn now to a brief consideration of the post–Civil Rights era
consensus about the notorious ending of *Huckleberry Finn*, in which Tom's
torturous freeing of an already free man is often read as a satiric farce
about race relations in the 1870s and early 1880s, when the limited reforms
instituted by Reconstruction were systematically dismantled with the
approval of many Northerners and Southerners.

I believe that it is a mistake to ask whether the Tom Sawyer-dominated
episodes exploit racist stereotypes for humor or undercut them through irony
and satire. Such a question implies we have an either/or choice in assessing
the cultural work (or cultural damage) accomplished by Twain's novel.
Rather, we should attend to the ways in which the last chapters of the novel
enact doubleness and duplicity in ways that can never be reduced to a single
way of interpreting their meaning. In their own demonic way, they complete
the novel's cultural work of making Huck's identity-split representative of the
nation's.

One key to the final chapters may be found in the meaning of Tom's phrase "letting on" to describe his plans for "helping" Jim. (Tom's term "evasion" (241; chapter 39) has been much discussed, but "letting on" has not, with the important exception of Forrest Robinson [174–78], who reads both these terms in the context of post–Civil War America.) For Tom, "letting on" signifies not just to say one thing and mean another, but it also becomes a systematic way of lying shared by a group. Case-knives shall be called pick-axes, and torture benevolence. Listen to Tom: "Things being so uncertain, what I recommend is this: that we really dig right in, as quick as we can; and after that, we can let on, to ourselves, that we was at it thirty-seven years." And here is Huck's endorsement of Tom's plan: "Letting on don't cost nothing; letting on ain't no trouble; and if it's any object, I don't mind letting on we was at it a hundred and fifty year." Such a consensus to wink to each other while lying Huck calls being "full of principle" (220, 222, chapter 35).[7]

Critics who want to defend Twain's ending as satire of Federal policy toward blacks after 1876 may point to many instances of Twain's contemporaries engaging in Tom Sawyer-like double-speak. Reversing the Civil Rights Acts of 1866 and 1875 that were high-water marks of Reconstruction, for instance, U.S. Supreme Court justices argued in 1883 that racial segregation was constitutional because such acts did not reenslave. Writing for the majority, Justice Bradley began by limiting the relevance of the XIIIth Amendment to the U.S. Constitution:

> The XIIIth Amendment relates only to slavery and involuntary servitude (which it abolishes), and, although, by its reflex action, it establishes universal freedom in the United States, ... yet such legislative power extends only to the subject of slavery and its incidents, and the denial of equal accommodations in inns, public conveyances, and places of public amusement (which is forbidden by the sections in question), imposes no badge of slavery or involuntary servitude upon the party but at most, infringes rights which are protected from State aggression by the XIVth Amendment.

According to such reasoning, the XIIIth Amendment effectively rendered itself moot once it abolished slavery; it cannot have any legal standing in the slave-free society that it brings into being. Such a narrow reading of the Amendment's meaning of course directly assaulted the Civil Rights Act of 1866, which, in the words of the legal scholar Charles Lofgren, "testified to the contemporary [Reconstruction-era] understanding that the Thirteenth

Amendment empowered the national government to strike directly at discrimination based on race" (75). Bradley then used the allegedly limited scope of the XIIIth to suggest that the XIVth Amendment is extremely narrow as well—making it apply to State laws only, not individual acts of discrimination that occur within the States. The convoluted syntax of the final part of the indented quotation above mirrors Bradley's convoluted logic; rights may simultaneously be infringed *and* protected because Bradley implies that individual acts and acts of a State legislature normally exist in entirely separate spheres.

Given such contortions, it is worth looking again at the actual wording of the XIVth Amendment to the Constitution, passed as part of the post–Civil War Reconstruction reforms. It prohibits "any law which shall abridge the privileges or immunities of citizens of the United States; nor shall any State deprive any person of life, liberty, or property, without due process of law; nor deny to any person within its jurisdiction the equal protection of the laws." For Bradley, reading narrowly, this means that if States do not pass laws openly abridging a resident's "privileges or immunities" (except for convicted criminals), then the XIVth Amendment's guarantees have not been violated.

> Civil rights, such as are guaranteed by the Constitution against State aggression, cannot be impaired by the wrongful acts of individuals, unsupported by State authority in the shape of laws, customs, or judicial or executive proceedings. The wrongful act of an individual, unsupported by any such authority, is simply a private wrong, or a crime of that individual; an invasion of the rights of the injured party, it is true, whether they affect his person, his property, or his reputation; but if not sanctioned in some way by the State, or not done under State authority, his rights remain in full force, and may presumably be vindicated by resort to the laws of the State for redress.
>
> Majority Opinion, Civil Rights Cases, 109 U.S. 3 [1883]

In short, Bradley's majority opinion did more than just claim that Congressional civil rights laws prohibiting racial discrimination were unconstitutional. He argued that any claim of racial discrimination was merely a "private wrong" unless it could be proven that such acts were explicitly sanctioned by the State legislature. Further, his decision forbade state or national legislatures from passing laws protecting individual rights, or Congress from requiring prosecution and penalties for individual acts of discrimination in the States. The dissenting justice in the case, John M. Harlan, fully recognized what had been accomplished by the majority ruling: "we shall enter upon an era of constitutional law, when the rights of freedom and American citizenship cannot receive from the nation that efficient protection which heretofore was unhesitatingly accorded to slavery and the rights of the master" (quoted by Lofgren, who adds that the decision "stripped the national government of the authority to protect the central constitutional principle of equality of citizenship" [76]).

From the 1883 "Civil Rights Cases" evisceration, it was not a large step, legally, to the 1896 *Plessy v. Ferguson* decision accepting "Jim Crow" state laws as constitutional. All that had to be done to achieve such a shift was to play further word-games narrowing even more the meaning of "State-sanctioned" infringement of private rights. Charles Lofgren again: "In the course of these [1883] comments, Bradley defined the scope of the rights that private action could not abridge as including those pertaining to an individual's 'person, *his property, or his reputation.*' It was almost as if [Bradley] foresaw and wished to counter the due process argument that Homer Plessy's counsel later raised," which argued that Plessy's ability to pass for white was both a right and valuable property (73–74; Lofgren's italics). In Bradley's construction the burden of proof would be on the plaintiff to show not only that an act of discrimination was sanctioned by the State, but also that it seriously damaged one's property or reputation, not merely inconvenienced one from staying in an inn, riding in a certain car on a train, being educated at a school, etc. Laws mandating segregation in public facilities and conveyances could indeed be justified as an honest and practical solution to the race problem that *protected* the individual rights and reputations of blacks and white alike via "separate but equal" facilities. Jim Crow was validated by the Supreme Court in 1896, but the legal reasoning and evasions justifying it had begun to be defined—or perhaps we should say "let on"—over a decade earlier, while Twain was working on his ending to *Huckleberry Finn*.[8]

Parodic of Reconstruction and post-Reconstruction policies toward blacks *Huckleberry Finn* may be, but in Twain's working notes to the novel he unselfconsciously listed on the same page new ideas for using Jim *and* new ideas for asserting his copyright powers as author. Revealingly, Twain's assertion of those ownership rights merge quickly into what sounds exactly like Tom brainstorming new plots to "free" Jim, or the King and the Duke coming up with ways to exhibit Jim for money or—most grotesquely of all—to sell a new "medicine."

> Publish this in England & Canada the day before the first number of it appears in ... Century or N.Y. Sun—that, makes full copyright.

Turn Jim into an Injun.

Then exhib him for gorilla—then wild man &c., using him for 2
shows same day.

Nigger-skin (shamoi) for sale as a pat med [patent medicine]

Tell me some mo' histry, Huck. (Blair and Fischer *Huckleberry
Finn*, 757; see 750 for ms. photograph)

Twain's plot in the second half of *Huckleberry Finn* indeed outdoes both
the King and the Duke and Tom in the ingenious ways it markets comedy
by silencing, stereotyping, painting, and threatening to dismember Jim.
Twain's satire, if that is what it is, is thoroughly complicit with what it
satirizes, not morally separate. In Huck's narrative there is no safe space
or safe language indisputably transcendent and free from the lies we may
tell ourselves about our own motives. The novel will certainly not disturb
our complacency if we too easily come to consensus that the ending
should be read as *either* safely controlled satire and critique *or* as complicit
racist humor. Only when these possibilities are made to share the same
space on the "raft" of meaning we construct may we truly experience
how Huck's fall from whiteness and then his confused attempts to put on
again—that is, let on—the mask of whiteness is a national story, not just
the tale of an orphaned child. Such is the sobering truth that Huck's "mo'
histry" tells us.

If critical narratives of Huck's eternal lighting out from the corrupting
influences of civilization were prime movers in the canonization of this
novel in the post–World War II era, perhaps for Twain's world-wide
readers in the twenty-first century the mo' history of Huck's and Twain's
ambivalent mimicry well captures the contradictions of whiteness as
it is currently being investigated. Not coincidentally, during the same
postwar period U.S. studies itself appears to be shifting from a dominant
narrative centered in New England exceptionalism to ones that emphasize
the paradoxes of the colonial and postcolonial condition, including the
instabilities of whiteness as a cultural construction. Twain's novel could
only with a good deal of ingenuity be made essential to narratives of the
Puritan origins of the American self, but Huck's crisis of whiteness makes
inescapable his relevance to colonial and postcolonial narratives of U.S.
identity.[9]

IV

Huck really is Charles William Allbright after all—haunting *us*. The raft is a floating colonial contact zone. The only question is, how will we on our raft respond to him once we uncover him in "our" space? As we meditate on our predicament, we should recall two of the items that Huck finds in the floating cabin that, as he eventually learns from Jim, held the corpse of his father (chapter 9). One of the items is well-known; indeed it has become the most famous part of Huck's visual identity—the "boy's old speckled straw hat" that Huck appropriates as his own. This hat, which Huck doffs to us in the famous illustration by E. W. Kemble that ends the novel, is the easy symbol of Huck's eternal innocence and integrity—what Twain, in making suggestions to his publisher regarding the book's illustrations, defined as follows: "Huck Finn is an exceedingly good-hearted boy, & should carry a good & good-looking face" (Blair and Fischer, *Huckleberry Finn* xlvii). But Huck also "borrows" something else from the haunted house that must be seen as equally essential to his identity: "a couple of masks made out of black cloth" (47). 'Terpreting one last time, I'd say that these twinned masks well stand for Huck's doubleness, which is also Twain's and that of the postcolonial U.S. Their blackness reflects (via illegibility, or disguise) the unsolvable enigma of who Huck "really" is and who he might become in his eyes and in our own. We cannot read the raftsmen's passage properly, much less *Huckleberry Finn* itself, unless we learn that Huck always wears a mask, even when naked.[10]

The tension between Huck's folksy hat and black masks should become a part of our cultural memory, eternally shadowing us with our own duplicities, what we have repressed or denied or idealized. Twain's best novel is indeed a tragicomedy of the unspeakable that we must embrace. Muddy and roiling with the convoluted and constantly changing conflicts at the heart of our cultural landscape, and yet also somehow majestic, giving us a vista of our possibilities we can discover nowhere else, Twain's *Huckleberry Finn* is the Mississippi of our literature.

NOTES

1. For accounts of the complex textual history of the raftsmen's passage, see Beidler, Hirst, Doyno xvi and 377–78, and Arac 139–42. For the "mo' histry" quotation, see the Blair and Fischer edition of *Huckleberry Finn*, 757. Quotations from the novel will be from the Oxford University Press edition edited by Emory Elliott, but for convenience I will also cite by chapter number.

2. One anomaly in Morrison's *Playing in the Dark* that has not received enough commentary is Morrison's elision of Ralph Ellison's essays on American literature and American memory, which in myriad ways prefigure her key insights, including those on Twain. Why should Ellison's ancestral presence in Morrison's project be so occluded? Morrison's book has a relationship toward current "whiteness studies" that is somewhat analogous to the relation between Said's *Orientalism* and postcolonial studies. Key anthologies of essays in whiteness, studies include Roediger's *Black on White*; Hill's *Whiteness: A Critical Reader*; Kincheloe, et al., *White Reign: Deploying Whiteness in America*; and Najmi and Srikanth's *White Women in Racialized Spaces*. The intersection between U.S. whiteness studies and postcolonial studies is too vast to cite here, but see Pratt and Bhabha. Some of the most influential individual volumes that focus on the U.S.: *Racial Formation in the United States: From the 1960s to the 1980s* by Omi and Winant; *White By Law* by Haney-López ; and books by Lott, Roediger, Dyer, Frankenburg, and Babb. A key early survey of whiteness studies was Fishkin's "Interrogating Whiteness"; for a more recent overview of intersections between postcolonial theory and whiteness studies, see Singh and Schmidt 35–38 and 55n36. An incisive critique of whiteness studies is Wiegman's. Of course, it is naïve to consider critical projects making whiteness visible an invention of the 1990s. Both the post-Reconstruction era and the post-1960s period featured major cultural studies published just when the meanings of "race" in the public sphere were in crisis. Contemporary cultural studies work on "whiteness" in the U.S. should therefore be read in the context of earlier writings by Albion Tourgée, Ida B. Wells-Barnett, José Martí, W. E. B. Du Bois, and many others.

"Whiteness Studies" has had some effect on Twain studies, perhaps most notably through Fishkin's work, but see also work by Lott and Jones. Jones understands Huck's contradictory ways of seeing Jim to be linked to a crisis in Huck's own identity, which Jones valuably calls "white double-consciousness"; I disagree with a number of other conclusions that Jones makes about the novel, however.

3. Twain made this famous comment many years after finishing *Huckleberry Finn*, in 1895, as notes for himself while introducing the novel's story to an Australian audience. The famous phrase is as follows: "a book of mine where a sound heart & a corrupt conscience come into collision & conscience suffers defeat." For the full notebook entry and commentary, see Blair and Fischer, *Huckleberry Finn* 806–07.

4. Regarding this "painting" of Jim, Lott comments: "Jim's appearance surely recalls the art of blackface at the same time that it explodes the very idea of racial performance. Twain no doubt means to lampoon the racial thinking behind forms such as blackface when he has the duke tell Jim [to perform like a wild beast].... Savage injuns and A-rabs too are invoked here as figments of the white supremacist imagination" ("Mr. Clemens" 140).

5. For connections between Twain and ex-slave narratives, see Beaver; MacKethan; Rampersad; Fishkin, *Lighting Out*; and Wieck 20–39. In general, these approaches focus on Jim more than Huck and ignore the "Raftsmen's Passage"; indeed, the one serious disagreement I have with MacKethan's excellent essay is that she suggests excising the Raftsmen's Passage brought the novel more into alignment with ex-slave narrative conventions. No ex-slave narrative provides such detail about how an accomplice aided the escape as Twain's novel does, and the above approaches, in their understandable focus on Jim's story, slight the implications ex-slave narratives could have for narrating *white* identity—an issue that I am arguing *Huckleberry Finn* foregrounds.

6. Huck's language about proper behavior in chapter 16 never calls it "white" directly; he uses terms such as "conscience" and "show" that emphasize both appearances

and how proper behavior is culturally constructed: a white "body that don't get started right when he's little, ain't got no show" (85). Ironically, the only direct reference to Huck's whiteness in the chapter is Jim's, who praises Huck as a "de on'y white genlman dat ever kep' his promise"—a phrase that the scene as a whole shows Huck links to being a despised white "Ab'litionist" (82–83).

7. There is another, possibly different, employment of "letting on" in *Huckleberry Finn*. After Jim breaks his teeth on brass candlestick pieces smuggled into his food, Huck comments: "Jim he never let on but what it was only just a piece of rock or something like that that's always getting into bread, you know ..." (224, ch. 36). This could be Huck revealing he knows Jim too is playing Tom's game, pretending brass is stone. But Huck's double negative could also mean that he believes Jim ignorant. The latter reading would certainly fit with many instances where Huck suggests a trick works best when the victim is fooled, not in on the joke. As Huck comments, "when Jim bit into it, it most mashed all his teeth out, and there warn't ever anything could a worked better" (224). In such a reading, interestingly enough, "never let on but what it was" means something like "never understood; he thought it was...." If so, though, Huck's use of "letting on" here to signify ignorance, not knowing deception, ironically rebounds against its user. In the "Evasion" chapters Huck normally implies that the line between "letting on" and self-deception is clear, but this instance suggests it is more unstable than Huck admits.

8. A more thorough discussion of the implications of the *Slaughterhouse* and "Civil Rights" cases, *Williams v. Mississippi*, and *Plessy v. Ferguson* and other legal decisions for the literary historian is Sundquist's, in *To Wake the Nations* 234–70 and 338–43. Sundquist focuses primarily on the relevance of these rulings for reading Twain's *Pudd'nhead Wilson*.

9. Regarding the guilt and ambivalence beneath Huck's masks of mimicry, two of many earlier critics who make a congruent point to mine are Holland and Robinson. Consider Robinson: "while Huck is aware enough of his bad faith to be ashamed of its effects, he is too much a product of the dominant culture to face it for long, and thus, perhaps, to deal with it. Instead, he flees from himself, seeking oblivion in the solitude of 'the Territory ahead,' just as he sought it before in the concealment of the snake-skins, and again, later, in his rebirth as Tom Sawyer" (207). It is perhaps also necessary to note here that in contemporary postcolonial theory "postcolonial" refers not to a temporal but to a metaphysical state. That is, not solely to the period after a colony is granted independence but also to any moment that calls into question the master narratives seeking to regulate the interactions of a "superior" civilization and race with an "inferior" one.

10. Compare another of Twain's working notes for the novel: "Wouldn't give a cent for an adventure that ain't done in disguise" (C-12, Blair and Fischer, 748 and 756). Interestingly, Twain also later joked that "Huck is two persons in one," though he meant it differently than I do here. (Twain wanted to publish a statement that Huck was an accurate portrait of the boyhood identities of two pompous newspaper editors who criticized his novel; see the Bradley et al edition of *Huckleberry Finn*, 285–86.) For a fine discussion of pairings and doublings in *Huckleberry Finn* read as an encoding of "twain," see Wieck 102–07. See also Wieck 82–92 for a superb short essay on various meanings that accrue around the objects Huck and Jim find in the floating house, including those black masks.

WORKS CITED

Arac, Jonathan. *Huckleberry Finn As Idol and Target: The Functions of Criticism in Our Time*. Madison: University of Wisconsin Press, 1997.

Babb, Valerie. *Whiteness Visible: The Meaning of Whiteness in American Literature and Culture*. New York: New York University Press, 1998.

Bhabha, Homi. *The Location of Culture*. New York: Routledge, 1994.

Beaver, Harold. "Run, Nigger, Run: *Adventures of Huckleberry Finn* as a Fugitive Slave Narrative." *Journal of American Studies* 8 (1974): 339–61.

Beidler, Peter G. "The Raft Episode in Huckleberry Finn." 1968. *Adventures of Huckleberry Finn: An Authoritative Text, Backgrounds and Sources, Criticism*. 2nd ed. Ed. Sculley Bradley, Richmond Croom Beatty, E. Hudson Long, and Thomas Cooley. New York: Norton, 1977. 241–50.

Chadwick-Joshua, Jocelyn. *The Jim Dilemma: Reading Race in Huckleberry Finn*. Jackson: University Press of Mississippi, 1998.

"Civil Rights Cases." U.S. Supreme Court. 109 U.S. 3. 1883.

Doyno, Victor. "Foreword to the Text." *Adventures of Huckleberry Finn: The Only Comprehensive Edition*. New York: Random House, 1996. xii–xvii.

———. "Textual Addendum." *Adventures of Huckleberry Finn: The Only Comprehensive Edition*. New York: Random House, 1996. 365–418.

Dyer, Richard. *White*. New York: Routledge, 1997.

Elliott, Emory. "Introduction." *Adventures of Huckleberry Finn*. New York: Oxford University Press, 1999. vii–xlvii.

Ellison, Ralph. *The Collected Essays of Ralph Ellison*. Ed. John F. Callahan. New York: Random House/Modern Library, 1995.

Fishkin, Shelley Fisher. "Interrogating 'Whiteness,' Complicating 'Blackness': Remapping American Culture." *American Quarterly* 47 (1995): 428–66.

———. *Lighting Out for the Territory: Reflections on Mark Twain and American Culture*. New York: Oxford University Press, 1996.

———. *Was Huck Black? Mark Twain and African-American Voices*. New York: Oxford University Press, 1993.

Frankenburg, Ruth, ed. *Displacing Whiteness: Essays in Social and Cultural Criticism*. Durham, NC: Duke University Press, 1997.

Haney-López, Ian. *White by Law: the Legal Construction of Race*. New York: NYU Press, 1996.

Hill, Mike, ed. *Whiteness: A Critical Reader*. New York: NYU Press, 1997.

Hirst, Robert H. "A Note on the Text." *Adventures of Huckleberry Finn*. Mark Twain Library Edition. Ed. Walter Blair and Victor Fischer. Berkeley: University of California Press, 1985. 44–51.

Holland, Laurence. "'A Raft of Trouble': Word and Deed in *Huckleberry Finn*." *American Realism: New Essays*. Ed. Eric Sundquist. Baltimore: Johns Hopkins University Press, 1982. 66–81.

Jones, Rhett S. "Nigger and Knowledge: White Double-Consciousness in *Adventures of Huckleberry Finn*." Leonard, Tenney, and Davis 173–94.

Kincheloe, Joe L., et al., eds. *White Reign: Deploying Whiteness in America*. New York: St. Martin's Press, 1998.

Ladd, Barbara. *Nationalism and the Color Line in George W. Cable, Mark Twain, and William Faulkner*. Baton Rouge: LSU Press, 1996.

Leonard, James S., Thomas A. Tenney, and Thadious M. Davis, eds. *Satire or Evasion? Black Perspectives on Huckleberry Finn*. Durham: Duke University Press, 1992.

Lofgren, Charles A. *The "Plessy" Case: A Legal-Historical Interpretation*. New York: Oxford University Press, 1987.

Lott, Eric. *Love and Theft: Blackface Minstrelsy and the American Working Class.* New York: Oxford University Press, 1993.

———. "Mr. Clemens and Jim Crow: Twain, Race, and Blackface." *The Cambridge Companion to Mark Twain.* Ed. Forrest G. Robinson. Cambridge: Cambridge University Press, 1995. 129–52.

MacKethan, Lucinda H. "Huckleberry Finn and the Slave Narrative: Lighting Out as Design." *Southern Review* 20 (1984): 247–64.

Mark Twain: A Film. Dir. Ken Burns. Warner Home Video, 2001.

Mensh, Elaine, and Harry Mensh. *Black, White and "Huckleberry Finn": Re-imagining the American Dream.* Tuscaloosa: University of Alabama Press, 2000.

Morrison, Toni. *Playing in the Dark: Whiteness and the Literary Imagination.* Cambridge: Harvard University Press, 1992.

Najmi, Samina, and Rajini Srikanth, eds. *White Women in Racialized Spaces: Imaginative Transformation and Ethical Action in Literature.* Albany: SUNY Press, 2002.

Omi, Michael, and Howard Winant. *Racial Formation in the United States: From the 1960s to the 1980s.* 2nd ed. New York: Routledge & Kegan Paul, 1994.

Pratt, Mary Louise. *Imperial Eyes: Travel Writing and Transculturation.* New York: Routledge, 1992.

Rampersad, Arnold. *"Adventures of Huckleberry Finn* and Afro-American Literature." Leonard, Tenney, and Davis 216–27.

Robinson, Forrest G. *In Bad Faith: The Dynamics of Deception in Mark Twain's America.* Cambridge: Harvard University Press, 1986.

Roediger, David R. *Towards the Abolition of Whiteness: Essays on Race, Politics, and Working Class History.* New York: Verso, 1994.

———, ed. *Black on White: Black Writers on What It Means To Be White.* New York: Schocken, 1998.

Said, Edward. *Orientalism.* New York: Vintage-Random House, 1978.

Singh, Amritjit, and Peter Schmidt. "On the Borders Between U.S. Studies and Postcolonial Theory." *Postcolonial Theory and the U.S.: Race, Ethnicity, and Literature.* Ed. Singh and Schmidt. Jackson: University Press of Mississippi, 2000. 3–69.

Smith, Henry Nash. "Introduction." *Adventures of Huckleberry Finn.* Boston: Houghton Mifflin, 1958. v–xxix.

Sundquist, Eric. *To Wake the Nations: Race in the Making of American Literature.* Cambridge: Harvard University Press, 1993.

Trilling, Lionel. "A Certain Formal Aptness." Introduction to *Adventures of Huckleberry Finn.* New York: Rinehart, 1948.

Twain, Mark. *Adventures of Huckleberry Finn.* 1885. Ed. Emory Elliott. New York: Oxford University Press, 1999.

———. *Adventures of Huckleberry Finn. The Works of Mark Twain.* Ed. Blair, Walter, and Victor Fischer. Vol. 8. Berkeley: University of California Press, 1988.

———. *Adventures of Huckleberry Finn.* 2nd ed. Ed. Sculley Bradley, Richmond Croom Beatty, E. Hudson Long, and Thomas Cooley. New York: Norton, 1977.

———. "A True Story, Repeated Word for Word as I Heard It." *Atlantic Monthly* (Nov. 1874). *Writings of Mark Twain: Definitive Edition.* Vol. 7. New York: Gabriel Wells, 1922. 240–47.

———. *A Connecticut Yankee in King Arthur's Court.* Ed. Bernard L. Stein. Berkeley: University of California Press, 1979.

————. *The Tragedy of Pudd'nhead Wilson, and the Comedy, Those Extraordinary Twins*. New York: Oxford University Press, 1996.

Wieck, Carl E. *Refiguring "Huckleberry Finn."* Athens: University of Georgia Press, 2000.

Wiegman, Robyn. "Whiteness Studies and the Paradox of Particularity." *boundary 2* 26.3 0999): 115–50.

BENNETT KRAVITZ

Reinventing the World and Reinventing the Self in Huck Finn

W hen Huck Finn reaches the "freedom" of Jackson's Island he believes he has fulfilled his American destiny by imposing his will upon the world. Indeed, Huck evaluates his situation when he arrives on the island as follows: "But the next day I was exploring around down through the Island. I was boss of it; it all belonged to me, so to say, and I wanted to know all about it; but mainly I wanted to put in the time" (64). After staging his own death, Huck arrives on the Island convinced he will be able to abandon civilization and refashion himself in a world of his own. Unconsciously, however, Huck has latched on to one of the most prominent American Dreams, one that appears—in Pierre Macherey's terms—in the margins or the "non-dit" of the text: the dream of domination in the guise of creating a new world, or settling a virgin land (85–88). By setting out to construct a new world—one in which he will become an active self-fashioner rather than the passive participant he had been in the Widow's "sivilized" world—Huck imagines he will be able to avoid the very conflicts Twain has assembled for him throughout the novel. Feeling "pretty satisfied," as he so often does at the beginning of a new adventure, Huck believes himself free of the major interpersonal conflicts that pursue him consistently throughout his quest. No longer will he have to resolve the dilemmas of freedom versus friendship, solitude versus solidarity, and Christian, Puritan conscience versus the natural, pagan values of the

From *Papers on Language & Literature* 40, no. 1 (Winter 2004): 3–27. © 2004 by the board of trustees, Southern Illinois University.

"noble savage." But Huck undermines himself in the very passage in which he claims to be "boss of it" all. Huck ends his rumination with the idea that he is "putting in the time." At the very moment Huck seems to control his world, he admits that his main objective is to keep busy and avoid the feelings of loneliness and solitude that attack him whenever Twain decides that Huck is feeling too satisfied.

The image of the virgin land in new-world and American ideology needs no introduction. From Columbus and the Puritans, through the destruction of the Native American tribes, new-world settlers have imagined a green, virgin space waiting to be taken over by yet another version of God's chosen people. Twain, it seems, was aware of this American fantasy, and the rich and complex themes of *Huck Finn* appear to revolve around this central "unsaid" theme. Though Twain may on occasion have disparaged American Indians in his writings, it does not mean he was unaware of or opposed to his ancestors' hegemonic behavior towards native Americans and even the European settlers who were not orthodox Puritans.[1] In an 1881 speech given to the New England Society of Philadelphia, Twain portrays an understanding of the initial American mission that would only begin to gain acceptability in the American mind close to a century later. The tolerance for the Other implicit in his treatment of America's "errand into the wilderness" should remain a lasting testimonial to Twain's attitude toward one civilization impinging itself upon another in the name of freedom:

> My first American ancestor, gentlemen, was an Indian—an early Indian. Your ancestors skinned him alive, and I am an orphan. Later ancestors of mine were the Quakers William Robinson, Marmaduke Stevenson, et al. Your tribe chased them out of the country for their religion's sake; promised them death if they came back; for your ancestors had forsaken the home they loved, and braved the perils of the sea, implacable climate, and the savage wilderness, to acquire the highest and most precious of boons, freedom for every man on this broad continent to worship according to the dictates of his conscience—they were not going to allow a lot of pestiferous Quakers to interfere with it. Your ancestors broke forever the chains of political slavery, and gave the vote to every man in this wide land, excluding none!—none except those who did not belong to the orthodox church. Your ancestors—yes, they were a hard lot; but nevertheless, they gave us religious liberty to worship as they required us to worship, and political liberty to vote as the church required; and so the bereft

one, the forlorn one, am here to do my best to help you celebrate them right. (Geismar 112)

Much like Huck Finn, Twain in the above passage has claimed to be an orphan, suggesting that he, too—despite the difficulties in doing so—has the right to strike out and create an alternative self and world of his own.[2] Because of the critique of America's Puritan settlers, Twain's ideology, or the way he imagines he lives in relation to his society, allows him to dissociate himself from his new-world origins. By the very fact that the author, Samuel Clemens, has become the implied author, Mark Twain, he has successfully become an "orphan" through his art. But Twain's Puritan pessimism undermines his "meditation on (American) origins" (Macherey 240) and will not allow Huck to succeed in the same type of dissociating mission. Huck may believe that he can "boss" it all, and as an orphan seeks his fortune in "virgin" territory, but Twain has other ideas in mind.

The notion of the "virgin land," or New World, is well substantiated in the text of *Huck Finn*. From the very moment that he decides to escape from the cabin in which his father imprisoned him, Huck assumes that his own initiative will be enough to fashion a world of his own. But the means Huck uses to escape from captivity is part of the floating debris that belongs to the world he is so desperate to leave behind:

> I noticed some pieces of limbs and such things floating down, and a sprinkling of bark; so I knowed the river had begun to rise. I reckoned I would have great times, now, if I was over at the town. The June rise used to be always luck for me; because as soon as that rise begins, here comes cord-wood floating down, and pieces of log-rafts—sometimes a dozen logs together; so all you have to do is catch them and sell them to the woodyards and the saw mill. (53–54)

From the very beginning, Huck's quest to "light out" into the new will be determined by his attachment to the old. He is, indeed, resourceful enough to "kill" his pig-like, natural "self" and escape from the grasp of Pap. He is unable, however, to avoid relying on the materials of the world he "abandoned" that seem magically to appear in the river. Far from arriving from some "virgin" untouched place in the world, the wood and the raft are recovered and reconstituted cultural materials of a civilization that Huck desperately seeks to leave forever.

Whenever Huck succumbs to his own ambition, and actually believes he is his own creator, Mark Twain reminds him that civilization is always ready to encroach on his "virgin" territory.[3] In the scene described earlier, when Huck is busy "bossing" Jackson's Island, his dream of domination is destroyed as he discovers the remains of a campfire. Immediately the dangers of his civilization are reified, as Huck hears a conversation between outlaws on the run. Huck loses his self-confidence but decides to discover exactly who has disturbed his paradise.

Huck never discovers the identity of the mysterious outlaws, but the text does offer him consolation. What will relieve his anxiety and solitude is his encounter with Jim. From this point on, the pair will embark upon a journey into "virgin" territory together. Though they will never succeed in their quest—to refashion their selves in a new world—their solidarity and friendship will serve as a buffer against all the dangers society casts in their path.

That the text does, indeed, engage the possibility of finding "virgin" territory and thus reinventing the world is suggested by Twain's parodic treatment of that most famous "encounterer" of new worlds, Christopher Columbus. When Jim and Huck discover a wrecked ship on the river, and decide to "borrow" whatever supplies might come in handy, Huck imagines how Tom Sawyer would feel were he to participate in their adventure:

> "I can't rest, Jim, till we give her a rummaging. Do you reckon Tom Sawyer would ever go by this thing? Not for pie, he wouldn't. He'd call it an adventure—that's what he'd call it; and he'd land on that wreck if it was his last act. And wouldn't he throw style into it?—wouldn't he spread himself, nor nothing? Why you'd think it was Christopher Columbus discovering Kingdom-Come. I wish Tom Sawyer was here." (97)

By combining the machinations of Tom Sawyer and Christopher Columbus, the implied author deconstructs the notion of Huck and Jim's virgin adventure in a number of ways. First, we once again find the pair exploring would-be new worlds on a shipwreck from the very civilization Huck and Jim seek to avoid. Second, that they intend to "borrow" things suggests that there is nothing new or original in their plan. The parody of Columbus also signifies that Huck and Jim's explorations have been relegated to the absurd. Third, Huck and Jim discover to their dismay that the wreck is still tightly bound to civilization. They encounter a gang of robbers who plan to execute one of their own. In order to escape from their predicament, they are forced to abandon the robber to his death. Last, and perhaps most important, is the connection drawn between Columbus and Tom Sawyer. The latter is a romantic who does everything by the book. He relies on the written word to make his way in the world and learn new things, yet he almost always gets things wrong. Indeed, at his romantic worst, he would like to follow the written advice on the subject, and "steal" Jim out of slavery—in a particularly brutal and cruel fashion—even though he knows that Jim has already been set free (304–10). But the wrecked ship, named the *Walter Scott*, suggests the destruction of romance.

Huck and Jim discover many "riches" in the trunk the gang had stolen from the wreck, such as boots, blankets, books, a spyglass and three boxes of "seegars" (109). They are quite pleased with their efforts because they do not realize that they have fallen into what might be called the "Robinson Crusoe" syndrome. Robinson Crusoe, that earlier settler of "virgin" land, also failed to notice his inability to create anything new; he always depended upon the artifacts of his former civilization to build his new world. As Pierre Macherey describes it, Defoe initiates the theme of "man on an Island" (240). The Island becomes the "indispensable setting, the scene for an ideological motif which was only beginning to emerge; the meditation on origins" (240). Indeed, many of the conflicts that Huck and Jim encounter have something to do with "meditation on origins," of ideals such as freedom, friendship, solidarity, solitude, and the fashioning of the self.

Though Huck and Jim experience danger, separation, escape from death, and Jim's capture and reintroduction to slavery, Huck does not abandon the idea of reaching that "virgin" land with Jim. Planning to liberate Jim from the Phelps' farm, Huck suggests the following plan to Tom Sawyer:

> "My plan is this," I says. "We can find out easy if it's Jim in there. Then get up my canoe to-morrow night, and fetch my raft over from the Island. Then the first dark night that comes steal the key out of the old man's britches, after he goes to bed, and shove off down the river on the raft, with Jim, hiding daytimes and running nights, the way me and Jim used to do before. Wouldn't that plan work?" (294)

Ironically, Tom agrees that the plan would succeed but rejects it because it would be too "easy" to free Jim in such a manner. Tom believes a more appealing way involves suffering and humiliation for Jim. That, after all, is the way the "book" says it is supposed to be done. So even in Tom's romantic terms, Huck and Jim will not be allowed to continue as they "used to do before." Their search for a new world down the river is doomed to failure.

Huck's final attempt to find a world of new origins is expressed at the novel's end. After completing his adventures, Huck learns that Jim had previously discovered Pap's dead body, something that would seem to offer Huck a chance at a new beginning, a realistic chance to fulfill the role of "orphan." With that very freedom, however, Huck finds himself trapped once again in the grasp of civilization:

> Tom's most well, now, and got his bullet round his neck on a watch-guard for a watch, and is always seeing what time it is, and so there ain't nothing more to write about, and I am rotten glad of it, because if I'd knowed what a trouble it was to make a book I wouldn't a tackled it and ain't going to no more. But I reckon I got to light out for the Territory ahead of the rest, because Aunt Sally she's going to adopt me and sivilize me and I can't stand it. I been there before. (366)

Huck has yet to solve the conundrum of self-fashioning in a new world. He is still being pursued by the old, and there is no apparent respite from it. He has discovered exactly how difficult it is to create an authorial voice, become "author of his book," and reinvent his self and his world. Despite his relief at his father's death, Huck is disturbed by Tom's civilized practice of "always seeing what time it is." A romantic quest like self-fashioning is only possible in an environment in which time stands still, much like Twain's portrayal of the Mississippi River in antebellum America. Indeed, everything that we have learned about Huck has come from his efforts at being the "author" of his own identity. Yet he now admits that the work was too difficult and he will no longer pursue his authorial dreams.[4]

Perhaps that is why his quest for self-fashioning seems to have run its course. The pull of social convention and intrusion is still overwhelming, which is why the novel cannot have a happy ending. Yet the fear of becoming "sivilized" is still intimidating for Huck, so he opts to "go for howling adventures amongst the Injuns, over in the Territory" (365). In terms of the "virgin" land or creating a New World, Huck will be joining the American effort that effectively ended Native American resistance to the total colonization of the continental United States by its white citizens.[5] Indeed, Huck will thus become implicated in the wholesale slaughter of the Native tribes. Whether Huck will become an active participant or seek to escape its horrors in a raft the reader cannot know. What is clear, however, is that Huck will not find the "virgin" land he seeks among the Indians in the already settled Territory.[6]

* * * *

Though Huck and Jim both set out on the raft to reinvent themselves, their personal agendas are very different. While Huck seeks to "boss" it all, Jim merely seeks to become his own master, though his strategy is determined by Twain's parodic treatment of the black as American Gilded-Age capitalist. Despite his resolve to rise from rags to riches, Jim's economic maneuvers—as he explains to Huck—have been dismal failures:

> "Wunst I had foteen dollars but I tuck to specalat'n en got busted out."
>
> "What did you speculate in, Jim?"
>
> "Well, fust I tackled stock."
>
> "What kind of stock?"
>
> "Why, live stock. Cattle, you know. I put ten dollars in a cow. But I ain' gwyne to resk no mo' money in stock. De cow up n' died on my han's."
>
> "So you lost the ten dollars."
>
> "No, I didn' lose it all. I on'y los' 'bout nine of it. I sole de hide en taller for a dollar en ten cents."
>
> "You had five dollars and ten cents left. Did you speculate any more?" "Yes. You know dat one-laigged nigger dat b'longs to old Misto Bradish? Well, he sot up a bank, en say anybody dat put in a dollar would get fo' dollars mo' at de en' er de year. Well, all de niggers went in, but dey didn' have much. I wuz de on'y one dat had much. So I stuck out for mo' dan fo' dollars, en I said 'f I didn't git it I'd start a bank myself. Well o' course dat nigger want' to keep me out er de business, bekase he say dey warn't business 'nough for two banks, so he say I could put in five dollars en he pay me thirty-five at de en' er de year." (71–72)

Jim's first disappointment in the American capitalist system comes from investing in the "stock" market. Despite the reader's expectation that the stock market would signify an institution such as Wall Street, Twain undermines that notion by replacing it with "live" stock. Jim, the slave capitalist, instinctively understands that market, because he himself has been a victim of a "live stock" economy: one that relies on the institution of slavery.

Jim's woeful economic saga continues. The so-called bank he invests in goes "bust." His final ten cents are given away to the poor, since Jim is sure his kindness—according to the preacher in his friend Balum's church—will be returned a hundred times. He is left without a cent but still considers himself rich because, as he puts it, "'I owns myself, en I's wuth eight hund'd dollars. I wisht I had de money, I wouldn' want no mo'" (73). Jim's riches, then, come from reinventing himself as his own master, something he will attempt to substantiate and legitimize in the eyes of white society as he travels to the "north" with Huck in search of a new frontier.

That Jim is involved in a quest for self-reinvention is accentuated throughout the novel. Though Jim is often metaphysically lost, Twain provides him with a number of strategies to embark on his search for a new identity. He often does not know who or where he is, but Jim is able to succeed in the world instinctively. "'Say—who is you? Whar is you'" (23) Jim exclaims when he hears Huck and Tom approaching at the beginning of chapter two. Jim and Huck, if not Tom, will discover at least partial answers to these questions together. When Huck decides to play a mean trick on Jim, pretending never to have left the raft after having been thrown overboard, Jim repeats the existential questions that guide him in his search for freedom: "'Well, looky here, boss, dey's sumf'n wrong dey is. Is I *me* or who is I? Is I heah, or whah is I? Now dat's what I wants to know'" (119).

As in most of the questions posited by *Huck Finn*, Jim will receive only limited answers. He will become a free man, but not through any actions taken by him, Huck, or Tom. Miss Watson's deathbed manumission of Jim has more to do with a guilty conscience and her salvation in the next world than admirable human enterprise. And the "fog" surrounding Cairo will cause Jim to seek his freedom sailing south into slave country. For Mark Twain, the initiatives of no man, white or black, can overcome the pessimistic notion that human determination counts for little in the making of human history. Thus, Jim is released from the bondage of slavery, though not because of any action of his own. Miss Watson, as "Deus ex machina," frees Jim to soothe her Christian conscience. As Roy Harvey Pearce has remarked, "*Huckleberry Finn* teaches us ... that whereas utopianism is possible, utopians are not" (313–14).

Perhaps the greatest weapon the author grants Jim on his journey of liberation is that Jim is labeled "white inside" (345). Though easily understood as the ultimate racist statement, "white inside" also contains the potential to undercut many of the prejudicial notions that whites held concerning blacks, whether slaves or ex-slaves. Huck is led to view Jim as "white inside" when the latter nobly offers to risk his freedom and watch Tom until a doctor arrives to treat Tom's bullet wound. Huck also finds Jim to be very much like whites when Jim decides that his first act as a free man, as reported by Huck, would be to save "money and never spend a single cent, and when he got enough he would buy his wife, which was owned on a farm close to where Miss Watson lived; and then they would both work to buy the two children, and if their master wouldn't sell them, they'd get an

Ab'litionist to go and steal them" (124). But the most moving rendition of "white inside" is manifested when Jim agonizes about his children, especially his mistreatment of his daughter Elizabeth. After the duke and the king join them, and Jim completes his night shift guarding the raft, Huck notices Jim's depression:

> When I waked up just at day-break, he was setting there with his head down betwixt his knees, moaning and mourning to himself. I didn't take no notice, nor let on. I knowed what it was about. He was thinking about his wife and children, away up yonder, and he was low and homesick; because he hadn't ever been away from home before in his life; and I do believe he cared just as much for his people as white folks does for their'n. It don't seem natural, but I reckon it's so. He was often moaning and mourning that way, nights, when he judged I was asleep, and saying, "Po' little 'Lizabeth! po' little Johnny! It's mighty hard; I spec' I ain't ever gwyne to see you no mo', no mo'!" He was a mighty good nigger, Jim was. (201)

Huck engages Jim in conversation and learns that Jim feels especially guilty for having beaten his daughter when she ignored his instructions only to discover that she had become deaf. Thus the measure of Jim's worth is presented in terms of his ability to imitate the white man's imagined values,[7] loyalty to and compassion for family and friends. If Huck had felt "ornery" and insignificant in the face of Providence (30), Jim is capable of the same emotion when he recalls his shabby treatment of Elizabeth. Twain has, perhaps for the first time in American fiction, created a round black character. Jim possesses a realistic range of human traits and emotions. By doing so, in the unsaid of the text, Twain has pointed to an intolerable ideological refutation that cannot be stated out loud. By presenting Jim as a family man *par excellence*, Twain has undermined the racist doctrine of retrogression: that is, the theory of the emancipated slave returning to his "natural" state of sexual and social bestiality supposedly inherent in African culture. Slavery, according to retrogressionist doctrine, had maintained a modicum of control over lascivious behavior, at least among slaves, if not their masters.

Retrogressionist beliefs had "distorted perception of Afro-American family life and sexual behavior and affected the most influential early-twentieth-century conceptualizations of the entire Afro-American experience" (Gutman 531). Because of emancipation, the myth that Black Americans lost the positive morals and restraints that slavery had perpetuated gained great prominence. That myth was useful for southern Bourbon political rhetoric that promised to save the South from political corruption, economic extravagance, and racial and sexual irregularities.

That myth became part of popular Gilded-Age culture in the North as well as the South. In the early 1880s, just about the time that *Huck Finn* was published, the *New York Sun* columnist Frank Wilkeson reported from St. Helena's Island, South Carolina:

> Almost without exception, the women of these Islands, who have negro blood in their veins, are prostitutes. It is a hopeless task to endeavor to elevate a people whose women are strumpets.... It is absolutely no disgrace for any black girl to have children before she is married. These people are devoid of shame. Their personal habits are so filthy, that I suspected that venereal disease was wide-spread among them. On inquiry of the physicians that practice among them, I found I was correct in my inference. The negroes are saturated with this deadly taint. This being the case, and free love in its vilest sense being practiced among them, it can readily be seen how widely diffused the ineradicable poison must necessarily be. (Gutman 532)

Perhaps to call this reporting is to exaggerate the point. Wilkeson—like many others who "reported" on the post-emancipation African-American plight—considered the ex-slaves' behavior to be an "ineradicable" poison, something that could not be changed. Those charges concerning the "peculiarities" of the Negro race were not limited to journalists. Nathaniel Shaler, who grew up in a family of Kentucky slaveholders and later became head of Harvard's Lawrence Scientific School, made similar arguments in an 1884 *Atlantic Monthly* article. Shaler was convinced, through his long experience growing up around Negroes, of the very "real dangers this African blood brings to our state":

> The peculiar monogamic instinct which in our own race has been slowly, century by century, developing itself in the old tangle of passions has yet to be fixed in this people. In the negro, this motive, more than any other the key to our society, is very weak. If indeed it exists at all as an indigenous impulse.
>
> The modern state is but a roof built to shelter the lesser associations of men. Chief of these is the family, which rests on a certain order of alliance of the sexual instincts with the higher and more human faculties. Next come the various degrees of human cooperation in various forms of business life; and then the

power of the will, that gives the continuity to effort which is the key to all profitable labor; and last but not least, the impulse to sexual morality. (Gutman 533)

Those lesser-developed people who are incapable of incorporating family values into their worldview threaten the structure of American society. Of course, the main point here is that because blacks were genetically "flawed" in terms of basic human morals, they were thought incapable of running their own affairs. A more likely explanation, aside from the obvious rationale for a desire to continue to dominate and exploit the blacks, was that the southern male attributed his own desire and lust for the black female to the black male who, after achieving independence, would now want to steal the Southern Belle away from his former enslaver.

For whatever reason the retrogressionist theories abounded, *Huck Finn* clearly takes issue with them. Rather than present only the single, monologic voice of the oppressor in the struggle between slave and slaveholder, Twain reconstructs the marginalized voice of the slave to subvert the hegemonic retrogressionist theory. Twain portrays Jim as noble, loyal, and the ultimate friend and family man. Twain takes issue with the major racial theories of his day, and those critics who are convinced only of the racist potential of the text and/or Mark Twain would do well to examine the "unsaid" of the text.[8]

Another tool that Twain provides for Jim on his quest for freedom is the latter's belief in the spirit world. In chapter two, Huck and Tom play a trick on the sleeping Jim—they remove his hat and place it on a tree limb—and when Jim awakes he assumes that "witches bewitched him and put him in a trance, and rode him all over the State, and then set him under the trees again and hung his hat on a limb to show who done it" (23). As Huck notes, "Jim was monstrously proud about it, and he got so he wouldn't hardly notice the other niggers." Indeed, Jim interprets his episode with the witches as having made him different from all the other slaves, and that experience not only enhanced his sense of self-worth but "infected" him with the romantic notion of self-fashioning:

> Niggers is always talking about witches in the dark by the kitchen fire; but whenever one was talking and letting on to know all about such things, Jim would happen in and say, "Hm! What you know 'bout witches?" and that nigger was corked up and had to take a back seat. Jim always kept that five-center piece around his neck with a string and said it was a charm the devil give to him with his own hands and told him he could cure anybody with it and fetch witches whenever he wanted to, just by saying something

to it;[9] but he never told what he said to it. Niggers would come from all over around there and give Jim anything they had just for a sight of that five-center piece; but they wouldn't touch it, because the devil had his hands on it. Jim was most ruined, for a servant, because he got so stuck up on account of having seen the devil and been rode by witches. (24)

As Huck observed, Jim was "most ruined, for a servant," because he had been infected by the positive, romantic spirit of the devil. In attempting to free himself from the constraints of slavery, Jim will rely upon that very spirit. But Jim does not succeed in freeing himself through his own efforts. In an ironic twist, Miss Watson, his owner, is the person who legally grants Jim his freedom. Twain presents the law as a fiction, neither able to keep Jim in captivity nor grant him anything other than legal manumission. Of course, physical manumission was for most slaves their *raison d'être*, yet from the moment Tom arrives with news of Jim's freedom, the text reduces Jim to minstrel caricature.

Jim's relationship with the devil, witches, and the spirit world is a curious mixture of domination of and submission to spirits. Jim, as we have seen, believes he has power over the witches and a special relationship with the devil. But he is also submissive to and fearful of the power that ghosts have; Jim believes that ghosts primarily appear for vindictive purposes. After Huck explores Jackson's Island and discovers that Jim has intruded upon his "virgin" territory, his greeting causes sheer terror in Jim:

He bounced up and stared at me wild. Then he drops down on his knees, and puts his hands together and says: "Doan hurt me—don't! I hain't ever done no harm to a ghos'. I awluz liked dead people, en done all I could for 'em. Yo go en git in de river agin, whah you b'longs, en doan' do nuffin to Ole Jim, 'at 'uz awluz yo' fren'." (67)

Unlike Huck, who has explained that he "don't take no stock in dead people" (18), Jim certainly does. Jim is well aware of the double-edged potential that ghosts held for the slave population of the south. Double-edged, because a slave's ghost could be a potent source of vengeance against white injustice, or a white man's ghost could appear to protect or punish a slave. Though belief in spirits probably did more to reinforce white hegemony than to subvert it, the spirit world did offer relief from the agonies of slavery. Kentucky slaves often appealed to magic and witchcraft to "prevent their masters from exercising their will over the slaves." One slave, Henry Bibb, used roots and powders suggested by a conjurer to ward off floggings and to change his owner's "sentiments of anger to those of love toward [him]" (Gutman 278).

Twain, it appears, was familiar with the pervading belief in spirits as a source of great power in Southern American slave culture. He understood that the spirit world could be used in both positive and negative fashions. These beliefs were so widely held that one former slave, Tom Windham, was not above reminiscing about his encounter with that most mythical of presidents, the spirit of "old father" Abraham Lincoln. "'I've seen him since he been dead too, I got a gun old Father Abraham give me right out o' his own hand at Vicksburg. I'm goin' to keep it till I die too. Yes ma'm, I know they is spirits'" (Rawick 11). Windham uses the spirit of the Great Emancipator to protect him from the turmoil of his society, but the manipulation of spirits could serve other aims as well. In general, this type of Black folklore was used, in Claude Lévi-Strauss' terms, to smooth over the cultural contradictions of slave society.[10] Black folklore taught the ways of the world, how it was possible to fear and perhaps love a slave owner, and, most important, how to get along in the white world as a slave. As Eugene Genovese contends, slaves' attitudes toward their owners should be understood as a dialectic between accommodation and resistance to the demands of a slave society. But this dialectic took place within an overall acceptance of white hegemony.[11]

In his desire to survive as a "state prisoner"—as Tom Sawyer defines Jim's role while the boys plan his escape from the Phelps' farm—Jim relies on the spirit world to chart his path into the unknown world of freedom. In chapter nine, Jim and Huck discover a dead body in a frame house floating down the river. Later, Jim refuses to discuss the dead man with Huck, for fear "it would fetch bad luck; and besides, he said, he might come and ha'nt us" (79). One aspect of the "hant" stories told by the slaves suggested that angry white slave owners could reach out beyond the grave to inflict suffering on insolent slaves. One such slave, who, like Jim, decided to ignore the terrible consequences of failure and to escape from his master, was Lewis Clarke. Though he was brave enough to risk brutal punishment and sale to the deep South for attempting to flee north, Clarke still feared his dead owner: "'I was actually as much afraid of my old master when dead as I was when he was alive. I often dreamed of him, too, after he was dead, and thought he had actually come back again, to torment me more'" (Gorn 556). Jim, who is in a similar situation to that of Clarke, knows better than to upset the spirit of a potentially angry white ghost with foolish speculation. He uses his culture's familiarity with the workings of the spirit world to avoid unnecessary confrontation with the powers that be.

*　*　*　*

As previously noted, Jim manifests both Christian virtue—especially when he aids Huck and Tom in life-threatening situations—and pagan belief in spirits in his search for a new identity in free society. Huck Finn will also have to maneuver between the Christian and pagan worlds before he can finally "remember" his name and sign his manuscript, "Yours Truly, Huck Finn." Initially, Huck assumes that nothing would be easier than to abandon his Christian, civilized self. At the conclusion of *The Adventures of Tom Sawyer*—which Twain uses as his starting point for *Huck Finn*—Huck decides to return to the widow and become "respectable" so that Tom will accept him in his gang of robbers. But in order to join Tom's gang, Huck was asked to nominate a family member for execution should Huck foolishly divulge any of the gang's secrets. Huck designates Miss Watson as the member of his "family" to be killed, in effect, killing his Christian conscience.

In Huck's meditation on origins, he finds very little of value in the Christian world. He is all "cramped up" by his new clothes, and the Widow cries over him, calling Huck "a poor lost lamb, and ... a lot of other names too, but she never meant no harm by it" (18). Strange customs abound in the Christian world of the Widow and Miss Watson. People are forced to "grumble a little over the victuals" before they are allowed to eat. Huck is forced to learn something about the Bible, but despite his initial interest, as soon as he discovers that Moses is dead he becomes bored. Huck thinks he will be able "to take no stock in dead people" as he forges a new identity for his self (18). If heaven is filled with people like the Widow and Miss Watson, Huck would much prefer the "bad" place. Indeed, Huck is unable to "pray a lie," so his chances of getting to heaven are, in his view, remote.

When Huck does try to pray the results are unsatisfactory:

> Miss Watson she took me in the closet and prayed, but nothing come of it. She told me to pray every day, and whatever I asked for I would get. But it warn't so. I tried it. Once I got a fish-line, but no hooks. It warn't any good to me without hooks. I tried for the hooks three or four times, but somehow I couldn't make it work. (29)

In Twain's parodic treatment of the gospel according to Matthew, Huck will find it most difficult to join Jesus to become a "fisher of men" because he lacks a hook. In addition, by having Huck pray in a closet with Miss Watson, Twain parodies the notion of a Puritan retreat for women. For example, Sarah Osborn, the distinguished Puritan spiritual leader, finds her closet to be the proper sanctuary to commune with God:

Grace was for a few minutes drawn forth [illegible word] sensible, lively exercise; and I appeared to myself as a vessel which had been wind about and could by no means get forward, while wind and tide were against it. But, now, as there seemed to be a favorable gale, determined to weigh anchor, hoist sail, ply my work, and make all speed toward the desired haven.—But, alas! Ere I could get to my closet, to pour out my soul to God there, I seemed ... calmed again. (144)

In a position of weakness, "'driven by infirmity and want to conveniency,'" Osborn "retreats" to make her closet her bed. Yet from the supine position Osborn finds the "curtains drawd Except just to Let in Light" (Norton 527). From the "confines" of the closet Osborn is able to "avoid interruptions from family affairs ... [and finds the time] to read and write things of a religious nature" (527). Osborn, then, has made the closet, in the tradition of Virginia Woolf, a room of her own. But unfortunately for Huck, he cannot find a room of his own, especially in the confines of the civilized, Christian society of Miss Watson. Instead of the Puritan closet, Huck's retreat will be on the river, and much like Sarah Osborn, relief from the anxieties of civilization and the human condition will be for him, at best, temporary.

That Huck is not inspired by his sojourn in Miss Watson's closet is not his only problem with Christian belief. Huck asks the age-old agnostic, existential question concerning justice in the world for those who obey God's law. Perhaps Huck is even asking the essential question for heretics who believed in the duality of creation:

I says to myself, if a body can get anything they pray for, why don't Deacon Winn get back the money he lost on pork? Why can't the widow get back her silver snuff-box that was stole? Why can't Miss Watson fat up? No, says I to myself, there ain't nothing in it. I went and told the widow about it, and she said the thing a body could get by praying for it was "spiritual gifts." This was too many for me, but she told me what she meant—I must help other people, and do every-thing I could for other people, and look out for them all the time, and never think about myself... I went out in the woods and turned it over in my mind a long time, but I couldn't see no advantage about it anymore, but just let it go. Sometimes the widow would take me one side and talk about Providence in a way to make a body's mouth water; but maybe next day Miss Watson would take hold and knock it all down again. I judged I could see there was two Providences, and a poor chap

would stand considerable show with the widow's Providence, but
if Miss Watson's got him, there warn't no help for him any more.
I thought it all out, and reckoned I would belong to the widow's,
if he wanted me, though I couldn't make out how he was agoing
to be any better off then he was before, seeing I was so ignorant
and so kind of low-down and ornery. (29–30)

Huck is no more confused than any skeptic through the ages who asked, "If
God is good, from whence cometh evil?" He is able to answer that question
by applying the heretic, dualistic approach to religious belief. Specifically,
however, the project of individual spiritual preparation so common to the
Puritan experience seems to be an integral part of Huck's life.[12] But unlike
the Puritans, Huck imagines the possibility of two Providences, one that
he rejects outright, and one that might be suited to one as "low-down
and ornery" as he. So, it is not, as Huck would like to think, that he has
no connection to or use for Christian credo. His "heretical" Providence,
however, is one that allows Huck to free Jim from slavery and find Jim "white
inside."

Though Huck is not conscious of the fact, he travels down the river
with that spirit of compassion he absorbed from the widow's Providence.
Twain has often noted that the human conscience pursues humanity like
a "yellow dog," and Huck himself utters that remark after the tar and
feathering of the duke and the king. But his compassion emerges not only
from the guilt he feels at the two scoundrels' predicament, but also because
he learns from this episode that "human beings *can* be awful cruel to one
another" (291). And Huck, despite his occasional insensitivity to Jim, is not a
cruel boy. His conscience and compassion motivate him to help Jim, take the
king and duke aboard the raft, and foil their plan to defraud the Wilks sisters.
Huck's compassion will serve him well in creating a real friendship with Jim,
but Twain will not allow him to find a place in which he can feel "satisfied"
for a significant period of time.

*   *   *   *

As we have seen, the prime impediment to Huck and Jim's quest of
self-fashioning is the impossibility of reinventing the world and reinventing
the self. In the novel, the potential for reform is either dim or non-existent.
Despite the text's superficial support for the American ideal of "orphaning"
the self, and the Emersonian notion of becoming rather than being, Huck
and Jim are essentially impotent. Twain's Puritan pessimism casts great
doubt on humanity's ability to transcend the pettiness of human existence.

Sometimes Twain does so with humor and sometimes with viciousness, but the result is always stagnant.

The most obvious and humorous episode in *Huck Finn* that questions the human potential for reform occurs when Pap decides to repent his sins by giving up his "noble savage" lifestyle and abstaining from the "devil's brew." After winning custody of Huck—in Pap's terms, allowed to become the boss of his son—Pap goes on a drinking spree to celebrate his victory in the courts. The judge, who had given Pap custody of Huck, decides to "make a man of him":

> So he took him to his own house, and dressed him up clean and nice, and had him to breakfast and dinner and supper with the family, and was just old pie to him, so to speak. And after supper he talked to him about temperance and such things till the old man cried, and said he'd been a fool, and fooled away his life; but now he was agoing to turn over a new leaf and be a man nobody wouldn't be ashamed of, and he hoped the judge would help him and not look down on him. The judge said he could hug him for them words; so *he* cried and his wife she cried again; Pap said he'd been a man that had always been misunderstood before, and the judge said he believed it. The old man said that what a man wanted that was down, was sympathy; and the judge said it was so; so they cried again. And when it was bedtime, the old man rose up and held out his hand and says: "Look at it gentlemen, and ladies all; take a hold of it; shake it. There's a hand that was the hand of a hog; but it ain't so no more; it's the hand of a man that's started on a new life, 'll die before he'll go back. You mark them words—don't forget I said them. It's a clean hand now: shake it—don't be afeard." (42–43)

Ironically, the judge is partially correct in his estimation of Pap. Pap does not die "before he'll go back" to his "evil" ways, but he does manage to drink himself to death shortly afterward. Although Pap had supposedly left the "hog's" life and signed and kissed a pledge never to drink again, the judge soon finds him drunk on his porch with a broken arm. The judge, as Huck notes, "felt kind of sore. He said he reckoned a body could reform the ole man with a shot-gun, maybe, but he didn't know no other way" (44). Thus, in amusing fashion, Twain expresses his skepticism in regard to the possibility of reform.

But the most potent argument for the impossibility of reform is presented in the so-called "evasion" scene toward the novel's closure. Many critics have expressed their dissatisfaction about the collapse of the novel's moral stance.[13] Both Jim and Huck revert to grotesque caricatures once Tom arrives at the Phelps farm. Both lose the initiative they have displayed throughout their journey on the raft. Jim is once again a parody of minstrel blackface as he agrees to Tom's tortuous route to escape from slavery. He must be subjected to snakes, rats, and chains to make his impending escape more "real" and thus satisfying to Tom. Huck, having proved himself more creative than Tom throughout the novel, abandons his own initiative and meekly agrees to all of Tom's plans. And Tom, who seems to control his own fate, earns nothing but a bullet wound for his absurd attempt to free Jim the way "the book says." In the context of the text's pessimism, however, the ending is far from inappropriate. True reform has never been possible in the novel, despite the bond of friendship formed between Huck and Jim.

The quest for reinvention, then, of both the self and the world, has ended in failure. But through Huck's and Jim's "meditations on origins" friendship and solidarity have combined to mitigate the harsh reality of human existence. Perhaps Twain's most important contribution to American letters through *Huck Finn* is not, in Hemingway's tribute, that "all American literature comes from one book by Mark Twain" (22). Rather it is the mixing of black and white voices in a high-brow or low-brow cultural attempt to discover the similarity rather than the differences between oppressor and oppressed. In Jim's terms, if a Frenchman is a man, "'why doan' he talk like a man?'" (114).[14] Jim is interested in establishing the common denominator among men, most often through the freedom that comes from "owning" one's self. Huck, in contrast, is "willing to go to hell" for a friend because he believes that Jim is "white inside." He is unable to accept the equality of difference, but he is willing to ignore Jim's origins and establish equality based on his friendship with and love for Jim. Their "meditation on origins" has not left Huck and Jim with a coherent plan to fulfill their "self" ambitions. They have discovered, however, the only way to confront and to mitigate the horrors of the human condition: that is, the freedom of choice one acquires through solidarity and friendship with the other.

NOTES

1. James C. McNutt traces the development in Twain's writing vis-à-vis the American Indian. He notes that while Twain is vicious in his treatment of the Indians in *Innocents Abroad*, that antagonism is greatly mitigated in a later work, "Captain Stormfield's Visit to Heaven." McNutt believes that an attitude such as that of Leslie Fiedler's (*The Return of the Vanishing American* 1968), that Twain "'was obsessed by a hatred of Indians from the very beginning of his literary career,'" ignores the latter phase of Twain's thinking (224).

2. Hana Wirth-Nesher discusses the ideal of orphanhood in American literature in "The Literary Orphan as National Hero: Huck and Pip": "The loner, cut loose from

family responsibilities, is an inherent part of the romance of America, or the myth of eternal fresh starts.... Orphanhood in American literature is a clean slate, self-reliance, and often enchanted solitude that veers dangerously close to real loneliness."

3. The theme of Huck Finn as self-creator is introduced in the first page of the novel. We are told that our knowledge of Huck comes from having read a book by Mark Twain, that is, *Tom Sawyer*. Huck also tells us that Twain was occasionally guilty of telling "stretchers," but Huck implies that because he is able to tell his own story, *Huck Finn* will be different.

4. In "Huck Finn's Written Word," Steven Blakemore discusses Huck's difficulties with writing, claiming that "Huck is enslaved to but liberated in his language" (29). In "'Nobody but Our Gang Warn't Around': The Authority of Language in *Huckleberry Finn*," Lee Clark Mitchell contends that Huck styles his self through his "writing" (83–84).

5. The Territory refers to the area, originally part of the Louisiana Purchase, that was to become the State of Oklahoma. It had been reserved as Indian Territory in 1834 by the federal government. In response to pressure to open it to white settlement, the government allowed whites to settle the territory in 1889. In 1907 Oklahoma was admitted into the union.

6. Twain's sequel to *Huck Finn*, "Huck Finn and Tom Sawyer among the Indians," perpetuates the choices that Huck encountered in the original novel. Twain portrays both whites and Indians as murderers, but his representation of the latter is especially brutal. Twain completed 17 chapters but was unable or unwilling to complete and publish the book. Paul Delaney, in "You Can't Go Back to the Raft Ag'in Huck Honey!: Mark Twain's Western Sequel to *Huckleberry Finn*" (*Western American Literature* 11 [1976]: 215–29), claims that Huck did not resolve the conflicts he faced in *Huck Finn* in Twain's continuation. That the novel was never completed suggests that Twain was unwilling to allow Huck to "find" himself through the barbarous slaughter of others.

7. In the novel the superiority of white men's values is reduced to the absurd. White people engage in murder, mayhem, debauchery, thievery, and stupidity, so that "white inside" is doubly ironic.

8. For the view of *Huck Finn* as racist, see, for example, Ernest D. Mason's "Attraction and Repulsion: Huck Finn, 'Nigger Jim,' and Black Americans Revisited." Mason specifically notes that "Huck's feeling ... that Jim is essentially 'white inside' can hardly be distinguished from the racist refusal to associate anyone black with human decency" (37). Huck is only able to accept a "distant intimacy" with Jim, while their master–slave relationship is preserved. For an ambiguous view of the novel, see both Rhett S. Jones's "Nigger and Knowledge: White Double-Consciousness in *Adventures of Huckleberry Finn* (*Mark Twain Journal* 22 [1984]: 28–37), and Kenny J. Williams's "*Adventures of Huckleberry Finn* or Mark Twain's Racial Ambiguity" (*Mark Twain Journal* 22 [1984]: 38–41). The reassessment of the novel begins with Shelly Fisher Fishkins's claim, in *Was Huck Black? Mark Twain and African American Voices* (New York: Oxford UP, 1993), that Huck's voice is probably based on that of ten-year-old Jimmy, a black boy Twain described in an 1874 article. She does not argue that Huck is "black" but rather that Jimmy's speech pattern was used as a model for Huck's voice.

9. Huck and Tom had taken candles from Miss Watson's house to light their path in the garden. Tom had left five cents on the kitchen table in payment, and it is that "five-center" piece that Jim assumes the devil had left behind for him (23–24).

10. See *The Savage Mind*, where Lévi-Strauss portrays the development and propagation of myth in primitive society.

11. See the first chapter of Eugene Genovese's *Roll, Jordan, Roll: The World the Slave Made* (New York: Pantheon, 1974).

12. As Huck attempts to re-form himself and prepares for or invents the Providence he imagines would suit him, he relives, to an extent, the Puritan experience. Andrew Delbanco traces the "persistent sense of renewal and risk" that has attended the project of becoming American from Puritan times down to the present. The "extraordinary tenacity ... with which the Americans have clung to the belief that their lives can be radically renewed" may be the most singular characteristic of the Puritan culture and legacy (251). Sacvan Bercovitch notes a similar pattern in his interpretation of the American experience as he claims that early New England rhetoric "provided a ready framework for inverting later secular values—human perfectability, technological progress, democracy, Christian socialism, or simply (and comprehensively) the American Way—into the mold of sacred teleology." In Bercovitch's cultural analysis there exists a continuity, from the Great Awakening through the American Renaissance, Edwards through Emerson, that has contributed to the genre of auto-American-biography: "the celebration of the representative self as America, and of the American self as the embodiment of a prophetic universal design" (137).

13. See footnote 8 for critics who view the novel as racist. Steven Railton, in "Jim and Mark Twain: What Do Dey Stan' For?" (*Virginia Quarterly Review* 63 [1987]: 393–408), claims that the ending reduces the text to "trash" in Jim's terms. See also John Fraser's "In Defense of Culture: *Huckleberry Finn*" (*Oxford Review* 6 [1967]: 5–22) and Donald B. Gibson, who objects in "Mark Twain's Jim in the Classroom" (*English Journal* 57 [1968]: 196–202) to the stereotypical portrayal of Jim, most particularly at the novel's end. John Harris, in "Principles, Sympathy, and Doing What's Right" (*Philosophy: The Journal of the Royal Institute of Philosophy* 52 [1977]: 96–99), claims that Huck "collapses" on the issue of conscience. Ernest Hemingway, in *Green Hills of Africa* (New York: Scribner's, 1935) recommends concluding the novel before the "evasion" scene (22–23).

14. David L. Smith argues in "Huck, Jim, and American Racial Discourse" that "While Jim's response—that a man should talk like a man—betrays his ignorance of cultural diversity, his argument is perceptive and structurally sound. The humor in Huck's conclusion, 'you can't learn a nigger how (sic) to argue' arises precisely from our recognition that Jim's argument is better than Huck's" (8).

Works Cited

Bercovitch, Sacvan. *The Puritan, Origins of the American, Self*. New Haven: Yale UP, 1975.

Blakemore, Steven. "Huck's Written World." *American Literary Realism* 20 (1988): 21–29.

Delbanco, Andrew. *The Puritan Ideal*. Cambridge: Harvard UP, 1989.

Geismar, Maxwell, ed. *Mark Twain and the Three R's Race, Religion, Revolution—and Related Matters*. New York: Bobbs-Merrill, 1973.

Gorn, Elliot J. "Black Spirits: The Ghostlore of Afro-American Slaves." *American Quarterly* 36 (1984): 549–565.

Gutman, Herbert G. *The Black Family in Slavery and Freedom 1750–1925*. New York: Vintage, 1977.

Macherey, Pierre. *A Theory of Literary Production*. London: Routledge, 1989.

Mason, Ernest D. "Attraction and Repulsion: Huck Finn's 'Nigger' Jim, and Black Americans Revisited." *College Language Association Journal* 33 (1989): 36–48.

McNutt, James C. "Mark Twain and the American Indian: Earthly Realism and Heavenly Idealism." *American Indian Quarterly* 4 (1978): 223–242.

Mitchell, Lee Clark. "'Nobody but Our Gang Warn't Around': The Authority of Language in Huckleberry Finn." *New Essays on Huck Finn.* Ed. Louis J. Budd. New York: Cambridge UP, 1985.

Norton, Mary Beth. "'My Resting Reaping Times': Sarah Osborn's Defense of her Unfeminine Activities, 1767." *Signs* 2 (1976): 515–529.

Osborn, Sarah. *Memoirs of Mrs. Sarah Osborn.* Ed. Samuel Hopkins. Privately published ms. 1799.

Pearce, Roy Harvey. "'Yours Truly, Huck Finn.'" *One Hundred Years of Huckleberry Finn: The Boy, His Book, and American Culture.* Ed. Robert Sattelmeyer and J. Donald Crowley. Columbia: U of Missouri P, 1985. 313–324.

Rawick, George P. *The American, Slave: A Composite Autobiography.* Westport, CT: Greenwood, 1972.

Smith, David L. "Huck, Jim, and American Racial Discourse." *Mark Twain Journal* 22 (1984): 4–11.

Twain, Mark. *The Adventures of Huckleberry Finn.* New York: Oxford UP, 1996.

Wirth-Nesher, Hana. "The Literary Orphan as National Hero: Huck and Pip." *Dickens Studies Annual* 15 (1986): 259–273.

TODD GILES

"That Night We Had Our Show": Twain and Audience

Mark Twain was no stranger to drama. During his career he wrote eleven plays, collaborated on ten others, translated three from German, supervised the dramatization of six of his novels—*Adventures of Huckleberry Finn* among them—and began several of his other prose works as dramatic scripts. Twain also acted in Shakespearian parlor productions, worked on a burlesque of *Hamlet*, and joined the Players Club, a group of prominent New York theatre professionals. His affinity for the theatre was tempered, however, by his skepticism of theatergoers and more generally of any group of individuals gathered for a common purpose. He insisted that "men in a crowd do not act as they would as individuals. In a crowd they don't think for themselves, but become impregnated by the mass sentiment uppermost in the minds which happens to be en masse."[1] This sentiment is echoed in "The United States of Lyncherdom" (1901), in which Twain characterizes people's "commonest weakness" as "Moral Cowardice, ... the commanding feature of the make-up of 9,999 men in the 10,000."[2] Twain uses some of the devices of drama in *Adventures of Huckleberry Finn* to underscore the moral cowardice evident in both crowd reactions to violent public spectacles such as lynchings and audience reactions to staged entertainments such as plays and circuses.

In his depiction of Bricksville, Arkansas, Twain silhouetted the characteristics of crowd mentality evident in both public spectacle and mass

From *American Literary Realism, 1870–1910* 37, no. 1 (Fall 2004): 50–58. © 2004 by the University of Illinois Press.

entertainment. The events that Huck describes in the Bricksville episode (chapters XXI–XXIII) occur in the space of a mere sixteen pages and could easily be overlooked as a minor episode in Huck's adventures along the river. However, a closer reading reveals an intricate structural design. Twain uses the dramatic form of a three-act play as a structural code in the Bricksville episode to develop his views about mass mentality. The three chapters may be divided into three main "acts" that comprise a larger play that serves to stage Twain's attack on crowd mentality. There are no sharp divisions between chapters XXI–XXIII in relation to the three acts. That is, none of the acts is contained within a single chapter alone. For example, the acts that I will label "Boggs-Sherburn," "The Circus," and "The Revival" flow between the three chapters as a means of accentuating the blurred lines between spectacle and entertainment. Simply put, the Bricksville episode is a play within the larger narrative structure of the novel. To heighten the effect, Twain structures the episodes in such a way that the reader not only encounters the play as a whole, but also sees that each of the acts contains scenes that mirror the larger one.

Twain effectively blurs the lines between distinct types of events to show the reader that those generally considered specific to discrete types of venues, such as lynchings or plays, do in fact overlap when public viewing habits are taken into consideration. In the case of the Bricksville crowd, the audience who witnesses the cold-blooded murder of Boggs moves effortlessly between the roles of viewer and participant, as well as from one type of viewing event to the next. For example, they chidingly watch Boggs accost Sherburn, but when Sherburn reacts to Boggs by shooting him, they turn from disengaged spectators to justice-seeking lynchers before reverting back to passive viewers at the circus. This crossing of spectator boundaries is solidified by Twain through the repeated use of plot elements that occur in the same order in all three acts of the larger play. These elements include initial crowd responses, staged/performed actions, crowd reactions, speeches by prominent Bricksvillians, and finally crowd withdrawals, all serving to accentuate the blurring between different types of events.

A common device employed in many different art forms is repetition. Twain makes repetition an integral part of the structure of *Huck Finn*, particularly in the Bricksville episode. According to Victor A. Doyno, Twain's real interest was in "writing memorable episodes and frequently in doubling the incidents or repeating the basic situation in varied forms."[3] In an autobiographical entry dated 31 August 1906, Twain wrote of repetition, "If frequently used, nearly any precisely worded and unchanging formula will *eventually* compel laughter if it be gravely *and earnestly* repeated, at intervals, five or six times."[4]

Along with the structural device of repetition in *Huck Finn*, Twain also uses shifts in point of view to create an interesting dichotomy running throughout the Bricksville episode. These shifts occur when Huck reacts to what he reports as an outside narrator and when he reacts as an actual member of the crowd—in other words, Huck as detached observer versus Huck as invested participant. Huck the observer acts as the readers' eyes by providing stage directions, scene settings, and descriptions of the people's behavior that he witnesses. Huck the participant provides readers with the more internalized immediacy of the emotions that he feels, not as a detached recounter of events, but as a boy in the midst of intense and exciting happenings. It is also interesting to note that the role of the reader of the Bricksville episode is constantly in flux due to Huck's shifts in point of view. At one point the reader will be watching Huck the observer in the guise of a journalist watching a crowd watching an event (such as in the Boggs-Sherburn episode when Huck relates his gaze upon the loafers who are themselves watching dogs torture a sow), versus Huck the participant placing the reader in the position of outside audience watching an audience which includes Huck within it, watching an event.

Before Huck and company arrive at Bricksville, we see the king and duke rehearsing scenes from *Romeo and Juliet*, *Richard III*, and *Hamlet* as they float downriver. It is during these rehearsals that we first encounter Huck as gazer: "the way they laid on, and pranced around the raft was grand to see."[5] Huck tells the reader that the duke's rendition of Hamlet's soliloquy has "knocked the spots out of any acting ever I *see* before" (204). Once they arrive at Bricksville, Huck shows the reader a copy of the first of two play-bills that the duke has printed for their productions. It begins with the aptly phrased "Shaksperean Revival!!! Wonderful Attraction!" "Revival" harkens back to the king's portrayal of a reformed pirate at the religious revival in Chapter XX. The fevered pitch of the camp meeting is repeated shortly in the form of the lynch mob and the circusgoers. Both groups are stimulated like a pack of wild animals, until, as in the case of the revival-goers, "you couldn't make out what the preacher said, any more, on account of the shouting and crying" (197). Twain's repetition of similar scenes, with participants/viewers losing themselves in mass rapture, serves not only as an indictment of mass behavior, but also points out the similarities between public spectacles, mass entertainment, and religious practices.

Act I of the Bricksville episode, as seen through the eyes of Huck, takes place in the town's set-like streets, which are littered with unproductive gardens, haphazard fences, loafers, and muddy streets (which foreshadows the eventual fate of the king and duke with "mud as black as tar"). It is the introduction of the loafers that gives readers their first look at the crowd mentality which Twain condemns through the use of satire and the repetition of themes. In a scene that aptly foreshadows the entire section, Huck notes that

> The hogs loafed and grunted around, everywheres ... and pretty soon you'd hear a loafer sing out 'Hi! so boy! sick him, Tige!' and away the sow would go, squealing most horrible, with a dog or two swinging to each ear, and three or four dozen more a-coming, and then you would see all the loafers get up and watch the thing out of sight, and laugh at the fun and look grateful for the noise. (109)

The townsfolk are not only akin to the lazy hogs; they also double, as we shall see, as the pack dogs. Huck's description of the loafers serves two purposes: first, literally setting the stage, and second, showing readers the kind of men they will encounter throughout this section. The townsfolks' desire for relieving the mundane nature of their daily lives through spectacle-like entertainment enables the king and the duke to move effortlessly in their midst.

Like the loafers, the people mill around the streets in anticipation of the circus and take part in such degrading activities as drinking to excess and fighting before they are unwittingly, but more than willingly, treated to the spectacle of the drunken Boggs. This scene—part of Act I—begins as simple entertainment but builds to a tragic denouement, and like the hogs and dogs Boggs is baited by the onlookers merely for a good laugh. Twain introduces in each act the recurring scenario of laughter/anger/withdrawal in which the crowd participates. Boggs (the name perhaps a play on "saturation" and/or "mired") rides into town on his "monthly drunk" with the intention of picking a fight with Colonel Sherburn, who has apparently wronged him. Boggs is on the "waw path," inciting the crowd to laugh and catcall in response to his red-faced antics. Sherburn enters and, as Huck tells us, he is "the best dressed man in that town." Throughout the Bricksville episode it is the well-dressed men who know how to control their audiences, even if they themselves are members of it. The scene progresses with much "Injun"-like excitement; Boggs is shot in cold blood; and the town reacts. The reaction is not immediate, however. First, everyone must get a look at the dying Boggs (based on an actual shooting Twain witnessed as a child in Hannibal), followed by a play-like retelling of the events that they have just witnessed. The crowd needs the retelling of the murder to act as yet another diversion from the mundane, but more importantly, as a means of displacing the horrific events they have just witnessed. The murder requires a sequel to mute its moral and social implications.

Before the murder, Huck sees the loafers torturing dogs to death for entertainment, thus setting the stage for the mob mentality of the townsfolk as they go after Sherburn. As soon as the reenactments of the death have run their course, Buck Harkness, a member of the crowd, sends out the lynch call. The crowd, having turned from audience to actors themselves, "swarmed up the street," taking on the characteristics of the dogs chasing the sow, "a-whooping and yelling and raging like Injuns, and everything had to clear the way or get run over and trompled to mush...." "It was awful to see," Huck tells us, even though he himself is temporarily caught up in the frenzy (215). The mob, as Twain shows us, is a privileged organization with admittance requiring white flesh and a phallus. Huck, floating between boyhood and manhood, is able to accompany the mob unnoticed, but throughout the ordeal he retains his own more privileged position as an observer.

Describing the mob's route, Huck says, "Children was heeling it ahead of the mob, screaming and trying to get out of the way; and every window along the road was full of women's heads, and there was nigger boys in every tree, and bucks and wenches looking over every fence." The readers too are cast outside of the privileged mob and are, like the on-looking bucks and wenches, the unprivileged others in the eyes of the justice-seeking mass. The lynch mob's adoption of a self-proclaimed policing role stems from the people's need for the guise of respectable entertainment that we see repeated throughout the episode. For example, the mob needs to seek retribution on Sherburn for killing Boggs; they castigate the outlandish circus drunk; and they attempt to rid the stage of the king and duke by pelting them with rotten produce once the entire town has been taken in by the "Revival."

The crowd, thinking they are cleansed of any implication of complicity (their inaction during the shooting) by witnessing a replay of the Boggs murder, are now free to avenge Boggs' death, but as we shall see, it is Sherburn who avenges the crowd's weakness in the name of individual fortitude. Once they reach their destination, Sherburn, as actor/preacher, steps out onto his stage-like roof and presents a condemnatory dramatic monologue vehemently aimed at the mass of people who have come to kill him. Sherburn's speech has been read by scholars as a masked soliloquy-like rant by Twain in which he rails against the crowd's self-deception, cowardice, and stupidity. All Sherburn has to do to show his superiority over the crowd is stand silently, holding them dumbfounded by his gaze, controlling their every move through his mere presence. The crowd stands helpless, silently admitting their guilt, as they did before the lynch call, waiting to be ushered from one spectacle to the next. Before being ushered along, though,

Sherburn castigates them for their inability to act as individuals. "The idea of you lynching anybody! It's amusing," Sherburn says. "The idea of you thinking you had the pluck enough to lynch a *man*! ... Why, a *man's* safe in the hands of ten thousand of your kind—as long as it's daytime and you're not behind him" (216). As individuals they are cowards, and even as a mob they are unable to carry out their supposed moral convictions. In reality, their convictions play second fiddle to their fear of being castigated by their neighbors. Sherburn's moral stance is steeped in the dialogue of the western ideal of self-reliance and individualism that Twain so admired, a trait that Sherburn's fellow Bricksvillians fail to exhibit. Sherburn sends the crowd on its way deflated but perhaps grateful to learn that their cowardice is normal, thus exonerating them of any individual moral flaws.

In one of the fragments that Twain deleted from *What is Man?* the "Young Man" declares that "Moral courage is that great quality which enables a person to stand up for the right, at cost of popularity, caste, esteem,—sometimes at cost to fortune, liberty, or life."[6] The "Old Man" responds that people's moral stands are often selective, depending not only on what they favor but on public sentiment as well. Despite this argument, Twain at heart apparently believed that men like Sherburn, while a literary character, did exist. The young man's statement that "not more than one person in half a million" possesses moral courage recalls the point Twain would make in "The United States of Lyncherdom" that nine-tenths of men exhibit moral cowardice, leaving room, however slight, for a man of exemplary courage like Sherburn.

In Act II, "The Circus," the scene immediately shifts from the failed lynching to public entertainment without a chapter change in the text. Just as the scene shifts, so too does the crowd move from one spectacle to the next, from would-be murderers to gleeful spectators. Once again Huck sets the stage, which is in marked contrast to the muddy streets and townspeople whom he first encountered as they arrived in town earlier that afternoon. Although Huck uses words like "lovely," "gentle," "wavy," and "graceful" to describe the circus—in contrast to "lazy," "drawly," "gaping," and "yawning" to describe the loafers from the previous episode—the reader soon sees just how much the entertainment of the circus mirrors the spectacle of the murder and attempted lynching. Through his command of language, in both instances Huck relates the mood of the scenes by presenting them through different types of reportage. In Act I, he observes Bricksville through the eyes of a detached observer who is nearly disgusted by the rundown condition of the town and its lazy inhabitants. In Act II, he is enamored with the whirling motion and excitement of the circus performers. In other words, his language is flat and matter-of-fact in the first instance, fluid and colorful in the second.

For example, in the first act, Huck refers to the loafers who "had on yellow straw hats most as wide as an umbrella," whereas in the second he watches "every lady's rose-leafy dress flapping soft and silky around her hips, and she looking like the most loveliest parasol" (207, 219).

Act II is filled with references to the Boggs-Sherburn episode which precedes it. There is a clown who "carried on so it most killed the people," followed by the introduction of a seemingly drunken Boggs-like braggart in the audience who claims that he can ride a horse "as well as anybody that ever was" (220). At this point we get a near replay of the earlier Boggs-Sherburn scene with the crowd (not quite the audience yet) egging on the drunken audience member. They begin by laughing at him but his saucy remarks in return "stirred up the people, and a lot of men begun to pile down off the benches and swarm toward the ring, saying "Knock him down! throw him out!" The ringmaster gets the attention of the crowd by saying that he hopes there will be no disturbance—just as Sherburn warns Boggs—and offers to allow the drunk to show his riding skills if the crowd agrees. "So everybody laughed and said all right," Huck reports. The crowd's laughter can be seen as another incidence of self-cleansing, just as the re-witnessing of the murder scene served to distance the viewers from any implication due to their own inaction. Also reminiscent of the earlier episode is the fact that both incidents contain two men attempting to rein in the drunkards before they come to harm through their unseemly actions. The braggart, "with two circus men hanging onto his bridle," mounts the horse and a whirlwind of action proceeds as Huck once again comments: "the people [were] just crazy. It warn't funny to me, though; I was all of a tremble to see his danger." So again, even though Huck is a part of the crowd and sees what the crowd sees, he still maintains his individuality as the crowd works through the laughing/anger/withdrawal scenario. Though distinct from the mass, he is still taken in by the scene, as he fails to realize that he has just witnessed a staged production in the greater play of the circus. Again, too, there is a scene within an act within the larger play.

"Well, that night we had our show," Huck tells the reader in Act III, "The Revival"; but since the original program of the "Shaksperean Revival" failed to provide high-culture through the production of *Romeo and Juliet*, *Richard III*, or *Hamlet*, the king and duke are forced to resort to low entertainment and creative marketing to further bilk the citizens of Bricksville.[7] Before act three proper begins, however, Huck shows the reader another playbill. This time, the reader sees firsthand LADIES AND CHILDREN NOT ADMITTED. "If that line don't fetch them," the duke says, "I don't know Arkansaw!" (222). At this point Twain inserts the heading "Chapter XXIII." Again Twain lets the action shift from one event to the next without regard for chapter changes and so shows how the crowd makes the transition from spectacle to entertainment with little or no distinction.

Act III proper begins with Huck once again setting the stage for the reader by describing the scene, which is now an actual stage set. From an audience of twelve at the previous night's show to a "house ... jam full of men in no time," the production begins with "a little speech" by the duke, and again, we see the laughter/anger/withdrawal scenario. The king comes on stage and prances around "on all fours, naked; and he was painted all over, ring-streaked-and-striped, all sorts of colors, as splendid as a rainbow." The crowd "most killed themselves laughing.... [T]hey roared and clapped and stormed and haw-hawed till [the 'camelopard'] come back and done it over again" (223).[8]

The curtain falls and the townsfolk, changing from audience (viewing the spectacle) to crowd (being viewed by the reader through Huck), react angrily, calling for retribution against the frauds. "But a big fine-looking man jumps up on a bench" to retard the action (224). Like Sherburn and the ringmaster, he gives a speech and calms the crowd. The "sold" townsmen respond to the show not by following their initial desire to harm the troupe but by scheming to draw their neighbors into their embarrassment so they alone will not look like fools. "We don't want to be the laughing-stock of the whole town, I reckon, and never hear the last of this thing as long as we live," the man says. "What we want, is to go out of here quiet, and talk this show up, and sell the rest of the town!" (224). One cannot help but wonder if this crowd-controller is not the same Buck Harkness who sent out the lynch-call in Act I.

The king and duke brilliantly anticipate the reaction of the crowd, knowing that they can continue to play it until the town as a whole has been taken in. As a whole, no one individual would have to suffer humiliation. The production is repeated a second night, but during the third and final performance the house is packed with citizen "actors" trying, as Sherburn described earlier, to exert the "courage that's borrowed from their mass" (217). The crowd, made up of audience members from the previous two nights, enter the theatre with "pockets bulging" with "sickly eggs by the barrel, and rotten cabbages, and such things" (225). Sherburn's earlier recollection that he saw a single man stop "a *stage* full of men" and rob them is ironic here considering that the king and duke make a clean getaway with over four hundred dollars before the mob even recognizes that they have once again been "sold." In this act, as in the previous two, we again see Huck as both participant and observer. He describes the scene in detail, this time as both witness to the actions and accomplice (although unwillingly, but somewhat amusedly), but in the end he too is taken in when he finds that the king has been absent from the courthouse all along.

Like many of the modernists that followed him, Twain skillfully combined different genre to comment on the traits, not only of small-town America, but of mass mentality in general. The Bricksville episode can be read as a single play broken into distinct scenes to illustrate how blurred the lines between entertainment and actual tragedy may be.

NOTES

The author would like to thank Sherry Ceniza, Bryce Conrad, and John Samson for their input and encouragement.

1. Henry W. Fisher, ed., *Abroad With Mark Twain and Eugene Field* (New York: Nicholas L. Brown, 1922), p. 59.

2. Frederick Anderson, ed., *A Pen Warmed Up in Hell: Mark Twain in Protest* (New York: Harper & Row, 1972), p. 155.

3. Victor A. Doyno, *Writing Huck Finn: Mark Twain's Creative Process* (Philadelphia: Univ. of Pennsylvania Press, 1991), p. 102.

4. Quoted in Doyno, p. 240.

5. Mark Twain, *Adventures of Huckleberry Finn* (Berkeley: Univ. of California Press, 1985), p. 202. Subsequent references to this edition will be cited parenthetically.

6. Mark Twain, *What is Man? and Other Philosophical Writings*, ed. Paul Baender (Berkeley: Univ. of California Press, 1973), p. 495.

7. John D. Reardon, "'Shakespearean Revival!!!': Satire of American Elizabethans," *Mark Twain Journal*, 21 (Fall 1983), 36–38.

8. The play, which is billed as the "The King's Camelopard," is probably drawn, according to Walter Blair, from Poe's story in *Tales of the Grotesque and Arabesque*, "Four Beasts in One; or The Homocameleopard," as well as from the "Gyascutus hoax," in which two broke peddlers fooled a paying crowd into thinking that they were viewing an exotic beast, when in reality they were just looking at the decorated feet and hands of a man. See Walter Blair, *Mark Twain and Huck Finn* (Berkeley: Univ. of California Press, 1960), pp. 318–19.

STEPHANIE LE MENAGER

Floating Capital:
The Trouble with Whiteness
on Twain's Mississippi

In the antebellum slave market that was rigorously conducted on and along the Mississippi River, Mark Twain recognized a fundamental plot that he found still visible in his own post-frontier United States, where the promise of a free, unbounded space of nationalist imagining had finally dried up. The fundamental national plot Twain noted in the antebellum Mississippi's volatile market culture involved selling something that does not belong to you, the misappropriation of others' labor and sentience. Since the late eighteenth century, the river had been a primary conductor of commercial traffic, carrying, among more innocent commodities, slaves and slave-grown cotton. Imagining the great river highway, Twain identified our American pleasure with a commercial imperialism which perpetuated the piracy and slaving that had characterized the era of mercantile capitalism; in his Mississippi River fictions, he reproduces in miniature the volatile commercial space of the early modern oceans. For Twain, the North American West had not been about the political disinterest, domestic economy, and republican virtue long associated with agricultural settlement, from eighteenth-century European agrarian philosophy through Thomas Jefferson. The Mississippi River was the West that Twain returned to, again and again, because it was water and not land that could ever be settled. The river was a carrier of economic desire and troubled commodities that flowed beyond continental spaces, suturing the

From *ELH* 71 (2004): 405–431. © 2004 by The Johns Hopkins University Press.

U.S. to global networks of capital. Reading the *Adventures of Huckleberry Finn* (1885) against the unfinished novella *Tom Sawyer's Conspiracy* (1897–1899) transforms Twain's classic river novel into a profound, postnational critique of white mobility on the western frontier. As Twain rewrites *Adventures of Huckleberry Finn* through *Tom Sawyer's Conspiracy*, he reconnects the racial and spatial praxes of U.S. expansion, or manifest destiny, to an always international slave market that enabled the emergence of the United States' normative—white, middle-class—national character.

Mark Twain's West was never a Turnerian frontier, a "line of most rapid and effective Americanization" that healed sectional and racial conflict. Cultural historian Richard Slotkin has aptly described Mark Twain as a "post-frontier" thinker, although his use of this epithet is primarily limited to a chronological meaning. Slotkin suggests that Twain writes about the Frontier Myth when it is no longer possible to imagine "'real life' ... constituted (if it ever was) to provide farms, ranches, and gold mines to the first comers for no cost."[1] By Frederick Jackson Turner's definition, the frontier is essentially over once there is no longer a habitable region in the United States, or the territories it claimed, occupied by fewer than two people per square mile. I'd like to prescribe another use for the term "post-Frontier," which is similar to the pragmatic use of the term "postmodern." Rather than imagining particular moments in time when the idea of the frontier is superseded, I recognize "post-frontier" as the marker of a literary style and a political orientation that exists alongside frontier literatures and ideology as an ongoing critique of their limitations. Specifically, I recognize Twain as participating in the school of post-frontier U.S. history that Patricia Limerick has rather wryly named "expansion of the world market studies," a school that draws on the work of world systems theorists like Immanuel Wallerstein and Fernand Braudel.[2] Twain recognized the importance of a national and international market culture to the North American West long before the world had heard of global studies or the New Western Historians' radical recontextualizations of the United States's expansion as a continental nation. Amy Kaplan has offered a suggestive analysis of Twain's *Letters from Hawaii*, originally published in 1866 in the *Sacramento Union*, to argue that "the routes of transnational travel" first enabled Twain's exploration of U.S. race relations.[3] While the still so-called foreign territory of Hawaii may have contributed to the opening of the young Twain's racial memory, I think it crucial to emphasize that Twain made visible the intersections of U.S. race prejudice and international capital in fluid sites *within* the apparently domestic territory of the United States. Given the essentially international economies of many western places in the nineteenth century, it is not surprising that Twain's western writings link the regional economies of Nevada, California, and the Mississippi Valley to international circuits of capital and to cosmopolitan commodity forms that resisted the definition of capital, like those African Americans categorized as "chattel" or the Chinese "coolie" labor that played a crucial role in western construction industries.[4]

Twain's acknowledgment in *Life on the Mississippi* (1883) that the Mississippi River gave him a lifetime of literary material suggests how much the national popular culture that he generated in the late-nineteenth century owes to what we might call a water-based theory of culture, where U.S. nationalism is recognized as an effect of mobility and exchange, the basic terms of a commercial discourse dating back to the sixteenth century. Twain popularized a way of thinking about the United States's national culture and, more specifically, a way of thinking about westward expansion that both predates him, in early modern theories of mercantile empire that posit oceans as the primary sites of nation-building, and allows him to appear in sync with the New Western History and with contemporary theories of global empire as a fluid, "decentered and deterritorializing apparatus of rule," in the current terms of Michael Hardt and Antonio Negri.[5] My purpose here is not to dehistoricize Twain by forcing his work into contemporary paradigms. However, I do think that current understandings of "sovereignty" and "empire" as expressed through international or even transnational networks of capital and power can reopen the deeply resonant locale, the Mississippi Valley, which has lent an enduring popularity to Twain's work. Twain most successfully reimagined manifest destiny and U.S. national emergence in terms of the socioeconomic possibilities of a river that could not be contained as purely national space.

As Henry Nash Smith noted many years ago, in his classic *Virgin Land*, Southerners who had grown up imagining national expansion in terms of their region's extensive river systems were more likely to view the United States and the North American West as fatally linked to the international spaces that rivers emptied into—spaces like the Gulf of Mexico or the Pacific Ocean.[6] Twain's fellow Missourian, the Senator Thomas Hart Benton, argued up through the 1850s that the Pacific and those western rivers that touched it would enable a "coastal" western republic tending toward Asia but likely to separate from the United States because of the vast arid region that fell between the Mississippi River and the Rocky Mountains.[7] Even the dream of a transcontinental railroad could not easily shake Benton's faith in the greater—certainly the more international—possibilities of empire articulated through water. I think it important to delineate the origins of Twain's late-century cultural critiques in earlier southern economic and spatial praxes with which he was familiar. Twain's much discussed rants against imperialism, particularly the conquest of indigenous populations in the Philippines and the Congo, complement a more ambivalent interest in another form of empire that was commercial and not driven by colonialist or European-style bids for territorial domination. Twain's anti-imperialist rage interacts quite curiously with his lifelong obsession with U.S. business culture to produce a conflicted, insider's critique of market capitalism as it was expressed in the slave trade on the Mississippi River and in the market for precious metals in the Far West. The peculiarly double, regional and global, character of the Mississippi allowed Twain to envision continuity among early modern elaborations of commercial empire, like the international slave trade, U.S. expansion into the continental West, and later nineteenth-century imperial ventures outside the borders of the United States. As a writer whose favored setting, the Mississippi Valley, was characterized throughout the nineteenth century as both western and southwestern, Twain also teaches us the importance of recognizing that the West and the South once could be seen as a "single physiographic region" (an argument traceable to John C. Calhoun, among others) which was naturally articulated to international interests.[8] Twain's own career as a Mississippi riverboat pilot began in what might be characterized as a uniquely Southern and/or international imperial fantasy; his first trip down the Mississippi was meant to be the first leg in a journey to South America, where he hoped to prosper in the coca trade. Twain's cultural history is never one in which international contexts, or the international circulation of troubling commodities like slaves, figure as merely incidental to the United States's emergence as a settler nation, as they do in the influential late-century essays of Turner.

For Twain, the Mississippi River is simultaneously the landscape of an antebellum commercial culture whose vibrancy was underwritten by a barbaric slave traffic and the landscape of a late-century commercial culture deemed decadent by prominent cultural critics like Brooks Adams and Theodore Roosevelt. In the *Law of Civilization and Decay* (1896), Adams flatly stated that "commerce from the outset seemed antagonistic to the imagination" and predicted that cultures which had reached the commercial stage would remain "inert until supplied with fresh energetic material by the infusion of barbarian blood."[9] As is well known, Adams idealized the soldier and prescribed the renewal of military rather than commercial conquests. Troubled by Turner's prediction of the end of the frontier as a stimulant for national consolidation, Adams sought Indian wars abroad. Roosevelt found the *Law of Civilization and Decay* unsubtle, yet he essentially crafted his political persona in accordance with Adams's imperialist, militaristic ideal.[10] Twain's classic writings of the 1870s through 1890s predict and defy this kind of late-century embrace of conquest abroad, highlighting the emptiness of military honor and the potentially annihilating consequences of territorial war against the creativity of essentially commercial, speculator-trickster figures who reopen their small lives to alterity and possibility, figures like Tom Sawyer or Beriah Sellers in *The Gilded Age*. Yet by the end of his life, Twain could satirize the Adams-Roosevelt ideal without fully believing that he had championed superior ideas. Ostensibly a Republican, Twain conceived of Roosevelt as the worst president the United States had ever had. When he dictated his rambling biography to Albert Bigelow Paine in the first decade of the twentieth century, he slandered the president rather perversely, likening him to Tom Sawyer.[11] Finally, the productive and eminently commercial imagination of Tom Sawyer had gotten mixed up in San Juan Hill, the United States's imperial reach toward Asia, and what Twain deemed Roosevelt's deceitful pretense of limiting corporate greed.

In truth, those productive speculators whom Philip J. Fisher identifies as Twain's "world-makers," characters like Tom Sawyer, always had been tied to a systemic imperialism larger than San Juan Hill.[12] Their fellow travelers were the Duke and Dauphin and Tom Driscoll of *Pudd'nhead Wilson*, men who were not merely imaginative frauds but actual slave traders. Myra Jehlen has written that "it is impossible in the Mississippi River towns through which Huck and Jim journey to imagine being a hero," and that Jim's freedom is necessarily contradictory to Huck's because it includes communitarian commitment and "something very like a revolution." Freedom for Huck, in turn, is simply freedom from commitment, what Jehlen calls "pathlessness" and what she intends as a naive, liberal self-interest.[13] While the gentle Huck is not by design a slave trader, his embrace of a liberal *freedom from* puts him in the company of slave traders who cruelly, although not unexpectedly, sell his best friend. The amoral justice of the market is the nature of the river that fits Huck like a second skin. Reading the *Adventures of Huckleberry Finn* through Twain's later writings, including his retelling of *Huckleberry Finn* in the fragmentary *Tom Sawyer's Conspiracy*, denatures the white mobility that Twain also lived and often praised. When put into dialogue with each other, both narratives betray Huck's apparently heroic western travel as an iteration of the same international networks of capital and power that sponsored the slave trade.

By the time Twain began work on the river novella *Tom Sawyer's Conspiracy* in 1897, he wholly identified the United States's commercial culture with what Forrest G. Robinson has called a culture of "bad faith" where normative behavior involves exploiting others and, even more perversely, swindling yourself into believing that such exploitation is normal.[14] Twain originally imagined the plot of *Tom Sawyer's Conspiracy* to pivot around Tom's selling of a cork-blackened Huck into slavery and then stealing him out again for fun. This potential plot, which was ultimately abandoned, suggests the extent to which *Tom Sawyer's Conspiracy* begins a revisionist, even explosive, interpretation of *Adventures of Huckleberry Finn*, where it could be said that Huck had played Tom's "nigger."[15] Certainly not one of the other sequels Twain wrote to his successful boys' novels attempts the kind of metacriticsm that *Tom Sawyer's Conspiracy* achieves. Perhaps the plot of Tom selling a minstrelized Huck finally offered too cutting a critique of the earlier novel. In the version of *Tom Sawyer's Conspiracy* which Twain left unfinished in 1899, Tom does not sell Huck for scandal and laughs. Instead, Tom himself plays the parts of slave, slave trader, and slave thief. In brief, Tom "blacks up" to impersonate a slave so that he can sell himself to a local trader, Bat Bradish, and then scare the villagers of St. Petersburg by having himself fictitiously run off by "ablitionists." This ruse does provoke terror in the village when Jake Flacker, detective, identifies the faux abolitionists (Tom and Huck) as "members of Burrell's gang," an allusion to the legendary slave-stealing ring of John Murrell.[16] As Tom and Huck are repeatedly and mistakenly cast as "niggers," abolitionists, and slave thieves, Twain plays with the question of which misidentification proves most true. Of course, this question has troubled many readers of the *Adventures of Huckleberry Finn*.

I. DENATURING WHITE MOBILITY

Huck's venture down the Mississippi River is a kind of speculation as well as an act of emigration by which Huck hopes to elude his abusive father and gain ownership of himself. The trip is a calculated risk that places Huck, historically, in the company of the many poor but climbing whites who emigrated to the Mississippi Valley from the 1820s through the 1840s. In a small way, Huck tests the concept of manifest destiny, the promise that providence will look after those who keep moving farther from where they started, toward yet to be consolidated territory whose apparent openness allowed antebellum boosters like John L. O'Sullivan to speak of the nation's infinite expandability.[17] As Turner would assert in his nostalgic revisitation of manifest destiny in the 1890s, "America has been another name for opportunity.... Movement has been its dominant fact."[18] But in Twain's river fictions the Mississippi River and the culture of the river make plain that nature does not necessarily complement the emigration of white Americans into western lands that do not belong to them, that the generalized and (for Euro-Americans) happy concept of white mobility must be understood in relation to historical contingencies that denature it. The success of the class of person Huck represents, the poor-to-middling whites who came to farm along the Mississippi or work in its thriving carrying trade, was subject to many changeable factors, perhaps most crucially the physics of the river itself.

The "June rise" which initiates Huck and Jim's downriver journey represents a belated spring thaw that would have opened the season of navigation on the Mississippi River. Steamboat carriers depended upon a succession of rises, issuing from various tributaries, to provide the six-foot stage necessary for transporting full cargoes.[19] Just on the other side of the seasonal rises that facilitated trade and allowed western farmers access to markets, the flood signaled financial collapse. Historian John W. Monette notes that there were twelve significant Mississippi floods from 1820 to 1840.[20] Floods washed away the wood yards necessary for fuelling steamboats, buried boat landings deep in mud, and destroyed crops and homes. In *Life on the Mississippi*, Twain represents the Mississippi flood as a moment of transition in which socioeconomic status might shift radically, down or up. Some canny speculators managed to convert unpredictable river levels into capital. "When the river is rising fast, some scoundrel whose plantation is back in the country, and therefore of inferior value, has only to watch his chance, cut a little gutter across the narrow neck of land some dark night, and turn the water into it, and in a wonderfully short time ... the whole Mississippi has taken possession of that little ditch, and placed the countryman's plantation on its bank, quadrupling its value."[21]

As a carrier of the booms and busts of the nation's market economy, the Mississippi was described by Andrew Jackson as a domestic alimentary canal that found its mouth through New Orleans. It was conceived as the center of the American West and, it was hoped, proof that the American West would someday be central to the world. "Every Man of the western Country turns his eyes intuitively upon the mouth of the Mississippi," Jackson noted, "Blocked up, all the fruits of his industry rot upon his hand—open and he carries on a trade with all the nations of the earth."[22] Twain, writing to his friend Ann E. Taylor in 1857 from New Orleans, recognized that city's centrality through the cosmopolitan crowd that gathered at its overstocked markets. Of New Orleans's French market, Samuel Clemens wrote: "I thought I had seen all kinds of markets before—but that was a great mistake—this being a place such as I had never dreamed of before.... Out on the pavement were groups of Italians, French, Dutch, Irish, Spaniards, Indians, Chinese, Americans, English, and the lord knows how many more different kinds of people."[23] While working temporarily as the St. Louis correspondent to the *Muscatine Journal* in 1855, Twain delivered similar encomia on St. Louis's "brisk" levees and cultural connections to far-flung ports. "A panorama of Australia, China, and the Japanese Expedition, is now on exhibition at Wyman's Hall," he reports, "which far exceeds anything of the kind in beauty, interest, excellence, and truthfulness to nature.... One portion of this painting in particular, (and it was all good)—a sun-set scene in China—was enchantingly beautiful: even more so than Muscatine sunsets in summer."[24] The mere comparison of the sunsets of Muscatine, Iowa, to the sunsets of anywhere, China, performs a startling imaginary geographical linkage between a relatively small western river port and the Pacific Rim. Even ex-slaves took pride in the thriving commerce of the river and the stimulating worlds that gathered in its primary ports. In his memoir, the St. Louis barber and former slave James Thomas recalled with pride the New Orleans port of the 1830s and 1840s as a rival to New York, handling the transport of "horses, cattle, hogs, mules, corn flower" and, in what appears almost as an afterthought, "occasionally a crowd of blacks."[25] The slave market in New Orleans was the biggest in the country by the 1840s, moving slaves from the Atlantic seaboard and upper south into the cotton frontiers of Mississippi, Arkansas, and Texas. Meanwhile, Caribbean islands like Cuba had become depots for international slave ships whose West African cargo might be smuggled into the U.S. through scarcely nationalized western territories like Texas.

The nationalist pride normally inspired by the sight of traffic on the West's greatest market road was problematized by the sight of slave cargoes being moved against their inclination toward the same southwest that even Henry David Thoreau would indicate held a magnetic attraction for Euro-American bodies.[26] Whatever one's politics, the transformation of humans into freight imaged the opposite of providential destiny; it was anti-emigration. In the chapter of *Uncle Tom's Cabin* titled "La Belle Rivière," Harriet Beecher Stowe depicts genteel women travelers attempting to reconcile themselves to the presence of a slave trader, Haley, and his human cargo aboard their Mississippi steamboat. "All [aboard] was full of life," Stowe remarks, "—all but Haley's gang, who were stored, with other freight, on the lower deck." One of the ladies dismisses the slaves as a "shameful sight" to be seen on the otherwise heroic river.[27] In a famous letter to his friend Mary Speed, the young Abraham Lincoln observed twelve chained slaves traveling downriver aboard a Mississippi boat. Considerably agitated by the sight, Lincoln sought comfort for himself in the apparent cheerfulness of the slaves amidst "these distressing circumstances.... One whose offense for which he had been sold was an overfondness for his wife, played the fiddle continuously."[28] By allowing the substitution of the slave's music for his inevitable if undetectable grief, Lincoln aestheticizes this scene, transmuting it into a valediction.[29]

The presence of slaves in river traffic imaged the social death characteristic of all speculative risk, and in *Adventures of Huckleberry Finn* this slave presence disrupts the confirmation of national ambition normally offered by river travel. When Huck says, "No'm. Killed a nigger" (*H*, 279), in answer to Aunt Sally Phelps's question of whether or not any person was hurt when a steamboat that he claims carried him to Arkansas blew a cylinder head, he voices the novel's only specific reference to the slave cargo and slave boatmen who were visible on boats like the ones remarked by Lincoln, Thomas, and Stowe. As John Seelye has noted, Huck's river is unrealistically empty.[30] Perhaps this is because explicit reference to the "shameful sight[s] to be seen" on the river (in Stowe's phrase) would have utterly destroyed the illusion of pastoral idyll that makes *Adventures of Huckleberry Finn* such a frustratingly divided book. Other human sacrifices to the greater economy of the Mississippi Valley who would have been visible in river traffic in the era of Huck's travels include Creek (Muscogee) Indians, who were being transported across the river in order to open prime Alabama cotton land to white settlers.[31] European immigrants traveling aboard the riverboats made another species of live freight, confined in the often disease-ridden deck quarters, which were also home to livestock, slaves, bales of hay, and baggage. Cholera, yellow fever, and other deadly diseases fomented in these filthy deck quarters, and sick travelers were sometimes forced to disembark on unpopulated river islands by steamboat captains who hoped to prevent the spread of disease in riverside towns.[32]

If Twain fails to mention outright the less pleasing species of traffic that must have been observable to him from the time of his childhood through his young adulthood as a steamboat pilot on the Mississippi, he nevertheless alludes to the domestic slave trade and its presence on the river in *Adventures of Huckleberry Finn*, albeit in a deeply ironic fashion. After all, Jim travels downriver to be sold in Arkansas, the cotton frontier, despite Huck's belated efforts and good intentions. As many critics have noted, Twain's portrayal of Jim's sale well after the Civil War had cancelled the commodity value of African Americans should have provoked only small anxieties; circa 1885, when *Adventures of Huckleberry Finn* was published, readers knew that Jim would be free eventually.[33] Yet the dramatic irony built into the novel by its historical distance from the slave problem does not free the narrative from a broader nervousness about race. There are many ways of talking about racial discomfort in the novel, including the representational problem of minstrelsy, which Eric Lott has addressed most powerfully and which I will touch upon in a quite different way. Lott recognizes Huck's great compliment to Jim that Jim is "white inside" (*H*, 341), a compliment inspired by Jim's refusal to escape when Tom has been shot during the boys' raid on the Phelps's home, as "the crowning statement on the centrality of blackface's contradictions to Twain's imagination." Blackface imagery in Twain's work allows the exercise of the imperialist psychological orientation Homi Bhabha calls "ambivalence," where the mind of the colonizer is haunted by the difference of the colonized even when most readily aware of their humanity. The black who is "white inside" reassures the colonizer that "they must be versions of 'us,' caught in a cycle of mimicry ... and yet perennially unable to make the grade."[34]

Twain reasserts the internal whiteness of Jim in the late novella *Tom Sawyer's Conspiracy*, where Huck goes so far as to say that Jim is "the whitest man inside that ever walked" (*T*, 214). At the same time, the terms "white nigger" (*T*, 203) and "counterfeit nigger" (*T*, 211) are ascribed to the Duke, who has been passing himself off as a slave in order to be sold for profit by the King. The same troubled term, "white nigger," is ascribed to Tom, who was also hoping to profit in gossip by selling and stealing himself as a slave. Tom recognizes the Duke as another "white nigger" when he sees him sleeping in the cabin of the slave trader Bat Bradish. Tom's means of identifying a blackface minstrel are predictable enough; he informs Huck that you tell a "white nigger" by the palms of his hands ("the inside of a nigger's hands ain't black") and by the way he talks in his sleep ("he hasn't learned to talk nigger in his sleep, yet" [*T*, 204]). Predictable as Tom's racist epistemology is, it accrues surplus meaning from the larger narrative of *Tom Sawyer's Conspiracy*. Here the "white nigger" is an uncomfortable, imperfect inversion of the "black" who is white inside. "White niggers" can easily wash up to visible social personhood but their transracial play reveals that they have no proper inside, not the individuating map of the palm nor the unself-conscious "nigger talk" that Twain seems to have identified with authenticity, beginning in 1874 with his first narrative written in African American dialect, which is significantly titled "A True Story."

By making one of his central, most beloved characters, Tom Sawyer, into a defamiliarized sign of white racial privilege—a figure both "white" and "nigger" at the same time apparently because he sees his only partially successful performance of blackness as preferable to remaining unexceptionally white— Twain offers a primitive version of what is now known as critical whiteness studies.[35] By naming Tom himself as the problematic sign of whiteness, the exemplary "white nigger," Twain allows us to think about how whiteness also works as a sociological and epistemological problem in the earlier fictions where Tom appears. Through Tom, Twain breaks whiteness away from the constellation of mobility, property, and nature, the constellation of Euro-American virtues that had underwritten U.S. manifest destiny and conferred a national-racial character upon the North American West that even in the 1840s seemed mythic, in the Barthesian sense, dehistoricized, and apparently inevitable. In *Tom Sawyer's Conspiracy*, Tom Sawyer's race is a conspiracy, exceptional in a historically particular, unnatural way that exposes the geopolitical space of the Mississippi as likewise unnatural, caught up in a proliferation of the commodity-form that threatens to cancel even the most apparently essential human values. Unlike Jim's "blackness," which is filled with a culturally validated whiteness equivalent to personhood, Tom's "whiteness" is empty insofar as he is a "nigger" or nonperson—as that pejorative and abusive term implies. Tom's "white nigger" enactment is nakedly appropriative; again, he does it to sell himself and to create a juicy scandal in the village. Tom's racial play indicates Twain's experimentation with whiteness as an appropriative and empty sign reminiscent of the "eating the other" that bell hooks has identified with late-twentieth century white cooptations of black styles and bodies.[36] More significantly, Tom's incorporative whiteness is clearly written as an effect of colonial structures which are still in place in the time about which Twain writes, the 1840s: Tom appropriates "nigger" status so that he can actively engage in the domestic and always international slave trade that had shifted the meaning of "nigger" from the relatively neutral negro to "slave" by the eighteenth-century.[37] It is important to recognize that in *Tom Sawyer's Conspiracy*, Tom's peculiar minstrelsy does not include an imitation of the falsely perceived behavioral characteristics of African Americans, in other words an embrace of what we might now recognize as romantic racialism. Rather, Tom's minstrelsy in the novella includes a ham performance of whiteness itself, where whiteness is conceived as the institutionalization of European colonialism through the slave traffic.

The *Adventures of Huckleberry Finn* is less cynical than the fragmentary *Tom Sawyer's Conspiracy*, but it too interrogates what we might call the white race problem. Floating on a raft that precariously supports his worldly possessions, Huckleberry Finn reenacts the anxieties that the slave traffic inspired in antebellum whites, whose skin privilege depended largely upon their ability to hold property, black property in particular. Howard Horwitz has remarked that white nervousness about the alienability of property and the implicit slipperiness of liberal selfhood contributes to Huck and Jim's peculiar interest in kings.[38] *Adventures of Huckleberry Finn* is heavy with a fear of white social death, a kind of white nonpersonhood roughly equivalent to what Twain later identifies as the status of the "white nigger." This devalued status threatens not only poor whites. Even Huck, with his unclaimed monies in Judge Thatcher's safe and his precariously floating slave charge, is not exactly poor. His position is reminiscent of middling speculators and small riverside plantation owners. No matter how vigorously mapped or patrolled by slaveholders, the entire Mississippi Valley remained, at least imaginatively, a landscape of risk for white investors in slaves and riverside lands.

II. ECONOMIC AND RACIAL DRIFT

As slave values soared in response to rising demand for cotton in the 1830s and again in the 1850s, the domestic slave trade which was conducted upon the Mississippi River reminded slave owners that their slaves' value as commodities depended upon their mobility, an attribute which could be used against owners if it were acknowledged that, in the abolitionist Theodore Dwight Weld's terms, slaves were "property *with will*."[39] When Jefferson Davis lobbied for the Fugitive Slave Act of 1850 as a Senator from Mississippi, he claimed that the value of riverside properties was compromised because of the easy access to slaves that the river afforded thieves and abolitionists, who were also called "slave-thieves." Davis argued: "Those like myself, who live on the great highway of the West, the Mississippi River—are most exposed [and] have a present and increasing interest in this matter."[40] Although incidents of slave escape from the Mississippi Valley, especially the southwestern border states of Mississippi, Louisiana, and Alabama, were in reality quite low, slave owners imagined that the river beckoned slaves with the promises of riverboat thieves and abolitionists who would steal them only to resell or exploit them elsewhere. The river imaged, for speculators in slaves as well as riverside lands, the social death of bankruptcy if not a metaphorical slavery to the commodities that constituted wealth.[41]

Like slave property, Mississippi Valley real estate played a crucial role in the development of identities both within and beyond the region. The land booms of Kentucky and Tennessee in the 1790s were followed by early nineteenth-century booms in Mississippi, Louisiana, Alabama, and Arkansas. The Mississippi River threatened the value of this land as much—in reality, more—than it threatened local slave values. The southwestern humorist Thomas Bangs Thorpe, writing for *Harper's New Monthly Magazine* in 1855, warned investors away from riverside properties, as "untold acres of rich land, forming the banks, annually cave into the stream."[42] In Herman Melville's metaphysical critique of the market culture of the Mississippi, *The Confidence-Man* (1857), a Missouri plantation owner named Pitch attributes his distrust of Emersonian nature to the loss of a riverside farm—"ten thousand dollars' worth of alluvion, thrown broad off upon the waters."[43] In the *Adventures of Huckleberry Finn*, Twain represents the uncertainty of land values in this volatile riverine environment in his depiction of Bricksville, a destitute town on the Mississippi "that has to be always moving back, and back, and back, because the river's always gnawing at it" (*H*, 183). This same town hosts the torture of street pigs and dogs and the casual murder of a drunk, Boggs, by a merchant, Sherburn, which results in the formation of a lynch mob. The sudden and irrevocable destruction perpetrated by the river upon this town creates a social climate in which equilibrium is sought through reciprocal acts of annihilation. The assumption made by the denizens of Twain's Bricksville that growth contains within it the possible cancellation of presence is an assumption taught by the river. This same assumption fueled the anxious speculative economy of the Mississippi Valley, where "the parasitical nature of white freedom," to quote Toni Morrison, was evidenced in both the spectacle of slave traffic and in scenes of receding properties.[44] Mississippi Valley property holders' imperfect grasp on riverside lands and slaves that seemed eager to defy them made whiteness a particularly unstable category on and along the river.

Drifting and floating on the raft proves to be a politically ironic movement in *Adventures of Huckleberry Finn*, a parody of manifest destiny in which providential protection is denied to the earnest white boy who initially rejoices in the naturalness of his travel. The river sensually joggles Huck and seems to fit him so well he can even smell the passage of time in it. "Sometimes moonlight, sometimes storms, and we a floating along, talking, and singing, and laughing," Huck reflects (*H*, 270). But of course Huck and Jim's gentle floating makes them targets for theft and easy prey to river pirates like the Duke and King. Even Huck describes floating as a mobility which denies agency when he, in a canoe, and Jim, on the raft, drift past the Ohio River in a thick fog. Jehlen describes this moment as the point in which "freedom" in the novel is sundered, and Jim's freedom as revolutionary reform loses to Huck's liberal freedom from emplottedness.[45] Certainly the missing of the Ohio nixes Jim's escape. Yet at this same moment in the novel Huck narrates a frightening loss of control, a literalized environmental determinism in which his body recognizes itself as at odds with the nature that once seemed to have been poured into it "like melted wax," to borrow Ralph Waldo Emerson's simile for the interpenetration of self and world.[46] Floating past the Ohio River cancels Jim's freedom and complicates Huck's illusion of freedom as he realizes that the weather runs contrary to his intentions and that he is not, at least not wholly, natural. Implicitly, there is a rend in Huck's normativity here, if not in his racial normativity per se. Huck recalls in an anxious past-present tense: "[First] I know I'll run into a bank or a tow-head or something; I got to set still and float, and yet it's a mighty fidgety business to have to hold your hands still at such a time" (*H*, 100). The surrender of craft signified by Huck's holding of his hands prompts his further reflection upon how floating does not even feel like moving. It offers a somatic image of the anti-emigration suggested to more acute minds by the appearance of slave cargoes on the river. "No, you feel like you are laying dead still on the water; and if a little glimpse of a snag slips by, you don't think to yourself how fast you're going, but you catch your breath and think, my! how that snag's tearing along" (*H*, 100). Of course, it is significant that immediately after experiencing this loss of control over his own mobility Huck attempts to reassert mastery over Jim by cruelly pretending that Jim imagined their separation.

Huck's problem of ownership is not really the problem of a poor child, but rather the problem of any slaveholder—a large and inclusive class—who might desire to imagine his household as an autonomous unit, as in the Aristotelian *oikos*, that is unaffected by market forces. Walter Bern Michaels has made a complementary argument about *Uncle Tom's Cabin*, where he suggests that the real spectacle of horror is not slavery per se, but the imperfect nature of white mastery of purportedly domestic, patriarchal economies.[47] For Twain, the Mississippi River is a field of desire in which capital is continually broken up, moved, or transformed. Riverside lands tumble into flood waters, slaves occasionally stow away on steamboats or disappear at the hands of abolitionists and slave thieves, who are the same people for slaveholders. The movement of the water and the things it carries is unpredictable. Huck identifies the river in the moderate flood-stage of the June rise in which his journey begins as a theater of floating capital, capital that takes the rather innocent form of unclaimed driftwood and unmanned rafts. Even to Huck, his chosen form of movement, drift, signifies a ready vulnerability to appropriation. Moreover, a raft is a thing that he has learned is easy to take. Early in the novel, Huck and Pap gather "part of a log raft—nine logs fast together" to sell as firewood in Hannibal (*H*, 39). The occasional canoe floating on the river represents a more speculative venture, insofar as it is difficult to see if a canoe is really unmanned. When Huck first glimpses the canoe that will take him to Jackson's Island, he "just expected there'd be somebody laying down in it, because people often done that to fool folks, and when a chap had pulled a skiff out most to it they'd raise up and laugh at him" (*H*, 38). Huck himself lies down in the canoe as he drifts past the dock at Hannibal, but it is nighttime and, fortunately, no one attempts to board him. These floating rafts and canoes that are given to Pap and Huck by the river suggest that capital naturally flows where it is most needed, that the river indeed may approximate a distributive justice.

Yet this commercial ideal is repeatedly undermined, as I have suggested. Its most obvious antitheses are the Duke and King, who rig the river system with phony handbills creating false values and unnatural desires. The Duke and King advertise themselves as "tragedians" and Jim as a "fugitive" from Louisiana (*H*, 194, 174). Their false papers set the market flowing in directions Huck could not have anticipated from his childhood experiences waiting for what the spring rises might bring. The advertisement the Duke prints up in Bricksville for Jim allows the frauds, as finders, to hold Jim and sell him; the legendary slave thief John Murrell used a similar ruse, an allusion Twain would have known and that links Huck and Jim, once again, back to the river's most famous pirate. In *Tom Sawyer's Conspiracy*, the Duke and King again attempt to hold Jim with spurious papers. In this later narrative, Jim is accused of murdering the local slave trader and about to be tried for murder. Informed of this dire situation by Tom and Huck, the frauds imagine that they might still profit from Jim if they can produce a "requisition for Jim from the Governor of Kentucky" claiming that he is already awaiting trial for murder in that state. They will then take Jim and sell him further downriver. "All bogus, you know," the Duke confides in Huck, "but the seals and the paper, which is genuwyne—and on them papers we can go and grab Jim wherever we find him and there ain't anybody can prevent it" (*T*, 224). Paper is more fluid than water, it seems, and generates a more efficient and predictable, if less just, capital flow. In *Tom Sawyer's Conspiracy*, the printer's craft also plays a role in Tom's creation of the trumped up scheme that lands Jim, once again, between a public hanging and sale to the deeper South. Tom prints one hundred and fifty fake handbills for the "white nigger" that is actually himself so that he can pass himself off as a slave to the local slavetrader and villagers.

By the time Tom's handbills establish him as a slave, the point is moot. The trader, Bat Bradish, is about to be murdered, and Jim is about to be accused. Jim is the only man in St. Petersburg with a reasonable motive for killing the trader because Bradish had convinced Miss Watson to sell him "las' summer" (*H*, 168) in the fictive time-space of *Adventures of Huckleberry Finn*. But, again, Jim is falsely accused. The slavetrader was really killed by a pair of "white niggers," the King and Duke. Since their initial encounter with Huck and Jim the frauds have been making money by selling themselves as slaves, and Bradish had gotten in the way of one of their schemes. Tom figures out that the Duke, not Jim, is the "nigger" who killed Bradish. "Ain't it curious?" Tom remarks to Huck on their common cause with the frauds. "They got in ahead of us on our scheme all around: play counterfeit nigger like we was going to do" (*T*, 211). Other than the implicit query "ain't it curious," Tom and Huck offer scant commentary on why the once oppositional roles of "speculator" and "nigger" seem to have merged. Early in the planning stages of the conspiracy, Tom answers Huck's complaint that no black man will want to participate in their scheme by saying simply, "There's a lack—we've got to supply it" (*T*, 174). The lack, in part, is that Jim is now legally free and no longer eligible to enact Tom's sadistic plots. Clearly one of the interrogations Twain makes in this novella is what happens to masters—or, more broadly, what happens to white folks—when there are no longer slaves to entertain them. The simple answer is that they try to become slaves and entertain themselves: minstrelsy. The more complicated problem here is why impersonating a slave requires selling yourself to a trader and then stealing yourself away from him to "to get up a sweat in the town" (*T*, 173). It is as if, one year after the *Adventures of Huckleberry Finn* in the fictional time-space of Twain's oeuvre, the principal characters of that novel are trying to compensate desperately for the loss of speculative energy that fueled their earlier and more successful plot.

Without an active domestic slave market and slave commodities circulating within it, the suspense and poignancy of the *Adventures of Huckleberry Finn* would be nil. Even at the end of the novel, when Tom finally reveals Jim's legal freedom, Jim is effectively deglamorized by being paid forty dollars in wages for his performance as a fugitive slave. Tom's paying of wages to Jim is one of the many dull notes in the novel's anticlimactic, unsatisfactory conclusion. Jim's worth, in every sense of that word, was greater to the novel while he was a slave. His actual monetary worth as a slave ranged from eight hundred dollars, which is what Miss Watson collected on him, to the two-to-three hundred dollars that would be paid finders who encountered him on the road. As a slave, Jim is white treasure. Huck recognizes that Jim can't sit up on the raft in the daylight because of the excitement he will provoke in white onlookers: "[People] could tell he was a nigger a good ways off" (*H*, 62). The fact that Jim, like a celebrity, cannot be seen in public, makes Huck, too, potentially famous or infamous.[48] White people can't stop talking to Huck about Jim. "There's two hundred dollars on him," a boy tells Huck after Jim has been sold in Pikesville to Silas Phelps. "It's like pickin' up money out'n the road ... they ain't no trouble 'bout *that* speculation, you bet you" (*H*, 267). Judith Loftus, the woman who sees through Huck's lame disguise as a girl, tells Huck that Jim has been traced to Jackson's Island and then describes Jim as sure money. "Does three hundred dollars lay around every day for people to pick up?" (*H*, 70). In *Adventures of Huckleberry Finn*, the distinction between "money" and "people" is initially clear: "people" is white, "money" black. Once Jim really is free, there can be no compensation to the white world of the Mississippi Valley for the excitement, the glamour, the possibility of undeserved advancement signified by a black body adrift on the river.

As many abolitionists and, later, politicians who considered compensating slaveholders for the loss of slave capital in the event of emancipation came to acknowledge, there really was no way to account for the tremendous value of slaves to white Americans. Some politicians, like Henry Clay, could name a price; in 1839, Clay estimated on the Senate floor that twelve hundred million dollars in slave capital would have to be compensated if emancipation occurred.[49] Years later, in 1855, Emerson suggested that, while no price would be high enough, still the nation should try to pay itself back for the loss of its slaves. In Emerson's metaphysical politics, drawing the larger circle was theoretically important, even if the circle never got finished because the arc of desire, as in this case, was simply too large. "If really the matter could come to negotiation and a price were named," Emerson lectured, "I do not think any price founded on an estimate that figures could tell would be quite unmanageable. Every man in the land would give a week's work to dig away this accursed mountain of sorrow once and forever out of the world."[50] Emerson could not have predicted the theatrical compensation staged in *Tom Sawyer's Conspiracy*, where it becomes clear that the loss of the slave, or of the particular slave Jim, has to be addressed by a novel performance of whiteness. What the "nigger" had been to the "white" was an idea of value detached from labor, a natural resource and treasure, white gold. The gold and silver rushes of the Far West that were Twain's first successful literary topic figure as merely a pallid afterthought to the international slave rush. It was the transatlantic slave trade that first allowed the American West to imagine itself as the future center of the world.

III. STEALING THE CIVIL WAR

At the end of *Tom Sawyer's Conspiracy*, which is not quite a conclusion because the text is fragmentary, Tom states before a judge that Jim is not guilty of murder. Then Tom recounts, in his typically stylish cant, the essential plot of his conspiracy. When the fragment simply stops, it has become clear that Tom has both saved Jim from the gallows and rendered him obsolete. What Tom reveals is what the reader already knows: everyone acting in this plot is actually white. Jim's testimony in court is cursorily summarized and irrelevant. Jim's voice is reduced in *Tom Sawyer's Conspiracy* to an evasive "mumbling" (*T*, 171). The minstrel behaviors that vaguely represent Jim throughout the novella are so exaggerated as to be grotesque.[51] Twain either really doesn't care about Jim anymore by the time that he writes *Tom Sawyer's Conspiracy*, or he is elaborately acting out a disowning of this once rather carefully rendered character as a perverse self-reproach. Curiously, Twain asks us to believe that Tom created the conspiracy that is the primary plot of the novella in response to a request from Jim, as if it were really Jim, not Tom, who motivates the "white nigger" plot. Supposedly Jim rejected two prior plots Tom dreamed up. The first plot was called "civil war"; the second, "revolution" (*T*, 165, 167). To be nice to Jim, Tom abandoned these alternatives, showing a generosity that Huck lavishly praises without questioning why a former slave who is living in a slave state might tell a white

220 Stephanie Le Menager

boy that he desires neither civil war nor revolution. Perhaps even the reader is not meant to ask these questions.

At any rate, Twain distracts us with Huck's almost shocking statement near the beginning of the novella that Tom has "countermanded the Civil War" (*T*, 167). This indeed would be Tom Sawyer's greatest evasion. For achieving it, Huck thinks Tom ought to be compared to "Harriet Beecher Stow and all them other second-handers [who] gets all the credit for starting that war and you never hear Tom Sawyer mentioned in the histories ransack them as you will, and yet he was the first one that thought of it" (*T*, 167). What a premise: that Tom thought of the Civil War first, and then tossed the idea aside. So Tom should be famous for not bringing the slavery struggle to a head, while Stowe has been credited with injecting it, irrevocably, into the popular culture and history of the United States. It is impossible not to wonder what, if anything, Twain meant by playing with the idea that Tom might be the anti-Stowe, the figure who depopularizes an earnest, if limited, antebellum dialogue about freedom and supplants that dialogue with a racial mystery by which no one profits, and a black man, again, is locked up. Was this pale anti-Stoweism what Twain, when affected by what he called the "deep melancholy" that visited him in the later years of his career, conceived of as Tom's contribution, or even as his own contribution, to the national imaginary after the Civil War?[52]

In the "Chapters from My Autobiography," which Twain published in the *North American Review* in the first decade of the twentieth century, Twain begins his self-description with a genealogy in which his ancestors figure as "pirates" and "slavers," the sorts of characters Tom modeled in play. "Back of the Virginia Clemenses," Twain recounts, "is a dim procession of ancestors stretching back to Noah's time. According to tradition, some of them were pirates and slavers in Elizabeth's time. But this is no discredit to them, for so were Drake and Hawkins and the others. It was a respectable trade, then, and monarchs were partners in it. In my time I have had desires to be a pirate myself. The reader—if he will look deep down in his secret heart, will find—but never mind what he will find there; I am not writing his Autobiography, but mine."[53] The associational reach of Twain's *Autobiography* suggests that he actually was writing the reader's autobiography, too, or at least an ethnobiography of European America. His leap from biblical progenitors to pirates and slave traders neatly encapsulates the nineteenth-century United States's compromised version of modernity, where eschatological idealism competed with a brutal international history to tell the story of the world from here. Twain confides that he prefers to recognize himself in the pirate, who is implicitly synonymous with the slaver; piracy and slaving is the seat of our American pleasure.

This glib, unsettling, Tom Sawyerish message reasserts itself in the last installment of the *Autobiography* that Twain published before he died, which ends with a silly anecdote, the sort of shtick which Michael J. Kiskis notes as having found its way back into Twain's *Autobiography* from his earlier work on the stage.[54] Twain tells a story about how, when he was in desperate need of three dollars rent money in the late 1860s, he stole a dog from the celebrated Indian fighter Nelson A. Miles, sold it to a stranger for three dollars, then reclaimed the dog (refunding the stranger's money), and returned the dog to Miles for a finder's fee of three dollars. "I went away with a good conscience, because I had acted honorably; I never could have used the three that I sold the dog for, because it was not rightly my own, but the three I got for restoring him to his rightful owner was righteously and properly mine, because I had earned it.... My principles have remained to this day what they were then."[55] This is a strange note on which to leave the world, inasmuch as it can be seen as an ending. What is really odd, I think, is how generalized this bit about selling what does not belong to you had become in Twain's writings, both fictional and autobiographical. In private and public letters, Twain accused almost all of his former publishers of misusing copyright and profiting by his imagination, which he was quite certain did not belong to them. Then there are the memoirs and fictions where ex-slaves (Jim and Roxy in *Pudd'nhead Wilson*) are sold by men who do not own them, or white boys sell themselves as something other than what they are, or claim jumpers profit from mines not rightfully theirs. Finally there are the figures of international imperialist infamy, those who bought and sold countries, like the Philippines, that never belonged to them. It is significant that General Miles, who supposedly had helped capture Geronimo, figures in Twain's apparently absurdist bit about selling the dog. Twain recognizes that the romantic pirate of child's play, the Indian fighter, and the historical slaver are one. For Twain, piracy, land theft, slavetrading, "selling what does not belong to you," offers not just a precondition of modernity, but also a precondition of comic imagination and, implicitly, of knowledge. His ethnobiography betrays a peculiarly contemporary recognition of the United States as situated in a rich and perilous transnational context: international piracy and slavery produce the Americas; and international piracy and slavery produce Twain's American West, a geopolitical imaginary where, because of the cosmopolitan Mississippi River, a stereotypically western openness is never far from the twisted circuits of human capital that defined the political economy of the circum-Caribbean South.

NOTES

1. See Richard Slotkin, *The Fatal Environment: The Myth of the Frontier in the Age of Industrialization, 1500–1590* (1985; reprint, Middletown, CT: Wesleyan Univ. Press, 1986), 61, 518.

2. Patricia Nelson Limerick, "The Adventures of the Frontier in the Twentieth Century," in *The Frontier in American Culture: Essays by Richard White and Patricia Nelson Limerick*, ed. James R. Grossman (Berkeley: Univ. of California Press, 1994), 78. Limerick's use of the phrase "expanding world market studies" is not flattering and suggests the verbal gymnastics historians undergo to avoid acknowledging themselves as heirs to Frederick Jackson Turner's frontier hypothesis. At the same time, this intentionally deflating phrase identifies for me some of the most powerful historical and literary historical work on the North American West that has been published in the past twenty years, including Richard White's *The Middle Ground: Indians, Empires, and Republics in the Great Lakes Region, 1650–1515* (Cambridge: Cambridge Univ. Press, 1991); James F. Brooks's *Captives and Cousins: Slavery, Kinship, and Community in the Southwestern Borderlands* (Chapel Hill: Univ. of North Carolina Press, 2002); and Limerick's own *The Legacy of Conquest: The Unbroken Past of the American West* (New York: W. W. Norton, 1987).

3. Kaplan brings a crucial dimension to Twain criticism by emphasizing that "Twain's career, writing, and reception as a national author were shaped by a third realm beyond national boundaries: the routes of transnational travel, enabling and enabled by the changing borders of imperial expansion." I simply don't think that it is necessary to go outside of the continental U.S. to find this "third realm." My interest in defamiliarizing the continental claims of the nineteenth-century U.S. requires a rereading of the continent, particularly the West, as never quite as clearly domestic as it appears in nineteenth-century expansionist and frontier rhetorics. See Amy Kaplan, "The Imperial Routes of Mark Twain," in *The Anarchy of Empire in the Making of U.S. Culture* (Cambridge: Harvard Univ. Press, 2002), 51.

4. Limerick has written of U.S. westward expansion that "[t]he events of western history represent, not a simple process of territorial expansion, but an array of efforts to wrap the concept of property around unwieldy objects" (71).

5. See Michael Hardt's and Antonio Negri's preface to *Empire*, xii. Kaplan contends that Hardt and Negri make unnecessarily fine historical distinctions among nineteenth-century U.S. imperialisms and late twentieth-century articulations of global Empire. See Kaplan's introduction to *Anarchy*. John Carlos Rowe has also emphasized that the long history of U.S. imperialism need not be thought about in terms of territorial domination and settlement, but rather as a continuous effort to establish political-economic spheres of influence throughout the world. *Literary Culture and U.S. Imperialism: From the Revolution to World War II* (New York: Oxford Univ. Press, 2000), 7–9.

6. Henry Nash Smith most pointedly addresses the Southern tendency to think in terms of world empire, articulated through the oceans and intracontinental waterways, in his discussion of Thomas Hart Benton and in his address of southern responses to the yeoman ideal. See Smith, *Virgin Land: The American West as Symbol and Myth* (1950; reprint, Cambridge: Harvard Univ. Press, 1978), 19–35, 145–55.

7. Benton's strongest claims for a separate western coastal republic appear in an early series of editorials, written between 1815 and 1819, for the *St. Louis Enquirer*. See Benton, *Selections of Editorial Articles from the St. Louis Enquirer*, microfilm (1844; reprint, New Haven, CT: Research Publications, Inc. 1975), 43–44. Smith discusses

Benton's longstanding focus on western water routes and his resistance to the idea of a transcontinental railroad (30–31).

8. John C. Calhoun, discussed in Smith, 148.

9. Brooks Adams, *The Law of Civilization and Decay: An Essay on History* (1896; reprint, New York: Alfred A. Knopf, 1951), 58, 61.

10. Theodore Roosevelt recognized Adams's nostalgia for a militaristic, feudal-patriarchal economy as simplistic, primarily because this nostalgia neatly excised the realities of slavery and peonage. Roosevelt, "Law of Civilization and Decay," in *American Ideals and Other Essays, Social and Political*, vol. 2 (New York: Charles Scribner's Sons, 1906), 183.

11. Twain's choicest rantings about Roosevelt were excised from Albert Bigelow Paine's biography and reprinted by Bernard DeVoto in Twain, *Mark Twain in Eruption: Hitherto Unpublished Pages about Men and Events*, ed. DeVoto (1922; reprint, New York: Grosset & Dunlap, 1940). The creation of future values that Twain once associated with economic speculation and the telling of tall tales has become quite dangerous in Twain's version of Roosevelt's America, as Twain juxtaposes Roosevelt's self-generated accounts of his bear hunts to his warmongering off the coast of Japan.

12. See Philip J. Fisher, "Mark Twain," in the *Columbia Literary History of the United States*, ed. Emory Elliott (New York: Columbia Univ. Press, 1988), 630. Fisher has eloquently described the speculator as Twain's culture hero, the ideal figure for a new country in which future values must be energetically projected. Fisher writes that "the world in which [Twain] moves is one in which people buy each other's useless worthless shares and all get rich together on faith. They float together in the insubstantial air of a society of massive credit, debt, risk and collapse." This almost casual optimism about the social value of speculative floating falters at the conclusion of *Adventures of Huckleberry Finn*, where Fisher acknowledges, "Tom Sawyer stages his heartless phony rescue of Jim [and] a speculative reality is evoked and then collapsed, but not without real wounds" (627). The perennial problem posed by the conclusion of *Adventures of Huckleberry Finn* is, essentially, the problem of reconciling Twain's lifelong obsession with U.S. business culture with the cynicism, anti-imperialism, and even anti-Americanism that is also present in his work as early as the 1860s.

13. Myra Jehlen, "Banned in Concord: *Adventures of Huckleberry Finn* and Classic American Literature," *The Cambridge Companion to Mark Twain*, ed. Forrest G. Robinson (Cambridge: Cambridge Univ. Press, 1995), 109, 110, 99. Jehlen writes in full:

> It is also impossible in the Mississippi River towns through which Huck and Jim journey to imagine being a hero. This in turn makes Sherburn a cold-blooded killer and Huck a saint (and Tom a fool). Let me repeat that as a saint, however, Huck is no more bent on social reform, no more optimistic about it, than is Sherburn. That is, his radical liberalism, not unlike Emerson's, is also conservative. He never reacts to social inequities by imagining them reformed; they appear to him as natural, ineluctable parts of a system as fixed as the system of nature. (109–10)

14. Forrest G. Robinson's reading of the effect of Tom Sawyer's speculations in St. Petersburg is in some sense a negative image of Fisher's; both equate the formation of community with willful self-deception, but they value such willful self-deception quite differently. For Robinson, Tom Sawyer provides the give in a rigidly conventional town, articulating in an almost purgative sense the hypocrisy that sustains local mores. So

although Tom figures as virtual embodiment of the will to deceive, he is also, as in Fisher's reading, crucial to community self-recognition. See Robinson, *In Bad Faith: The Dynamics of Deception in Mark Twain's America* (Cambridge: Harvard Univ. Press, 1986), 26.

15. Walter Blair traces Twain's development of the plot of *Tom Sawyer's Conspiracy* through a series of notebook entries, beginning in 1896:

> A notebook entry of 1896 shows Mark Twain hitting upon the idea of relating these [story fragments] to a plot which Huck would describe: "Have Huck tell how one white brother shaved his head, put on a wool wig and was blackened and sold as a negro. Escaped that night, washed himself, and helped hunt *for himself* under pay." A year later the author thought of using Huck himself as "the white brother": "Tom sells Huck for a slave." Some pages later in the notebook containing this entry, among items headed "For New Huck Finn," he writes "Huck," crosses it out, replaces it with "Tom" and concludes the sentence: "is disguised as a negro and sold in Ark for $10, then he and Huck help hunt for him after the disguise is removed." (Blair, "Introduction to *Tom Sawyer's Conspiracy*," in Twain, *Mark Twain's Hannibal, Huck and Tom*, ed. Blair [Berkeley: Univ. of California, 1969], 153).

16. Twain, *Tom Sawyer's Conspiracy*, in *Mark Twain's Hannibal, Huck and Tom*, 175, 171, 229. Hereafter abbreviated *T* and cited parenthetically by page number.

17. In an article in the *United States Magazine and Democratic Review* that followed on the heels of his famous assertion of the United States's "manifest destiny," John L. O'Sullivan argued that "the representative system as practically enjoyed in this country, will admit of an indefinite expansion of territory." O'Sullivan, "Territorial Aggrandizement," *United States Magazine and Democratic Review* 17 (October 1845): 244.

18. Turner, *History, Frontier, and Section: Three Essays by Frederick Jackson Turner* (1893; reprint, Albuquerque: Univ. of New Mexico, 1993), 1313.

19. Twain, *Adventures of Huckleberry Finn*, ed. Blair and Victor Fischer (1885; reprint, Berkeley: Univ. of California Press, Mark Twain Library, 1985), 37. Hereafter abbreviated *H* and cited parenthetically by page number.
These (and the following) general remarks about the importance of river levels come from Louis C. Hunter's standard history. See esp. "Techniques of Operation" in Hunter's *Steamboats on the Western Rivers* (Cambridge: Harvard Univ. Press, 1949).

20. John W. Monette, "The Mississippi Floods," in *Publications of the Mississippi Historical Society*, vol. 7, ed. Franklin L. Riley, (Oxford: Mississippi Historical Society, 1903), 427–713.

21. Twain, *Life on the Mississippi* (1883; reprint, New York: Penguin, 1980), 119.

22. Andrew Jackson, "Announcement to His Soldiers," 14 Nov. 1812, in Jackson, *Correspondence of Andrew Jackson*, vol. 1, ed. John Spencer Bassett (Washington, D.C.: Carnegie Institute of Washington, 1926–1935), 241–42.

23. Samuel Clemens to Ann E. Taylor, 1 June 1857, from New Orleans, Louisiana. In Twain, *Mark Twain's Letters*, vol. 1 (1853–1866), ed. Edgard Marquess Branch, Michael B. Frank, and Kenneth M. Sanderson (Berkeley: Univ. of California Press, 1988), 72.

24. See Clemens's two letters to the Muscatine *Tri-Weekly Journal* from St. Louis, on 5 March 1855 and 24–26 February 1855, respectively (*MTL* 1 [1855]: 55, 50–51).

25. James Thomas, *From Tennessee Slave to St. Louis Entrepreneur: The Autobiography of James Thomas*, ed. Loren Schweninger (Columbia: Univ. of Missouri Press, 1984), 116.

26. See the essay "Walking" (1862), which Henry David Thoreau originally gave as a lecture in the 1850s. In part inspired by a panorama of the Mississippi River, Thoreau offered his highly personal account of manifest destiny, declaring his own tendency to follow expanding circles in the direction of the southwest in his daily walks. See Thoreau's *Collected Essays and Poems*, ed. Elizabeth Hall Witherell (New York: Library of America, 2001), 239.

27. Harriet Beecher Stowe, *Uncle Tom's Cabin, or, Life Among the Lowly* (1852; reprint, New York: Garland, 1981), 199.

28. Abraham Lincoln to Mary Speed, 27 September 1841. Lincoln, *Abraham Lincoln: His Speeches and Writings*, ed. Roy P. Basler (New York: World Publishing Company, 1969), 131.

29. Saidiya V. Hartman comments on this letter, recognizing in it the assimilative effects of empathy:

> [T]he liberal extension of feeling to those shackled like a herd of cattle or strung together like a line of fish only serves to efface violence and circumscribe the captives' sentience through such attributions of contentment and evaluations of the bearable.... In order to understand the condition of the enslaved, Lincoln basically likens them to himself to address the human condition. The assimilative character of empathy can be blamed in part for this, for approximation overtakes the proximity essential to ethical conduct and the violence of this obliteration and assimilation is no less great, albeit of a different character, than the racist antipathy that can only envision the enslaved object as a dehumanized other. (Hartman, *Scenes of Subjection: Terror, Slavery, and Self-Making in Nineteenth-Century America* [New York: Oxford Univ. Press, 1997], 34 35).

30. John Seelye, *Introduction to Adventures of Huckleberry Finn* (New York: Penguin Books, 1985), xx.

31. For the larger context of the forced transport of the Creeks across the Mississippi, see Michael Rogin, *Fathers and Children: Andrew Jackson and the Subjugation of the American Indian* (1975; reprint, New Brunswick: Transaction Publishers, 1995), 144.

32. Hunter discusses the routes of immigrants and disease through the Mississippi Valley (419–41).

33. Examples of earlier criticism that points to the dramatic irony that affects both the narrative and reception of *Adventures of Huckleberry Finn* include Laurence B. Holland, "A 'Raft of Trouble': Word and Deed in Huckleberry Finn," *Glyph* 5 (1979): 68–87; and James M. Cox, *Mark Twain: The Fate of Humor* (Princeton: Princeton Univ. Press, 1966). Cox, in particular, argues that Twain reinvents the Southerner without cost, giving Huck the task of freeing a slave in the slave South once Emancipation has rendered that act clearly laudable and unnecessary. See Cox, 169–72.

34. Eric Lott, "Mr. Clemens and Jim Crow: Twain, Race, and Blackface," in *Cambridge*, 140. Homi Bhabha, quoted from Lott, "Mr. Clemens," 140.

35. A good summation of the current (at least pre-September 11) state of critical whiteness studies appears in *The Making and Unmaking of Whiteness*, ed. Birgit Brander Rasmussen, Eric Klinenberg, Irene J. Nexica, and Matt Wray (Durham: Duke Univ. Press, 2001). The work of David Roediger has been central in defining this field, from both black and white perspectives. See, for example *Black on White: Black Writers on What It Means to*

Be White, ed. Roediger (New York: Schocken Books, 1998). See also Theodore W. Allen's comprehensive *The Invention of the White Race: The Origin of Racial Oppression in Anglo-America*, 2 vols. (London and New York: Verso, 1994/1997).

36. bell hooks, *Black Looks: Race and Representation* (Boston: South End Press, 1992).

37. David L. Smith offers a useful gloss on Twain's use of the pejorative term "nigger" in *Adventures of Huckleberry Finn*.

> Most obviously, Twain uses "nigger" throughout the book as a synonym for "slave." There is ample evidence from other sources that this corresponds to one usage common during the antebellum period. We first encounter it in reference to "Miss Watson's big nigger, named Jim" (chap. 2). This usage, like the term "nigger stealer," clearly designates the "nigger" as an item of property: a commodity, a slave. This passage also provides the only apparent textual justification for the common critical practice of labeling Jim "Nigger Jim," as if "nigger" were a part of his proper name. This loathsome habit goes back at least as far as Albert Bigelow Paine's biography of Twain (1912). In any case, "nigger" in this sense connotes an inferior, even subhuman, creature who is properly owned by and subservient to Euro-Americans. (Smith, "Huck, Jim, and American Racial Discourse," *Satire or Evasion? Black Perspectives on Huckleberry Finn*, ed. James S. Leonard, Thomas A. Tenney, and Thadious M. Davis [Durham: Duke Univ. Press, 1992], 105)

38. Howard Horwitz has noted Twain's complex anxieties about the alienability of property, anxieties Horwitz explores most thoroughly in *Life on the Mississippi* but that he also recognizes in Huck and Jim's envy of the absolute sovereignty of kings. Horwitz's nuanced analysis of Twain's response to the Lockean construction of self through property has added depth to my own reading of Huck's inability to control his floating through the river market. Horwitz neatly summarizes the paradox of Lockean or, more broadly, liberal conceptions of selfhood: "Ideally, one is the inalienable master of oneself, and thus of one's labor and material property; but if identity is available only in terms of material property, which by definition is exchangeable, self and self-mastery are redefined ... revealed to be contingent—in every transaction." Horwitz, *By the Law of Nature: Form and Value in Nineteenth-Century America* (New York: Oxford Univ. Press, 1991), 87–114.

39. Theodore Dwight Weld, *American Slavery As It Is: Testimony of a Thousand Witnesses* (1839; reprint, Salem, NH: Ayer Company Publishers, 1991), 111. Weld deconstructs the absurd "chattel principle": "The idea of property having a will, and that too in opposition to the will of its owner, and counteracting it, is a stimulant of a terrible power to the most relentless human passions" (111).

40. Jefferson Davis quoted in Wilbur H. Siebert, *The Underground Railroad: From Slavery to Freedom* (New York: n.p., 1898), 312–13.

41. The historian Walter Johnson has shown, through his analysis of white Southerners daydreaming about slaves in their diaries and personal correspondence, the intimate dependency of slave owners not just upon slave labor but also upon the idea that slaves were commodities, accouterments or augmentations of white selfhood. Johnson, *Soul by Soul: Life Inside the Antebellum Slave Market* (Cambridge: Harvard Univ. Press, 1999). See esp. chap. 3, "Making a World Out of Slaves."

42. Thomas Bangs Thorpe, "Remembrances of the Mississippi," *Harper's New Monthly Magazine* 12 (December 1855): 27–28.

43. Herman Melville, *The Confidence-Man: His Masquerade* (1857; reprint, New York: Penguin, 1990), 131.

44. Toni Morrison, *Playing in the Dark: Whiteness and the Literary Imagination* (Cambridge: Harvard Univ. Press, 1992), 57.

45. Jehlen, 103.

46. "I—this thought which is called I—is the mold into which the world is poured like melted wax. The mold is invisible, but the world betrays the shape of the mold. You call it the power of circumstance, but it is the power of me." Ralph Waldo Emerson, "The Transcendentalist," *Selections from Ralph Waldo Emerson*, ed. Stephen E. Whicher (Boston: Houghton Mifflin, 1957), 195.

47. In short, Walter Bern Michaels finds that for Stowe the transfer of slaves due to a master's death or indebtedness reveals the horror of the market relation at the heart of an apparently paternalistic and personal economy. Michaels, *The Gold Standard and the Logic of Naturalism* (Berkeley: Univ. of California, 1987), 103–4.

48. Fisher discusses the inability of both Huck and Jim to appear in public as Twain's means of creating an experimental privacy apart from the "new public world" of the early twentieth century, when the marketing of public images made the construction of a private self a secondary, rather than primary, project in the cultivation of personality. See Fisher, *Still the New World* (Cambridge: Harvard Univ. Press, 1999), 140. I would simply suggest that Huck, unlike Jim, can appear in public, although his range of disguises is limited by his visible (or audible) origins in white poverty.

49. Henry Clay, quoted from William Goodell, *The American Slave Code* (1853; reprint, New York: The Arno Press, 1969), 34–35.

50. Emerson, "Lecture on Slavery," in *Emerson's Antislavery Writings*, ed. Len Gougeon and Joel Myerson (New Haven: Yale Univ. Press, 1995), 106.

51. Twain writes, in Huck's voice, that Jim "went on a mumbling to himself, the way a nigger does, and saying he wouldn't give shucks for a conspiracy that was made up out of just any kinds of odds and ends that come handy and hadn't anything lawful about it. But Tom didn't let on to hear; and it's the best way, to let a nigger or a child go on and grumble itself out, then it's satisfied" (*T*, 171). Here Twain, or Huck, is mocking Jim's literalism in regard to the definitions of "conspiracy," "insurrection," "revolution," and "civil war."

52. Twain, *Twain in Eruption*, 251.

53. Twain, *Chapters from My Autobiography*, ed. Shelley Fisher Fishkin (1906; reprint, Oxford: Oxford Univ. Press, 1996), 322–23.

54. Michael J. Kiskis writes that "as Twain relocated himself in autobiography, he became increasingly interested in the process of the story. He was excited by the series of autobiographical dictations (at least through 1906 and 1907) because of the emphasis on talk. Twain claimed that talk was at the heart of true autobiography and the reason for his enjoyment.... In effect, Mark Twain found himself facing his own beginnings as a storyteller: talk was the primary currency of his youth as he sat and listened to tales around slave kitchens, of his piloting days as he sat in wheelhouses, of his adulthood as he and Jim Gillis retold the story of the jumping frog as he stood night after night on the lecture platform." Kiskis, "Coming Back to Humor: The Comic Voice in Mark Twain's Autobiography," in *Mark Twain's Humor: Critical Essays*, ed. David E. E. Sloane (New York: Garland Publishing, Inc., 1993), 545.

55. Twain, *Autobiography*, 490–94.

Chronology

1835	November 30, Samuel Langhorne Clemens, sixth child of John Marshall Clemens and Jane Lampton Clemens, is born in Florida, Missouri.
1839	Moves with family to Mississippi River town of Hannibal, Missouri.
1847–1848	Father dies. Works as printer's apprentice.
1851	Publishes first-known sketch, "A Gallant Fireman," in Hannibal's *Western Union* newspaper, owned and edited by his brother. Works as a printer and editorial assistant.
1853–1857	Works as printer in St. Louis; New York; Philadelphia; Keokuk, Iowa; and Cincinnati.
1857	Becomes apprentice steamboat pilot on Mississippi River.
1859	Receives steamboat pilot license. Works on Mississippi until Civil War starts.
1861	Accompanies brother to the Nevada Territory, where brother has been appointed Secretary to the Nevada Territory. Works as clerk of the Territorial Legislature. Seeks to make money in mining.
1862–1865	Works as reporter and humor writer for several newspapers in Nevada and California. First uses *Mark Twain* as pseudonym. Publishes "Jim Smiley and His Jumping Frog," often seen as his earliest masterpiece.

1866	Correspondent in Hawaii for *Sacramento Daily Union*. Starts career as lecturer; becomes correspondent for the *Alta California*; leaves for New York.
1867	Travels to Europe and the Holy Land as correspondent for the *Alta California*. Publishes *The Celebrated Jumping Frog of Calaveras County and Other Sketches*.
1868	Lectures widely.
1869	Publishes the financially lucrative *The Innocents Abroad*.
1870	Marries Olivia Langdon in February. Son Langdon is born in November.
1871	Takes up residence in Hartford, Connecticut. Travels on extended lecture tour.
1872	Daughter Olivia Susan is born. Langdon dies. Publishes *Roughing It*.
1873	Spends time in Europe with family, the first of several stays there. Publishes *The Gilded Age* with coauthor Charles Dudley Warner.
1874	Daughter Clara is born. Moves into mansion in Hartford. Is in high demand as speaker.
1875	Publishes "Old Times on the Mississippi," a seven-article series in the *Atlantic Monthly*.
1876	Publishes *The Adventures of Tom Sawyer*.
1878–1879	Travels with family in Europe.
1880	Publishes *A Tramp Abroad*. Daughter Jane, called Jean, is born.
1881	Publishes *The Prince and the Pauper*.
1883	Publishes *Life on the Mississippi*.
1884–1885	Founds publishing company with Charles Webster. Travels on lecture tour with George W. Cable, a writer and civil rights advocate. Publishes *Adventures of Huckleberry Finn*.
1889	Publishes *A Connecticut Yankee in King Arthur's Court*.
1890	Mother and his wife's mother both die.
1891	Leaves Hartford and lives for most of the next decade in Europe.
1894	Publishes *The Tragedy of Pudd'nhead Wilson*. Business is declared bankrupt.
1895–1896	Travels on world lecture tour.
1896	Publishes *Personal Recollections of Joan of Arc*. Daughter Susy dies. Daughter Jean is diagnosed with epilepsy.
1897	Publishes *Following the Equator*.

1900	Returns to the United States, moving to New York City. Makes anti-missionary and anti-imperialist statements about U.S. actions in China and the Philippines.
1904	Wife dies.
1908	Moves to newly built mansion in Redding, Connecticut.
1909	Daughter Jean dies.
1910	Mark Twain dies in Redding, Connecticut, on April 21.

Contributors

HAROLD BLOOM is Sterling Professor of the Humanities at Yale University. He is the author of 30 books, including *Shelley's Mythmaking, The Visionary Company, Blake's Apocalypse, Yeats, A Map of Misreading, Kabbalah and Criticism, Agon: Toward a Theory of Revisionism, The American Religion, The Western Canon,* and *Omens of Millennium: The Gnosis of Angels, Dreams, and Resurrection. The Anxiety of Influence* sets forth Professor Bloom's provocative theory of the literary relationships between the great writers and their predecessors. His most recent books include *Shakespeare: The Invention of the Human,* a 1998 National Book Award finalist; *How to Read and Why; Genius: A Mosaic of One Hundred Exemplary Creative Minds; Hamlet: Poem Unlimited; Where Shall Wisdom Be Found?;* and *Jesus and Yahweh: The Names Divine.* In 1999, Professor Bloom received the prestigious American Academy of Arts and Letters Gold Medal for Criticism. He has also received the International Prize of Catalonia, the Alfonso Reyes Prize of Mexico, and the Hans Christian Andersen Bicentennial Prize of Denmark.

TOM QUIRK is Professor of English at the University of Missouri. He has authored titles and is the editor of *Mark Twain: A Study of the Short Fiction* and the Penguin edition of *Selected Tales, Essays, Speeches and Sketches of Mark Twain.* Also, he edited the *Mark Twain and His Circle Series* and is coeditor of *American Realism and the Canon.*

HARRY G. SEGAL teaches at Cornell University. Among other topics, he's interested in psychodynamic approaches to literary texts. His work appears in *Possible Selves: Theory, Research, and Application.*

CARL F. WIECK is Professor Emeritus in the Department of Translation Studies, Tampere University, Finland. He has published *Refiguring Huckleberry Finn* and *Lincoln's Quest for Equality: The Road to Gettysburg*.

JAMES S. LEONARD is Professor of English at the Citadel, where he has also been chair of the department. He has worked on several titles. He is the editor of *Making Mark Twain Work in the Classroom* and editor of the quarterly *Mark Twain Circular*. Also, he is the coeditor of *Satire or Evasion? Black Perspectives on* Huckleberry Finn.

SANFORD PINSKER is Emeritus Professor of Humanities at Franklin & Marshall College. He is the author of books about *The Catcher in the Rye* as well as of *Oedipus Meets the Press, and Other Tragi-Comedies of Our Time* and *Worrying about Race, 1985–1995: Reflections During a Troubled Time*.

SACVAN BERCOVITCH has been Powell M. Cabot Professor of American Literature at Harvard. He has authored many books and essays, such as *Prose Writing, 1820–1865* and *Prose Writing, 1940–1990*. He is the general editor of the multi-volume *Cambridge History of American Literature: 1590–1820*.

JEFFREY STEINBRINK is Alumni Professor of English and American Belles Lettres at Franklin and Marshall College. His published works include *Getting to Be Mark Twain* and he has spoken on Mark Twain in many venues.

MARY P. NICHOLS is a professor at Fordham University. She is coauthor of *Readings in American Government* and has also published a title on the films of Woody Allen. Additionally, she has written on literature, politics, and Greek and modern political thought.

PETER SCHMIDT teaches at Swarthmore College. He has published books on Williams and Welty and coedited the anthology *Postcolonial Theory and the U.S.*

BENNETT KRAVITZ is Senior Lecturer in the Department of English Language and Literature at the University of Haifa. He is the author of *Dreaming Mark Twain*.

TODD GILES is book review editor of the *William Carlos Williams Review*. He is a contributor to the *William Carlos Williams Encyclopedia*.

STEPHANIE LE MENAGER teaches English at the University of California, Santa Barbara. Her publications include *Manifest and Other Destinies: Territorial Fictions of the Nineteenth-Century United States.*

Bibliography

Arac, Jonathan. *Huckleberry Finn as Idol and Target: The Functions of Criticism in Our Time*. Madison, London: University of Wisconsin Press, 1997.

Arpaly, Nomy. "Moral Worth." *Journal of Philosophy* 99, no. 5 (May 2002): 223–245.

Balkun, Mary McAleer. *The American Counterfeit: Authenticity and Identity in American Literature and Culture*. Tuscaloosa: University of Alabama Press, 2006.

Bloom, Harold, ed. *Huck Finn*. Philadelphia: Chelsea House, 2004.

Bollinger, Laurel. "Say It, Jim: The Morality of Connection in *Adventures of Huckleberry Finn*." *College Literature* 29, no. 1 (Winter 2002): 32–52.

Boone, N. S. "Openness to Contingency: *Huckleberry Finn* and the Morality of Phronesis." *Studies in the Humanities* 31, no. 2 (December 2004): 173–188.

Boughn, Michael. "Rethinking Mark Twain's Skepticism: Ways of Knowing and Forms of Freedom in the *Adventures of Huckleberry Finn*." *Arizona Quarterly* 52, no. 4 (Winter 1996): 31–48.

Briden, Earl F. "Playing the Live Stock Market: Topical Humor in *Huckleberry Finn*." *ANQ* 9, no. 2 (Spring 1996): 14–16.

Chadwick-Joshua, Jocelyn. *The Jim Dilemma: Reading Race in Huckleberry Finn*. Jackson: University Press of Mississippi, 1998.

Coulombe, Joseph L. *Mark Twain and the American West*. Columbia, London: University of Missouri Press, 2003.

Deneen, Patrick J. "Was Huck Greek? *The Odyssey* of Mark Twain." *Modern Language Studies* 32, no. 2 (Fall 2002): 35–44.

Derwin, Susan. "Impossible Commands: Reading *Adventures of Huckleberry Finn*." *Nineteenth-Century Literature* 47, no. 4 (March 1993): 437–454.

Doyno, Victor A. "Huck's and Jim's Dynamic Interactions: Dialogues, Ethics, Empathy, Respect." *Mark Twain Annual* 1 (2003): 19–29.

———. "Presentations of Violence in *Adventures of Huckleberry Finn*." *Mark Twain Annual* 2 (2004): 75–93.

Graff, Gerald, and James Phelan, eds. Adventures of Huckleberry Finn: *A Case Study in Critical Controversy*. Boston: Bedford Books of St. Martin's Press, 1995.

Henrickson, Gary P. "Biographers' Twain, Critics' Twain, Which of the Twains Wrote the 'Evasion'?" *Southern Literary Journal* 26, no. 1 (Fall 1993): 14–29.

Horn, Jason Gary. *Mark Twain and William James: Crafting a Free Self*. Columbia: University of Missouri Press, 1996.

Horowitz, Howard. "Can We Learn to Argue? *Huckleberry Finn* and Literary Discipline." *ELH* 70, no. 1 (Spring 2003): 267–300.

Hutchinson, Stuart. *Mark Twain: Tom Sawyer and Huckleberry Finn*. New York, NY: Columbia University Press, 1998.

Jarrett, Gene. "'This Expression Shall Not Be Changed': Irrelevant Episodes, Jim's Humanity Revisited, and Retracing Mark Twain's Evasion in *Adventures of Huckleberry Finn*." *American Literary Realism* 35, no. 1 (Fall 2002): 1–28.

Johnson, Claudia D. *Understanding* Adventures of Huckleberry Finn: *A Student Casebook to Issues, Sources, and Historical Documents*. Westport, Conn.: Greenwood Press, 1996.

Kravitz, Bennett. "Reinventing the World and Reinventing the Self in *Huck Finn*." *Papers on Language and Literature* 40, no. 1 (Winter 2004): 3–27.

Leonard, James S., Thomas A. Tenney, and Thadious M. Davis. *Satire or Evasion? Black Perspectives on* Huckleberry Finn. Durham, N.C.: Duke University Press, 1992.

MacLeod, Christine. "Telling the Truth in a Tight Place: *Huckleberry Finn* and the Reconstruction Era." *The Southern Quarterly* 34, no. 1 (Fall 1995): 5–16.

Morley, Christopher. *Tom Sawyer and Huckleberry Finn*. London; Rutland, VT: J. M. Dent & Sons; Charles E. Tuttle, 1991.

Pardo García, Pedro Javier. "*Huckleberry Finn* as a Crossroad of Myths: The Adamic, the Quixotic, the Picaresque, and the Problem of the Ending." *Links and Letters* 8 (2001): 61–70.

Pinsker, Sanford. "Huckleberry Finn and the Problem of Freedom." *Virginia Quarterly Review* 77, no. 4 (Autumn 2001): 642–649.

Purdon, Liam O. "Huck's Rattlers and Narrative Sucker Bait in Twain's *Adventures of Huckleberry Finn*." *English Language Notes* 40, no. 2 (December 2002): 47–55.

Rao, E. Nageswara, ed. *Mark Twain and Nineteenth Century American Literature*. Hyderabad: American Studies Research Centre, 1993.

Rohrkemper, John. "Something Is Rotten in the State of—Missouri: Hamlet, Claudius, and Huckleberry Finn." *Midamerica* 28 (2001): 104–115.

Schmidt, Peter. "The 'Raftsmen's Passage,' Huck's Crisis of Whiteness, and *Huckleberry Finn* in U. S. Literary History." *Arizona Quarterly* 59, no. 2 (Summer 2003): 35–58.

Scott, Kevin Michael. "'There's More Honor': Reinterpreting Tom and the Evasion in *Huckleberry Finn*." *Studies in the Novel*, 37, no. 2 (Summer 2005): 187–207.

Shaw, Peter. *The Genteel Fate of* Huckleberry Finn. *Partisan Review* 60, no. 3 (Summer 1993): 434–449.

Tackach, James. "Why Does Jim Escape to Illinois in Mark Twain's *Adventures of Huckleberry Finn?*" *Journal of the Illinois State Historical Society* 97, no. 3 (Autumn 2004): 216–225.

Acknowledgments

"The Realism of *Huckleberry Finn*" by Tom Quirk. From *Coming to Grips with Huckleberry Finn*: 83–105. © 1993 by the curators of the University of Missouri. Reprinted with permission.

"Life Without Father: The Role of the Paternal in the Opening Chapters of *Huckleberry Finn*" by Harry G. Segal. From *Journal of American Studies* 27, no. 1 (April 1993): 19–33. © 1993 by Cambridge University Press. Reprinted with permission.

"Huck and Jim on the Mississippi: Going with the Flow?" by Carl F. Wieck. From *Refiguring Huckleberry Finn*: 70–81. © 2000 by the University of Georgia Press. Reprinted with permission.

"Huck, Jim, and the 'Black-and-White' Fallacy" by James S. Leonard. From *Constructing Mark Twain: New Directions in Scholarship*, edited by Laura E. Skandera Trombley and Michael J. Kiskis: 139–150. © 2001 by the curators of the University of Missouri. Reprinted with permission.

"Huckleberry Finn and the Problem of Freedom," by Sanford Pinsker. From the *Virginia Quarterly Review* 77, no. 4 (Autumn 2001): 642–649. © 2001 by the *Virginia Quarterly Review*, The University of Virginia. Reprinted with permission.

"Deadpan Huck: Or, What's Funny about Interpretation" by Sacvan Bercovitch. From *The Kenyon Review* 24, nos. 3 and 4 (Summer/Fall 2002): 90–134. © 2002 by Kenyon College. Reprinted with permission.

"Who Shot Tom Sawyer?" by Jeffrey Steinbrink. From *American Literary Realism, 1870–1910* 35, no. 1 (Fall 2002): 29–35. © 2002 by the University of Illinois Press. Reprinted with permission.

"*Huckleberry Finn* and Twain's Democratic Art of Writing" by Mary P. Nichols. From *Seers and Judges: American Literature as Political Philosophy*, edited by Christine Dunn Henderson: 17–32. © 2002 by Lexington Books. Reprinted with permission.

"The 'Raftsmen's Passage,' Huck's Crisis of Whiteness, and *Huckleberry Finn* in U.S. Literary History" by Peter Schmidt. From *Arizona Quarterly* 59, no. 2 (Summer 2003): 35–58. © 2003 by the Arizona Board of Regents, University of Arizona. Reprinted with permission.

"Reinventing the World and Reinventing the Self in *Huck Finn*" by Bennett Kravitz. From *Papers on Language & Literature* 40, no. 1 (Winter 2004): 3–27. © 2004 by the board of trustees, Southern Illinois University. Reprinted with permission.

"'That Night We Had Our Show': Twain and Audience" by Todd Giles. From *American Literary Realism, 1870–1910* 37, no. 1 (Fall 2004): 50–58. © 2004 by the University of Illinois Press. Reprinted with permission.

"Floating Capital: The Trouble with Whiteness on Twain's Mississippi" by Stephanie Le Menager. From *ELH* 71 (2004): 405–431. © 2004 by The Johns Hopkins University Press. Reprinted with permission.

Every effort has been made to contact the owners of copyrighted material and secure copyright permission. Articles appearing in this volume generally appear much as they did in their original publication with few or no editorial changes. In some cases foreign language text has been removed from the original essay. Those interested in locating the original source will find bibliographic information in the bibliography and acknowledgments sections of this volume.

Index

Action, motive vs., 8
Aliases, 20, 136
American humor, 75–76, 106–107
American vision, 1–3, 85–87, 172–176
Angel of Death, 105
Arac, Jonathan, 103
Argumentation, 62
"The Art of Fiction" (James), 24
Association, society and, 89
Aunt Sally, racism and, 7, 9, 56
Autobiography (Twain), 220–221

Bahktin, Mikhail, 110
Balcom, Editha, 121
Betrayal, 133–134, 150
Black-and-white fallacy, 55–64
Blackface imagery, 211–212
Black magic, 62
Bliss, Elisha, 89
Books, Huck and, 137
Boss term, usage of, 155
Bread, 143
Bricksville episode, 193–200

Calvinists, 47, 70, 101
Cannons, 47
Canoes, 44–45
Capitalism, 79, 177–178
Chattel slavery, 81, 83
Chérie (de Goncourt), 24
Children, success and, 31

Christianity, 70, 101, 184–186
Civil Rights Act, 161–163
Civil War, 158–159, 219–221
Columbus, Christopher, 174–175
Comedy. *See* Humor
Commerce, 203–204, 207–208
Compassion, 130, 131–132, 186
Confidence-Man (Melville), 77, 106
Conformity, Huck and, 96–97
Confrontations, 64–65
Con games
    disguises as, 136
    duke and king as, 138–139
    humor and, 76, 82–83, 88
    integrity of Huck as, 99–100
Congress, slavery and, 161–163
A Connecticut Yankee in King Arthur's Court (Twain), 90, 157
Conscience, 102–103
Constitution, slavery and, 161–163
Controversy, 68
Cord, Mary Ann, 156–157
Corruption, children and, 14
Count of Monte Cristo escapade, 27
Courage, importance of, 52
Cowardice, 9
Creation, 4–5, 185–186
Crowd mentality, 193–200
Cruelty, 12–13, 132
Crusoe, Robinson, 175
Culture, 3, 85–88, 104–105, 107, 205–206

Deadpan humor, 76–77, 79–81,
    106–108, 110–112
Deafness, 179
Death
    Angel of, 105
    causes of, 94
    fear of, 4, 95–96
    identification with, 149–150,
        154–155
    loneliness and, 33
    Mississippi River and, 47–48
    Pap and, 21, 33–34
    spirituality and, 182–183
    Tom and, 121
Deception, 137–139
Defiance, 49
Democracy, storytelling and,
    129–131
Descriptions, Huck and, 9–11
Desperation, 73
Deterministic principles, 89–90
Development, lack of, 98–99
Difference, recognition of, 108
Dilemmas, confrontation of,
    112–113
Disguises, 20, 136
Dog theft, 221
Douglass, Frederick, 63
Dreaminess, 34, 71, 135–136
Drift, economic and racial, 214–
    219
Duke and king
    cruelty and, 12–13
    deception and, 132, 138–139,
        200–201, 216–217
    slavery and, 52
    soliloquy of, 82
    travel with, 23
    Wilks girls incident and, 50–51
Dumas, Alexander, 98
Duplicity, ending and, 160–161

Economic drift, slavery and,
    214–219
Economic saga, 177–178

Education, 63, 130, 131–136
Eliot, T.S., 69
Ending, controversy over, 6, 27,
    38–39, 84–87, 160–164
Episodism, 18–24
Equivocation, Jim and, 60–61
Escape, 46–47, 85–86, 171–176
Evasions, Tom and, 71
Evasion scene, 186–188
Exaggeration, 19–20, 30
Excesses, Tom and, 124–125
Exegesis, 88–89
Exhilaration, paradox of, 112
Extremes, humor of, 107
Ezrahi, Sidra, 110–111

Facial expressions, 77
Fallacies, black-and-white, 55–64
False analogies, 56–59, 60–61
False dilemmas, 55–64
Family, Jim and, 179–180
Father figures
    changing nature of, 37
    footprints of, 34–35
    going against the flow and, 50
    issues surrounding, 28
    Jim and, 28, 36–37
    Judge Thatcher and, 35–36
    rivalry of with sons, 30–31
    slavery and, 157
    Tom Sawyer and, 33
Ferguson, Plessy v. , 163
Finn, Huck
    changes of, 154–160
    education of, 130, 131–136
    freedom and, 2–3, 4
    going against the flow and,
        49–50
    identity of, 29
    as metaphor, 18
    perspective of, 9–10
    prayers and, 142–144
    storytelling and, 136–144
    Tom Sawyer vs., 130
Folklore, humor and, 76

Footprints, sighting of, 34–35
Freedom
  betrayal and, 150
  drift and, 215–216
  escape and, 85–86
  fear of dying and, 4
  as goal, 152–153
  interpretation and, 103–105
  islands and, 171–176
  Jim and, 17, 21, 123, 135, 178
  loneliness and, 2–3
  meaning of, 67–73
  parasitical nature of, 151
  slavery and, 71–74
Frenchman scene, 56–59, 152
Freud, Sigmund, 108–109
Friendship, betrayal and, 133–134
Frontier Myth, 203–205
Funny, humor, 79

Genies, 135
Ghost story, 154
The Gilded Age (Twain), 81
Goodness, sympathy and, 131–132
The Great Dark (Twain), 81
Groups, Twain and, 193–200
Guilt, ghost story and, 154

Handbills, 216–217
Hants, 183
Hart, Bret, 89
Hat, straw, 165
Hemingway, Ernest, 27
Heroism, 15, 105
Hindsight, 77
History, humor and, 90, 110
Holocaust humor, 110–112
Hornets, shooting by, 120
Hostility, humor and, 110–112
"How to Tell a Story" (Twain), 75–76
Huck. See Finn, Huck
Huckspeech, 15
Humanity, 56, 91–93

Humor. See also Satire
  accidental, 15
  deadpan, 77–82
  denial of comic relief and, 113
  despair and, 110–111
  ending and, 164
  extremes and, 107
  Frenchman scene and, 56–59
  history and, 90
  interpretation and, 84–87, 101
  morality and, 105
  Phelps Plantation and, 90–94
  pranks and, 15
  slavery and, 81–82
  Twain on, 75–76
Humorous stories, 76
Hypocrisy, 70

Identity, 172–176, 177–183. See also Raftsmen's passage
Imperialism, commercial, 203–204, 206–207
Independence. See Freedom
Indians, 85, 172–173
Indigenous humor, 76–77
Interpretation, 77, 83–88, 101, 103–105
Irony, 57–58, 98
Islands, 44–46, 48, 171–176
Jackson's Island, 44–46, 171–176
James, Henry, 24
Jewish humor, 110
Jim
  conformity and, 49–50, 52
  dreaminess and, 135–136
  as father, 28, 36–37
  freedom and, 17, 21, 123, 135, 178
  as hero, 97
  race and, 57
  reinvention and, 177–178
  relationship with, 22, 133
  rescue of, 134–135
  slavery and, 52
  suffering of, 132, 133

treatment of, 140–141
tricking of, 60–61
Joints of culture, 104
Jokes, 60–61, 82–83, 133. *See also*
  Humor
Joy of being, 5–6
Judgment, vision and, 69
Judge Thatcher, 35–36

Knowledge, logic and, 22, 60–62

Ladd, Barbara, 159–160
Language, 56–59, 83, 102, 108,
  155–156
Leaves of Grass (Whitman), 1
Letter writing, 19–20
Lies, 3–4, 31–32, 68–70, 90–91
Life is Beautiful (Benigni), 111
Life on the Mississippi (Twain), 70,
  205
Lincoln, Abraham, spirit of, 183
Logic, 22, 34–35, 61
Loman, Willy, 73
Loneliness, 2–3, 32–33, 96
Lynching, 21
Magic, 62–65, 137–138
Manifest destiny, 215
Marx, Leo, 69, 72, 134
Masks, 165
Mass mentality, 193–200
Melville, Herman, Bloom on, 1
Minstrel-show darky syndrome, 57
Misreadings of novel, 68–70
Mississippi River
  commerce and, 203–204, 209–
    210
  death and, 47–48, 94–95
  departure from, 53
  escape and, 43–46
  going against the flow and,
    49–53
  rafts and, 46–47
  slavery and, 48–49
  style and, 105
  as thoroughfare, 48–49

Miss Lonelyhearts (West), 77
Mobs, 9, 193–200
Moby-Dick (Melville), 1, 8–9, 13–14
Morality
  cruelty and, 12–13
  Huck and, 56–58
  humor and, 90–92, 105
  Jim and, 64
  pseudomoralizing and, 14–15
  slavery and, 58, 133–134
  Twain on, 131
Morrison, Toni, 150–151
Mortification, 91
Moses, 137
Motive, action vs., 8
Multiculturalism, 104–105
Murderers, 132, 196–198
Myths, 47–48, 179–181

Narration
  democracy and, 129–131
  detachment and, 12–13
  Huck and, 18–21, 29–30, 136
  humor and, 80, 82–87
  Jim and, 64–65
  knowledge and, 55–56
  order of, 18
  realism and, 12–17
Nationalism, commerce and,
  210–211
Nature, goodness of, 131
New world, settlement of, 171–174
Notice, humor of, 82–83

Obenzinger, Hilton, 78
Oedipal struggle, 30–31, 33
Orwell, George, 67
Osborn, Sarah, 184–185
Outlaws, 174
Ownership, 216–217

Pap, 21, 33–34, 44, 186–188
Paradise, island as, 45–46
Paradoxes, 106–107, 112
Parody, 82, 83–84

Patterns, 21–22
Phelps farm escape, 38–39
Phelps plantation, arrival at, 90–94
Pikesville, 81–82
Pirates, 17
Platonism, 6
Plessy v. Ferguson, 163
Podhoretz, Norman, 103–104
Point of view, shifts in, 195
Power, 88–89
Pranks, adventure and, 15
Prayers, Huck and, 142–144,
  184–186
Prejudice, 7–8
Pretension, parody of, 83–84
Primary process thinking, 34–35
Pseudo-deadpan voice of Huck, 80
Pseudomoralizing, 14–15
Psychoformism, 29
Publication of *Huck Finn*, 24
Pudd'nhead Wilson (Twain), 81, 160
Puritan retreats, 184–185
Pynchon, Thomas, 106

Quicksilver, 47

Racism. *See also* Raftsmen's passage
  Aunt Sally and, 7, 9, 56
  economic drift and, 214–219
  ending and, 160–161
  family structure and, 179–181
  Huck and, 91–93
  Jim and, 57, 61
  mobility and, 208–214
  white inside and, 178–179
Raft, 46–47, 160
Raftsmen's passage
  commentary on, 149–152
  development of Huck and,
    154–160
  white racial panic and, 152–154
Rationalism, Huck and, 4–5
Realism, 7–12, 12–17, 20–22
Recognition, humor and, 80–81
Reconstruction, parody of, 161–164

Redemption, 111
Reform, impossibility of, 186–
  188
Reinvention, 177–183, 186–188
Religion, 70, 101, 142–144, 153,
  178, 184–186
Repetition, 11, 195
Rescue, of Jim, 134–135
Retrogressionist theories, 180–181
Rivalry, father-son, 30–31
Rivers, 203–204, 209–210. *See also*
  Mississippi River
Robinson, Forrest, 161
Robinson Crusoe (Dafoe), 45, 175
Romanticism, Tom and, 123, 130,
  131, 135, 175–176
Roughing It (Twain), 81, 119
Safety, in truth, 142
Satan, 70
Satire, 16–17, 71–72, 101, 124,
  161–163
Sawyer, Tom
  assistance from, 120, 134
  Christopher Columbus and,
    174–175
  Civil War and, 219–221
  differences of from Huck Finn,
    130
  racism and, 160–161, 212–213
  reintroduction of, 23–24
  satire and, 17
  shooting of, 119–125, 135
  storytelling and, 136–144
Seeing, understanding vs., 139
Segregation, 161–163
Self-affirmation, 16, 108–109
Self-defeat, ending as, 6
Sequels, 30–32, 38
Settlements, 85, 171–174
Shakespearean parody, 82
Shaler, Nathan, 180–181
Shootings, 119–125, 135
Sick jokes, 79
Sins, crimes as, 56
Skaz, 110

Slavery
   abolition of, 161–163
   economic drift and, 214–219
   education and, 63
   freedom and, 67–73
   going against the flow and, 51
   history and, 90
   Huck and, 55–56
   humor and, 81–82
   king and duke and, 52
   Mary Ann Cord and, 156–157
   morality and, 58, 133–134
   river commerce and, 210–212
   Uncle Tom's Cabin (Stowe) and, 72
Smallpox trick, 153
Smiley, Jane, 72
Snakes, 23, 87–88
Socialization, 103–104
Solomon, 83
Sons, fathers and, 30–31
Sophistry, 61
Southwestern humor, 78–80, 107
Speed, lack of, 46–47
Spelling, 20–21, 140
Spirit of the river, 3
Spirituality, Jim and, 181–183
Steamboat, description of, 153
Storytelling, 129–131, 136–144
St. Petersburg, 32–33
Straw hat, 165
Stretchers. *See* Lies
Style, as snapper, 102
Subversion, 73
Success, meaning of, 31
Suffering, sympathy and, 131–132
Superiority, reaffirmation of,
   152–153
Superstitions, 4–5, 135, 143,
   181–183
Suspects, Tom as, 120
Sympathy, goodness and, 131–132

Tall tales, 76, 78–80
Thoroughfares, rivers as, 48–49

Time, 3–4, 85
Tom. *See* Sawyer, Tom
Tom Sawyer, Huck on, 29–30
Tracking, rafts and, 45
Tragedy of man, 110–111
A Tramp Abroad (Twain), 16
Treasure Island (Stevenson), 24
Trickster, 104
Trilling, Lionel, 69
"A True Story" (Twain), 150
Truth, 68–70, 142. *See also* Lies
Twain, Mark
   audience and, 193–200
   descriptions of, 9–11
   Huck's relationship with, 37–38
   morality and, 131
   perspective of, 9–10
   self-description of, 220–221
   shooting of Tom Sawyer and,
      119–125

Uncle Tom's Cabin (Stowe), 72
Understanding, 7–12, 139

Victims, of river, 47
Virgin land, 171–176, 205–206
Vision, judgment and, 69
Volatility of perspective, 107

Walter Scott, 46, 51–52, 175
Water, culture and, 205–206
Wendell, Barrett, 92
West, Nathaniel, 77, 106
White inside, 63–64, 178–179, 212
White magic, logic as, 62–63
Whiteness, 150–151, 152–154,
   208–214
Widow Douglas, 32
Wilkeson, Frank, 180
Wilks girls incident, 50–51
Windham, Tom, 183
Women, 46
Wonham, Harry, 78
Working notes, 22